786

ll h₃

The Joel Goldsmith Reader

The
JOEL
GOLDSMITH
Reader

A Citadel Press Book
Published by Carol Publishing Group

Contents

Joel S. Goldsmith

Even in his own lifetime Joel Goldsmith was recognized as an authentically *American* mystic and religious teacher. His vision was most comprehensively expressed in a series of books whose message he referred to as The Infinite Way. These titles have sold more than two million copies both in the United States and abroad and each year additional translations are commissioned. Goldsmith has truly become a global phenomenon.

Born in New York City on March 10, 1892, in his youth he became a partner in his father's import business. Though raised in the Jewish religion he became interested in Christian Science when his father was helped by a Christian Science practitioner.

Shortly thereafter, as he himself described it, he "became reborn into a new state of consciousness." He then ventured out on his own, giving expression to his newly found vision in a series of books and lectures which became known as The Infinite Way writings.

From his home in Hawaii, Goldsmith wrote and lectured ceaselessly, amassing twenty-odd published volumes whose purposes were to help the reader establish a practical way of life which could lead to the discovery of *self* and awaken the awareness that it was possible to live *in the spirit.*

Many regard him as a twentieth-century embodiment of the school and spirit of Ralph Waldo Emerson and Walt Whitman. Above all he strove to affirm the reality of mystical experience and the possibility of a life lived in constant awareness of spiritual realities.

Joel Goldsmith never allowed himself to be referred to as "doctor" or "reverend," but simply as "mister," since he refused all offers of titles and honorary degrees, fearing that they might set up a barrier between him and his followers. It was also for this reason that he never encouraged an organization to develop to spread his thought. Rather, he taught his Infinite Way doctrine personally and directly by his lecture tours, his books and a monthly letter he mailed directly to those who requested it.

Joel Goldsmsith died on June 17, 1964, at the age of 72. He was in London on a lecture tour.

The Joel Goldsmith Reader

From

REALIZATION OF ONENESS

"Get Thee Hence, Satan"

———•———

It took a really great mystic to discover the secret of impersonal evil and devise the name "devil" or "Satan" for it. This devil or Satan, as it was first conceived, did not mean an opponent of God; it had no such meaning at all. Instead, it meant something in the nature of a tempter—not a power or a person, but a tempter offering temptation. The evil is never in us; it is the tempter that tempts us into sin, disease, death, lack, and limitation, and this tempter should be recognized at all times as the impersonal source of evil.

When the devil stood before Jesus in the wilderness tempting him to turn the stones into bread, Jesus answered, "Man shall not live by bread alone, but by every word that proceedeth out of the mouth of God."[1] Again Satan tempted the Master to cast himself down from the pinnacle of the temple, and Jesus' answer was,

[1]Matthew 4:4.

"Thou shalt not tempt the Lord thy God."[2] Once more Satan offered him temptation in the form of worldly glory, and to this, Jesus replied, "Get thee hence, Satan."[3] With this recognition of the devil as the impersonal source of evil, Satan left him.

From then on what do we hear about Satan as far as the Master is concerned? He does not appear any more. He seems to have faded out, right there and then. With that "Get thee hence, Satan," Satan is no more. The Master is alone, alone with God, consciously one with God, the victor, with full dominion. But the tempter, the devil, is gone; the temptation is gone.

Temptation Always Appears as a Person or a Condition

Every need for help for yourself or any call for help that comes from someone else should be recognized as a temptation, a temptation to be rejected. Even if it should be someone close to a hundred years, suffering from old age, remember that the claim of age has to do merely with the calendar. The calendar affects us only if we accept it, keep looking at it every day, and wondering what story it tells, instead of proving how impersonal it can be by commanding it to "get thee behind me, Satan."

Temptation will always come in the form of a person, a disease, a sin, or a lack. It will not come in the form of a man with a cloven hoof, or in the form of anyone or anything that can be identified. Often it comes in the guise of good, and we must be alert to recognize that sometimes good is as much of an evil as evil itself. Once we have learned to impersonalize every phase of good as well as of evil, however, we will not be fooled so easily, nor will we ever look at any person in an attempt to see what is in him that might be causing his difficulty.

Error has its rise in an impersonal source which in the beginning was called eating of the fruit "of the tree of the

[2]Matthew 4:7.
[3]Matthew 4:10.

knowledge of good and evil."[4] Anyone can begin to demonstrate harmony in his experience in proportion to his giving up the temptation to talk about one thing as good and another as evil, and in proportion to his realization that in a God-created universe there can be neither good nor evil: there can be only God, Spirit.

The biggest temptation that will ever come to us is to believe that one person is good and another evil, whereas no one is good and no one is evil. No human being, in his humanhood, can ever truthfully say that he is spiritual. To claim spirituality as a personal possession is egotism at its height. No one is spiritual; no one is perfect; and no one is evil: God is Spirit and only God is perfect; and evil is impersonal error.

The Belief in Two Powers is the Temptation

When it was revealed that man personally is not a sinner, but that there is a tempter called devil, or Satan, in some way this devil or Satan became known as, and understood to be, the opposite of God, the opponent of God, an enemy of God, something that God had to fight and get rid of. But be assured of this—and I say it only through revelation—God has nothing to fight at any time, no one to fight, and nothing to overcome. God *is*, and God is omnipotence, and besides God, there is none else. God has no battles. God has no enemies. God has no opponents. The devil can walk up and down the world parading its wares, but if everybody says, "No," to the temptation offered, that will be the end of the devil, and this, without any help from God. We do not need God to fight the devil for us. We need only the words, "No, get thee behind me."

Paul gave us another name for the devil or evil when he called it "carnal mind,"[5] although he, too, made the mistake that most modern metaphysicians have made of fighting the evil. Paul met

[4]Genesis 2:17.
[5]Romans 8:7.

with all manner of persecution—beatings and imprisonment—because he made the carnal mind "enmity against God."[5] Carnal mind is the "arm of flesh,"[6] or nothingness. It is a tempter that can tempt us to believe in a power apart from God, but it cannot make it so any more than the devil could make Jesus succumb to those temptations. No, carnal mind is a tempter; carnal mind is a claim of two powers; carnal mind is always presenting appearances of sin, disease, death, lack, and limitation; but these are nothing more than appearances. They are not reality.

For our purpose, we use terms such as devil, carnal mind, hypnotism, or mesmerism. As a matter of fact, one of the best words to use in describing evil is the word "appearance." Just as the illusion on the desert is not a thing or an entity but an appearance, so the evils that present themselves to us are not real: they have no identity; they have no substance; and they have no law. We may therefore look upon them as appearances.

The point that I would make is this: error did not have its rise in you or in me; it did not have its rise in wrong thinking; it did not have its rise in hate, envy, or jealousy. It had its rise in the acceptance of the belief that there are two powers. No man invented it or discovered it. This universal belief, which comes to us every minute of the day and night for acceptance or rejection, this belief in good and evil, this belief in two powers, is all there is to the carnal mind.

The Nothingness and Nonpower of Temptation

Is it consistent to declare God to be infinite and all power, and then in the same breath ascribe power to something else, giving it the power to cause disease, sin, or lack? If we are to love God supremely, it can only be because we accept God as the only power there is. How can anyone love a God that not only is not

[5]Romans 8:7.
[6]II Chronicles 32:8.

the only power, but is not even strong enough to take care of the devil in all these thousands of years? I do not believe that it is possible for anyone to love God with all his heart and soul while at the same time he believes in two powers,, regardless of how much he may mouth his love of God. One can love God only in the realization of the supreme nature of God's being, and that makes evil of no power.

In understanding God as being the only and all-power, having nothing with which to contend—no one and no condition— abiding in the supreme infinite nature of God's being, and then recognizing all these appearances as the "arm of flesh," or a temptation to believe in two powers, evil conditions will disappear and evaporate. They will come back, however, if we fasten the evil onto a person, that is, if we personalize. "Sin no more, lest a worse thing come unto thee."[7]

When we fight the devil, or carnal mind, we set up our own enemy, build it in our mind, and authorize it to stay there until something else gets rid of it. We have put it there, built it, called it carnal or mortal mind, and then given it evil propensities. Had we accepted God as Omnipotence, we would have said, "Carnal mind? Mortal mind? What of it? It must be that arm of flesh the Hebrew prophet was talking about that we do not have to war against. What we have to do is to rest in the Word."

We rest in the word that the carnal mind is not enmity against God. It is the "arm of flesh," a nothingness which must be understood to be an impersonal source of evil, impersonal, meaning without a person, without a you or a me. We are the person it is without—*when we impersonalize it.*

Devil, carnal mind, or mortal mind? It has only the power that universal belief gives it, and that is why we suffer from it without even knowing that it exists. But once we awaken, once we understand that the devil, Satan, mortal mind, or carnal mind is not power, but a suggestion offering itself to us for acceptance, we can say, "No," and then forget it.

[7]John 5:14.

Devil, carnal mind, or mortal mind has no existence. In all this world, it would be impossible to find a carnal mind, a mortal mind, or a devil. Then what is this devil, carnal mind, or mortal mind that we are talking about? It is the very thing that cast Adam and Eve out of the Garden: a belief in two powers. When we believe in two powers, we have a mortal mind or a carnal mind, and it can tear us to pieces; but we are free of it in proportion as we understand that God never made a power to destroy God or God's creation. God is the only creative principle of this universe, for God is omnipotence, omniscience, omnipresence, and therefore, there is no power of evil.

Stop Battling Error

Strange how, throughout the ages, religious men and women have dedicated their lives to the one purpose of overcoming the devil, and the devil has no power! The devil is nothing except what we decide to make it. The metaphysical world has made the self-same mistake. It will tell you that there is no devil or Satan: there is just mortal mind. Nevertheless, all kinds of quotations and affirmations are concocted to overcome this mortal mind, and thereby many sincere truth-students take a beating because of their belief in mortal mind.

All there is to what is called mortal mind is the belief in good and evil. There is no such thing as mortal mind as an entity; there is no such thing as carnal mind as an entity; there is no such thing as devil or Satan as an entity: there is only a universal belief in two powers, and that belief is the cause of every bit of discord and inharmony that has ever existed on the face of the earth.

In the degree that we fight or battle this so-called carnal mind or any of its individual forms and expressions, in that degree will we lose because we have created an enemy greater than ourselves, one with which God cannot help us because God has no knowledge of it. God is too pure to behold iniquity.

It was not the teaching of Jesus Christ to pray to God, "Please overcome my enemies! Please destroy my enemies! Please go out before me and slay these terrible people!" That is a superstitious and ignorant form of prayer, but certainly not enlightened Christian prayer. The overcoming has to be within us, and the overcoming that has to take place within us is our recognition of the truth:

> *I will never leave you, nor forsake you. If you go through the waters, you will not drown, and if you go through the fire, the flames will not kindle upon you.*

Why? Because they have no such power.

As we realize this, we shall understand why Jesus could forgive the woman taken in adultery, the thief on the cross, and Judas who betrayed him. He knew through divine revelation that these had no power.

"Destroy this temple, and in three days I will raise it up. . . . But he spake of the temple of his body."[8] This applies also to the body of our affairs, the body of our relationships, of our home, our work, and our supply. Certainly, depressions may come and deprive us of our savings, our wealth, and our investments, but they are only the body of supply: they are not supply. God is our supply, and if we lose what we consider to be the body of our supply, we can begin at once to build it again. There is no limit. There is no such thing as having only one chance, or even two or three. The only question is how much we ourselves are able to accept spiritual principles and then how much we practice them until they become a living force within our own being.

There Is No Power in the Discords of This World

I understand, of course, how difficult it is to look at the sins, diseases, and horrors of the world and not believe that there is

[8]John 2:19, 21.

power in them. It is possible to do this only after you feel within you a certain rightness about these principles and then are willing to put them into practice until such time as you witness the first healing as a result of the application of them.

The first time that anyone is healed through your realization that you have not appealed to God and have not expected truth to remove error, but have rested in the realization that there is only one power and that nothing has any power except what comes from above, you will know that you have witnessed these principles in action. Then you will have the courage to go on and on until you are able to do some of the greater works, because you have watched the enemy destroy itself; you have seen the appearances destroy themselves.

If God made all that was made and all that God made is good, then God did not make a carnal mind, a mortal mind, a devil, or a Satan, and it, therefore, has no existence except as a mental concept in human thought. If you would like to demonstrate how powerless a human concept is, close your eyes and build the biggest bomb you can possibly build. Build an atomic bomb and combine it with hydrogen and with all the forms of nuclear fission you have ever heard about, multiply it by a thousand, then throw it, and see how powerless it is to do anything. It is only a mental concept, and a mental concept has no substance; it has no law; it has no entity; it has no being. True, it has form, and that is why you can see it, but you can see it only in your mind as a mental image.

Once you begin to understand that the devil is a man-made entity formed in the mind of man, not in the mind of God, and that it has no law, no substance, no activity, no source, no avenue, and no channel, you nullify it. You have recognized it for what it is: temporal power, the "arm of flesh," nothingness.

It is with that realization that healing work begins. Actually, regardless of the name or nature of the problem with which you are confronted, you can be assured of this: it is nothing but a temptation of the devil coming to you for acceptance or rejection. This devil is nothing more nor less than the carnal mind, the human mind, which exists because of a belief in good and evil. When there is no belief in good and evil, there is no human mind any more, no carnal mind. You are then operating in, and through, and with the mind of God. It is only as long as there is a belief in good and evil that there is limitation, finiteness, negativeness.

The reason that healing is possible is because God is, and God constitutes this universe. God constitutes your being and mine, and that being is perfect. But because of a sense of separation we are mesmerized by the belief in two powers, and without our consciously knowing it, it becomes a part of our consciousness, and we respond to it in the same way that we do to the subliminal advertising that is thrown into the unconscious or subconscious.[9]

Error, a Mesmeric Sense of Reality

There is a God maintaining and sustaining the integrity of this universe, and it is perfect except when we see it "through a glass, darkly,"[10] except when we see it through a sense that has been to some extent mesmerized by the belief in good and evil. The healing lies in our realization that God's universe is intact, and therefore we are intact, for all that God is we are, and all that the Father has is ours. This that is appearing is just the product of mesmeric sense, but since it is not God-created, God-ordained, or God-sustained, it is a nothingness, the "arm of flesh."

As we abide in this truth of the unreal nature of evil, it begins to dissolve before our very eyes, because it does not exist as a person and it does not exist as a condition. It exists as a mesmeric influence, owing to our acceptance of the belief in two powers as real.

[9]For a complete discussion of this subject, see the author's *The Art of Spiritual Healing* (New York: Harper and Row, 1959), pp. 61, 62.
[10]I Corinthians 13:12.

A person is not evil even if he appears as the most ruthless and tyrannical dictator the world has ever known. He will be evil to us if we see him as evil, but he cannot be that to us if we see him as he is in his true identity and realize that the evil we are beholding is not an evil person: it is a mesmeric influence which is being accepted as reality. That is the secret. If we do not accept it as reality, it cannot operate against us.

As we sow, so shall we reap. If we believe that there is a sinful man, then sin can be committed against us. If we believe that there is a poverty-stricken man, poverty can knock at our door. If we believe that there is disease and death, we can experience them. *In the kingdom of God*, no man, woman, or child has ever died. There has never been a death since time began *in the kingdom of God*—never one. Passing from sight is part of the mesmeric influence. Those who are born must die; those who believe in birth must believe in death, for they are those who have not been able to see that this human picture is really immortal, eternal, and spiritual, but that it is seen falsely through the belief in two powers.

The beginning of wisdom is to know that God is, that God constitutes and is the substance of all that is, the life, the activity, and the law of all that is, and therefore this is an immortal and eternal universe, and we are eternal and immortal beings. Then that which we behold as a limited finite world, as evil in any form—sin, disease, lack, limitation, war, depressions, storms— we must understand to be the product of a universal mesmeric sense, that which was originally called devil but is now called carnal mind, or mortal mind. Because it never was of God, but was formed in the mind of man after the Fall of Man and his acceptance of two powers, it exists only as a mental picture, without power and without continuity. It thereby begins to fade and fade until it is no more.

Healing work is accomplished on that basis, but it is not accomplished by praying to God for help, by praying to God for employment, supply, activity, or any other kind of a gift. It is accomplished by realizing that the mind of God is actually our very mind, that all the capacities of that God-mind are our capacities, and that the picture that confronts us is a mesmeric picture, forever without law.

Healings take place, not because God has done us a favor and not because we have found some person we think is closer to God than we are. That is all nonsense. There is no one closer to God than we are. There are just those who have learned the nature and the origin of sin and disease and, thereby, knowing how to dissolve them.

If disease, sin, or any earthly condition were really a fact, a truth, or a being, God would have to be responsible for it, and the nature of it would be good instead of evil. It is not possible for God to be divided against Himself. It is not possible for an infinite Intelligence to act destructively against Itself or Its own creation. Therefore, we can accept that fact that God is perfection itself, and all that God has done and has made is good, and anything that God did not do or make does not exist. Neither sin, disease, death, storms, nor anything like that was ever made by God. They appear to us because of a universal belief in two powers, and our realization of that is the healing agency. Our realization of the nothingness of that which is frightening and confronting us as evil is the very presence and power that dissolves it, and nothing else will do it.

Breaking the Mesmerism

When we are faced with discords, inharmonies, unhappiness, lacks, and limitation, let us not go to God to try to get God to change these discords. Let us turn away from these, look right out into the world, and realize:

> *This is but a part of the universal mesmerism, trying to convince me that God is not on the field, that God is not my life and being, trying to convince me there are two powers on earth. But I know better. I know that there cannot be an infinite God and an evil power.*

Abiding in that word and letting that word abide in us, we break the mesmerism—not by might, not by power, but by understanding. Heaven cannot be taken by storm. We cannot gain heaven by might or by power, but only by an inner, silent, sacred communion, and that not for any purpose except for the joy of communing. When there is anything interfering with our well-being or that of someone who is looking to us for help, right there God is on the field. God is always present. We do not have to urge God to act in anyone's behalf. All we have to do is face the impersonal source of all evil and recognize its nothingness, its lawlessness, and then be still and watch—watch the carnal mind and its pictures pass away from us. It is only necessary to reassure ourselves that God is:

> *God is the substance of all form, and this world is perfect because it is God's world. If I am being faced with a picture of a dying person, a poor or sinful person, or an imprisoned one, that is the mesmeric activity of the carnal mind presenting this picture to me.*
>
> *How grateful I am that I have learned that there is no law in this picture to sustain it, no substance, no form, no activity, so it must dissolve!*

If we constantly have in mind these major principles, we must come to a complete conviction that God is, and this means that harmony is. It means that the entire kingdom of God is at peace and at-one with God. Then we realize that the only disturbance to our peace and harmony is caused by whatever it is that has convinced us that there are two powers. When we begin to understand that this belief is the fleshly mind, the "arm of flesh," or a nothingness, that is when the pictures of sense are dissolved.

That is why the person who does not rush out like a fireman to get his hat and coat to run to see the patient does the best work. The one who rushes to the scene will probably lose his case quickly because he has accepted the condition as a power. The mesmerism is broken by the person who can realize:

> *Nothing is going on in the kingdom of God about which I need to be disturbed, and what is going on to the human sense of things is not real, has no law to support it, and no power or continuity.*

In the silent contemplation of this truth, the mesmerism is broken, and along with it the picture disappears. That is how healing work is accomplished.

In our own being, let us be sure that we are not looking to God for something, that we have given up all thought or belief that we are going to get something from God that God is not already giving us. Rather let us understand that all that God is, is flowing now. All that God has is pouring forth now. God is. God is the same yesterday, today, and forevermore, so let us not annoy God! God is.

All the evils of this world are nothing but pictures in the mind, and when we know this they begin to dissolve. They begin to dissolve the very minute we know the nature of error. All evil functions as the universal carnal mind, the universal mesmeric mind, but since it is not law and has no law, since it is not being, since God did not ordain it, since God does not maintain it or sustain it, we do not fear it, nor do we fight it. We resist not evil. We put up our sword. We are at peace. God is.

Healing Comes Through a Realization of the Principles of
Impersonalization and "Nothingization"

Your healings will be miraculous, but only in proportion to your ability to impersonalize and "nothingize." It is not your patient who is responsible for his ills, nor is it anybody else. It is not your patient who is responsible for his nature or his character—or lack of it. It is only his ignorance of how to separate himself from these impersonal or devilish influences which come to him as temptations or suggestions but which, in and of themselves, are nothing until he accepts or believes them.

Spiritual healing has its foundation in God, but it is not a going to God for the healing, nor expecting God to do anything. It has its foundation in the realization that God never gives and God never withholds: God is forever being, harmonious being. Then follows your recognition of the fact that everything and anything of a nature unlike God belongs in the category of devil, Satan, or carnal mind, which is temporal power, nothingness.

In actual practice, you will come up against specific conditions such as infection and contagion which you will have to learn to handle in this impersonal way. Always, there are epidemics of one kind or another, and you will have to learn that these are not conditions of matter, nor are they conditions of weather: these are projections of the carnal mind, having no power.

The moment you try to deal with infection or contagion, you will fail because you will be on the *materia medica* level which operates from the standpoint of the power of germs, infection, and contagion. But you cannot do this. You can work only from the spiritual level, and that level knows the nothingness of what appears as destructive germs. We do not deny germs. I suppose in our human experience we could not live without them. What we do deny is the destructive nature of germs because God never empowered anything of a destructive nature to destroy His own creation.

You will also come up against hereditary diseases and beliefs. These must be dealt with in the same way. We were not born of the flesh. God is our only father; God is our only mother. That which is called human birth is not creation. Creation begins in the Invisible; it has its origin in God because God is the creative principle of all life, and therefore God is the only parent, and it is only from God that individual qualities can flow.

Then what of these evil qualities? They belong to that carnal mind which is no mind. Recognizing them as the carnal mind, they are thereby nullified. As long as you plant them in a man, as long as you blame them on his mother or his father, you are personalizing. You have to remove the belief in traits inherited from the parents and the grandparents and the great-grandparents. You have to stop believing that this person is this way owing to certain nationalistic, racial, or religious traits, because these traits all stem from the same source. They emanate from the carnal mind; and because their substance is the carnal mind, they are not power, they are not presence, they are not substance, they are not law.

Some of the evils you encounter will appear to you as forms that you may not recognize for what they are, and you may forget that these, too, have to be relegated to the carnal mind where they can be "nothingized."

In my thirty years of healing work, I have had the same problems to meet as every other practitioner. I have found, and you may have found this, too, that there are certain diseases that do not readily yield. However, not a single case that is called incurable really is incurable.

There is nothing impossible once you understand the nature of God and truly know the nature of error as an impersonal nothingness. But you have to be willing to stand with that principle until you can demonstrate it. Again, remember it is not because evil is nothing that it can be nullified. It is only in proportion as you can attain the consciousness of its nothingness that you can prove its nonpower. If the nothingness of evil could remove it, it would have been removed by now because it is nothing. But its nothingness will not remove it. It takes the enlightened consciousness of an individuasl. It takes the dedicated spiritual consciousness of an individual, and that is why there are so few healers in this age capable of doing the greater works. Anyone could do them if he would dedicate his life to this work, if he could drop other responsibilities and dedicate himself to study and to meditation until his spiritual nature so evolves that evil would automatically disappear at his approach.

There can be millions and hundreds of millions of persons who can be highly successful healers, but it is a life of dedication. The developing of the healing consciousness cannot be done in one's spare time. Yes, of course, the healing of colds, flu, or a little minor thing—that can be done. But in order to become a part of a world healing ministry and open up the rest of this world to the vision of living in God, there must arise out of society a group of persons who so want God and so want to bring God's government on earth that they dedicate themselves to this goal day and night.

ACROSS THE DESK

You will notice that each month The Infinite Way is now being given more and more recognition by the religious and educational worlds and, because of this, inevitably, you are going to be called upon to explain what The Infinite Way contribution is to the world.

To you, therefore, it must be clear that The Infinite Way reveals that:

> *1. There is a transcendental consciousness available to man here and now, which, when attained, results in the "dying daily" of the old man and the rebirth of the new man, the son of God. This transcendental or spiritual consciousness is the power of Grace in the experience of man, freeing him from the "law" and establishing his life under Grace.*

> *2. There are principles of life whereby this higher consciousness is attained.*

> *3. Through the spiritual discernment now possible, the nature of God as individual consciousness is revealed, the kingdom of God, and the secret of spiritual power.*

If all this is not clear to you, begin at once a serious study of *The Contemplative Life*[11] and of the following chapters in *A Parenthesis in Eternity*[12]: "Reality and Illusion," "The Nature of Spiritual Power," and "Living Above the Pairs of Opposites."

You cannot spend all your life *taking in*, but must rather expect to be called upon to *give out*, and you cannot give out more than you understand. What you understand of The Infinite Way is the measure of your demonstration of spiritual harmony. "Freely ye have received, freely give."[13]

[11]By the author. (New York, New York: The Julian Press, 1963).
[12]By the author. (New York, New York: Harper and Row, 1963).
[13]Matthew 10:8.

No And!

———•———

The secret of meeting error lies in knowing its nature. And the nature of error can be summed up in such words as "carnal mind," "suggestion," "appearance," or "hypnotism." The nature of error as hypnotism, or the carnal mind, can be illustrated in this way: If there were a plant in the room where you are now sitting and if someone hypnotized you, he could make you believe that, instead of branches, snakes were growing out of the flowerpot, and you would accept and believe it. Through hypnotic suggestion, the hypnotist has taken temporary control of your mind, and because you are apparently unable to act independently, you follow his suggestion to its logical conclusion. A fear of the snakes is set up in you; you run away from them and may even pick up a knife with which to chop off their heads—all this based on the belief that snakes are actually there.

No matter what you might do to those nonexistent snakes, you still could not change the fact that as long as you remain hypnotized you will see snakes. There is no possible way for you to be rid of those snakes except to become dehypnotized; there is no way to get rid of your fear of snakes except to become dehypnotized; there is no way to put up your sword except to become dehypnotized. In other words, as long as the hypnosis lasts, all the component parts of the picture are there, are they not?

Now just as it is possible to hypnotize you into believing that there are snakes in the room, so is it possible to hypnotize you into believing that there is a selfhood other than God in any place where you happen to be. As soon as you have been hypnotized into believing in a selfhood apart from God, you then logically accept all the beliefs regarding this selfhood: birth, growth, maturity, and ultimately death. There is only one way to be rid of the human picture, and that is to understand that there is no person and there is no selfhood other than God in the room or in any other place. But the hypnotized person will at once counter with, "How can you say that there is only God in the room?" And the answer is simple: there is only one Life, and that Life is God; there is only one Soul, and that Soul is God; there is only one Spirit; there is only one Law; there is only one creative Principle: God. What then can be present except God? Nothing!

The moment you see God *and*, you are hypnotized. The moment you see a mortal, material world, you are hypnotized; and from then on, there is no possible way to get rid of the appearance. That is the reason that even if you kill the snake over there in the flowerpot, two more will rise up to take its place. That is why with all the advances made in *materia medica* everybody still dies because everybody who is born must die. They do and they will. At best they may live a few more years, but that is all. People still die of pneumonia; people still die of tuberculosis; they still die of cancer; they still die of heart failure, and were a cure found for these something else would immediately replace them.

If you can agree that there is God, which means that you accept an infinite power of good, certainly then you must be able to understand that there cannot be error, disease, or death. In fact, not since time began has there ever been a single death *in the kingdom of God.*

So whatever you see in the nature of sin, disease, or death is a part of the hypnosis, and, furthermore, whatever you see as good humanhood is also a part of the same hypnosis. Even the healthy human being of thirty or forty will some day be an old human being of seventy or eighty. When you see a young, healthy person, therefore, you are just being fooled by an appearance of good. Until you can become dehypnotized to the degree that you know that there are not good human beings or bad human beings, that there are not diseased human beings or healthy human beings, but that there is only God, the one Life, the one Soul, the one Spirit, the one Substance, the one Law, the one Activity— until that time, you will have to experience death.

Judge Not After Appearances

No one can ever be dehypnotized as long as he is judging by appearances because the human mind with which he is judging is a state of hypnotism. In other words, in looking out from our eyes, we are looking out from a state of hypnosis in which our eyes are always going to see babies being born and old people dying; our ears are always going to be hearing about sin, disease, death, lack, and limitation. Until we are able to shut off those five senses and develop an inner discernment, we are always going to see, hear, taste, touch, and smell error.

If we look through our eyes at the people of this world, all we shall ever see are human beings, sometimes good, sometimes bad. The man and wife who love each other one day drive daggers into each other's hearts the next day. The parent who fondles the child one day reproaches him the next. It is the human picture, sometimes good, sometimes evil. That is what we shall always see, hear, taste, touch, and smell with the five physical senses.

The only way to be dehypnotized is to quiet the physical senses, to be still inside, and then spiritual awareness reveals the truth of being that enables us to see that which is not visible, to hear that which is not audible, to know that which is not knowable with the human senses.

A person with no musical appreciation listening to a symphony hears only a mass of dull monotonous noises, but a person with a developed musical consciousness listening to the same symphony hears harmony, melody, and rhythm. What does a person who has no art appreciation see when he looks at a beautiful painting? Daubs of paint! That is all—nothing more, nothing less—just daubs of paint that do not make sense. On the other hand, a person with an appreciation of art sees whatever it is that the artist had in mind, and appreciates the technique, execution, coloring, and the shading.

A person who knows nothing of sculpture looks at a statue, and what does he see? A piece of bronze or marble made into a statue which to him appears only as a very poor likeness. But the person with an artistic sense looks at it, and he sees the skill expressed by the line, form, and rhythm; he sees in it the flow in the artist's mind and hands. Such people are not seeing with their eyes: they are seeing through their understanding of music and art.

And just as no one will ever be able to understand a symphony or a piece of sculpture until he develops a certain measure of artistic appreciation, so no one will ever be able to understand the spiritual universe until he develops that inner spiritual consciousness, that which is called Christ-consciousness. It was Christ-consciousness which enabled Jesus to say to Pilate, the man who had the greatest temporal power of his day in Jerusalem, "Thou couldest have no power at all against me, except it were given theè from above."[1] How could Jesus make such a daring statement in the face of the great temporal power that Pilate wielded? It was only because he had the inner vision to see through to something beyond what the eyes could see and the ears

<hr>

[1]John 19:11.

could hear. He knew something that the human being could not know, and he proved it when he allowed himself to be crucified. They could crucify him, but they could not kill him. The Crucifixion and the nails had no power.

The Dehypnotized Consciousness Sees Reality

Dehypnotism is a state of consciousness that sees that which actually is: it is the ability to see, hear, taste, touch, and smell Reality; it is the ability to see sin not as sin, and disease not as disease, but rather to be able to separate these from the person and realize that we are dealing with a *false appearance* produced by the belief in a selfhood apart from God, a universal belief so powerful that it operates as law in our consciousness until we detect and cast it out, that is, until we know the truth which makes us free.

The only way this can be accomplished is through spiritual consciousness. First of all, we must know this: we cannot cure a disease—there is none; we cannot overcome poverty—there is none; we cannot overcome death—there is none. The only thing we can do is to recognize that we are not dealing with those appearances or suggestions as such: we are dealing with hypnotism.

Even a so-called mental cause for a disease is just as much an illusion as is the physical disease. If there is a mental cause for a physical disease, as is claimed in some teachings, the disease is no illusion, since it has a real cause. We, in The Infinite Way, believe that even a mental cause is as much of an illusion as the physical disease, since all there is to the human scene is of the nature of illusion. The mental cause is as illusory in its nature as the physical effect.

The truth is that all there is, is infinite God and Its creation. There is nothing else. To understand Reality, we must understand that Spirit alone is real, since Spirit is infinite. All that exists, then, must exist at the standpoint of Spirit and be under spiritual law. Therefore, we are not dealing with the physical effects of mental causes: we are dealing only with God manifesting Itself and expressing Its infinite harmonies, and with the appearance, suggestion, or claim of a universal belief in a selfhood apart from God, of a universe apart from God, and of a selfhood and universe subject to material and mental laws.

This Universe is Governed by Principle

Can you believe that there is God *and* sickness, too? Where would God be while someone is suffering? Human parents would never permit a child to suffer from a disease if they could prevent it. Would you let your child suffer? Then why do you think God would? It cannot be. *In reality,* there never has been a sick person or a dead one. Everybody who has ever lived from the beginning of all time is still alive—it could not be otherwise. Unless you accept this truth, you are really an atheist and believe that the world sprang up out of dust, that it is going to return to dust, and that there is no God.

But how can you believe that when you observe the law of like begetting like in operation: apples always coming from apple trees, cabbages coming from cabbage plants? That cannot be accidental; there must be a law. This is not an accidental world. There must be a principle behind it, and that principle is God. If there is a principle, is there ever an exception to the principle? In our system of mathematics two times two is four always, and there is never any exception to that. Does anything grow on apple trees but apples, or on orange trees but oranges?

There is a Principle governing the universe, and because there is a Principle, a divine Law, nothing is ever outside Its government or control, not any more than do the notes of the scale—do, re, mi, fa, sol, la, ti—change in their relationship to one another. No one note has ever crowded another off the scale. No one note has ever infringed upon another. No one note has ever taken anything away from another note.

It is exactly the same with the digits nought, one, two, three, four, five, six, seven, eight, and nine. They never get out of their rightful places; not one of them has ever taken anything from one of the others; not one has ever crowded the other out or drawn from another. Cooperation? Yes, they have cooperated for the common good.

If that is true of mathematics and true of music, how can it be other than true of man who was given dominion over mathematics and music? So, there never has been a man who crowded another man off the earth; there never has been a man who crowded another man out of his business. Never! Those pictures are a part of universal hypnotism, and if we can be made to believe that there is a mortal, material universe, we, too, are a part of this hypnotism. Hypnotism is the error, and we are the ones who have to correct it through the understanding that one with God is a majority. The moment a person knows the truth, or can turn to someone higher in consciousness who can know the truth for him, that "one on God's side is a majority,"[2] and that breaks the spell.

"Go, and Sin No More"

The mesmerism may be broken, but that does not mean that the dehypnotized person cannot soon get himself back into it again. If he does not conform to the higher vision, nothing is going to stop him from slipping right back into the same sin, the same disease, or a different one. Jesus said, "Neither do I condemn thee: go, and sin no more."[3] In other words,: "I release you and give you your freedom through my understanding of your spiritual nature, but do not go back and indulge in mortality

[2]Wendell Phillips, *Speech (November 1, 1859)*.
[3]John 8:11.

again." If a person who is healed does not change his mode of life, that is, if he goes back and "sins" again, he may find that a worse thing will come upon him.

The world misunderstands the meaning of the word "sin." It means not only getting drunk, committing adultery, or stealing: there is much more to sin than that. *Sin is really the acceptance of a material universe.* Just going back to the belief that there are human beings is the sin that throws a person back into disease and sin again. What the world might call sin—stealing, lying, cheating, and adultery—is of the same nature as disease: it is just another form of hypnotism.

Hypnotism is the Substance of All Discord

There is no difference between the hell called poverty and that called war, disease, or sin. One of them is no worse than another. They are all forms of one thing, and that one thing is hypnotism. In one man, hypnotism appears as some sinful thing or thought; in another, it appears as a diseased condition or thought; and in still another, it appears as poverty. The particular form makes no difference; it is all hypnotism. Take away the hypnotism, and none of these things would be there. There is only one error, and that is hypnotism.

If we can be induced to give treatments to persons—to treat them for nerves or for a mental cause for a physical disease, to treat them for resentment, hatred, jealousy, or anger, or if we can be made to treat them for cancer or consumption—we are not in the practice of spiritual healing: we are in *materia medica* because we are treating effects, whether the effect is a sin, a disease, or poverty, and if we do get rid of it, two more effects lift their heads.

Until we lay the ax at the root of the tree, which is hypnotism, we do not come out of the mortal or material state of consciousness. When we are able to see through the hypnotism, regardless of the name or nature of the sin, disease, or lack, our patient or student will experience harmony, health, wholeness, and completeness. If his trouble is nerves, he finds himself rid of nerves; if his belief is unemployment, he finds himself employed; if his claim is disease, he finds himself well. Why? Because of the practitioner's ability to see through the claim of hypnotism and realize God as the Principle of all that is.

Many times, however, even after a student understands hypnotism to be operating as the suggestion or appearance, he still believes there is a real condition to be destroyed. That is when we hear such expressions as, "Look what hypnotism is doing to me." But hypnotism is not an actual thing or condition. Hypnotism cannot produce water on the desert or snakes in the flowerpot. Hypnotism is itself no thing, no form, no cause, and no effect. Recognizing any form or appearance of error as hypnotism and then dismissing it without further concern is the correct way to handle all error.

Meditate on this idea of hypnotism as the substance of every form of the mortal or material universe that is appearing to you. When you see sin, disease, lack, and limitation, remember it is hypnotism presenting itself to you as what is called evil form. But then when you see beauty all around, the mountains, ocean, and sunshine, remember that these, too, are forms of hypnotism, only this time appearing to you as good forms.

This does not mean that we are not to enjoy the good of human existence, but rather that we are to enjoy it for what it is—not as something real, in and of itself, but because the reality, that which underlies all good, is spiritual, and must therefore be spiritually discerned. We enjoy the forms of good, knowing them to be temporary forms, not something to be stored up, not something to be put in bank vaults, but something to be enjoyed, and then we go on each day letting the manna fall afresh.

When confronted with the negative aspects of hypnotism, that is, the forms of sin, disease, lack, and limitation, the most important point to remember is that we are not to be fooled by them, not to be fooled into trying to reform evil or sinful persons, but always quickly to remember: "Oh, no! This is hypnotism appearing in still another form, hypnotism which, in and of itself, cannot be the substance, law, cause, or effect of any form of reality." Such a practice enables you to become a spiritual healer.

Never Try to Change a Person or a Condition

As you go further in the work and, through meditation, are able to rise to a point where you are above this world, then you will know me as I am, and I will know you as you are. That is how healings take place, and that is why I caution our students not to tell people that they must correct themselves, not to refuse patients because they do not seem to be doing what they think is right. That has nothing to do with the student. He must go within and see the person he is trying to help as God made him, and then the patient will soon conform "to the pattern shewed to thee in the mount."[4]

The world is hypnotized by person, place, and thing to such a degree that a good person, a good place, and a good thing become so pleasant and comfortable that everybody wants to enjoy these effects, and they do not want to go any higher than that. Such material pleasures and enjoyments cannot be a permanent dispensation, however, because no matter how much good a person may have, he still fluctuates between the pairs of opposites.

So again I say this to you: If you can be made to treat a person in an attempt to change him or give him more of this world's good, or if you can be made to fear war, a depression, or an atomic bomb, you are hypnotized. It is only a question, then, of what date will be placed on your tombstone. If, however, you can catch this vision, when the time comes for you to leave this world, you will step out into a transitional experience which will be higher and better than this one.

4Hebrews 8:5.

You cannot treat a person: you cannot treat a condition. To do that would be like trying to treat the snakes appearing in the flowerpot and saying, "I've got to get rid of my three snakes. As soon as I get rid of them, I'll be able to study better." Do you see how foolish that is? There are not any snakes, so you are never going to get rid of them. All you have to do is to get rid of the hypnotism!

When you really know and believe that—not just believe words—you will no longer have to study truth because the only purpose in studying truth is to learn that hypnotism is the only error, and when you have learned that, there is nothing more to study. All the rest is to be lived within your own being.

The minute you try to change or improve a disease or condition, you yourself are in the hypnotism because there is no disease or condition apart from the mesmerism or the hypnotism. To be ensnared, then, into trying to handle the condition would be but to make the whole situation worse.

Those who are reading or studying truth or who are using truth for healing, for supply, or for some other purpose will find that the more their minds are fixed on getting rid of the condition or on getting the healing, the more are their minds in the mirage of error. You must see that there is no human demonstration to make. There is only one demonstration, and that is gaining the realization of God.

When you have the realization of God, you have all: you have supply; you have immortal life, eternality, and infinity. You cannot demonstrate a home, a companion, a divorce, or a job: you can only demonstrate the presence of God, and that includes whatever the nature of the outward demonstration is to be.

There is No God "And"

Recognizing the hypnotism includes the demonstration of getting rid of whatever form it might take: the water on the road, the snakes in the flowerpot, or the cancer. But you cannot get rid of these separate and apart from getting rid of the hypnotism. Neither can you make a demonstration of home, employment, or health separate and apart from achieving the conscious realization of God, because there is no demonstration of good separate and apart from God.

There is no use treating person, place, or thing because all there is to error is hypnotism. There is no use seeking a demonstration of person, thing, or condition because there is no demonstration separate and apart from the realization of God. The realization of God includes all demonstrations. "Seek ye first the kingdom of God, and his righteousness; and all these things shall be added unto you."[5]

The important point to understand is that it is the same on the positive side as on the negative. On the positive side, it is demonstrating the consciousness of the presence of God; on the negative side, it is realizing that no matter what the form of error is, it is hypnotism, and hypnotism alone, which has no substance, law, cause, reality, or effect. These are the two sides of the picture.

The entire basis of The Infinite Way teaching is that there is not God *and*. There is not God *and* health, or God *and* strength, or God *and* immortality, or God *and* activity, or God *and* supply. There is only God manifesting *as*. You can take a block of mahogany, and out of it make a chair, a table, and a bench. But you do not have mahogany *and* a table *and* a chair *and* a bench: you have mahogany manifested or expressed *as* those pieces of furniture.

Therefore, when you think of God as the substance of the universe, you do not have God, the Substance, *and* a variety of forms: you have God appearing or *formed as* these forms, manifested and expressed as form. That is why, if you demonstrate God, you demonstrate every form as which God appears. You demonstrate God as health, as harmony, as immortality, and as supply. You cannot demonstrate God *and* these things, and you cannot demonstrate these things separate and apart from God because they are all God Itself formed.

There Is No Hypnotism "And"

This idea of no separation between the substance of a thing and the thing itself can also be applied to an understanding of all error as hypnotism. There is not hypnotism *and* a disease. There is not hypnotism *and* lack and limitation; there is not hypnotism *and* sin and death. There is only hypnotism *appearing as these pictures.* You cannot get rid of the sin, disease, or death separate and apart from the hypnotism, but when you have rid yourself of hypnotism, you are rid of all its various forms. The way to remove the effects of hypnotism is to understand hypnotism, not as a thing, but as no thing, no power, no presence.

Here you have the secret of living. When, through the senses, you observe life as it seems to be—as you see, hear, taste, touch, or smell it—you understand immediately that this is the product of hypnotism. Through your spiritual sense, however, you discern that right where this human, material, or physical sense seems to be is the spiritual, eternal, and immortal creation.

If you were to see a so-called evil appearance, a sinful, sick, dying, or dead appearance, you would probably be tempted immediately to know some truth that you hope would change the picture, or to think some thought that would heal, correct, improve, or reform it; whereas, if you saw normal human good, normal human wealth, harmony, wholeness, or prosperity, you would most likely accept that picture at its face value.

Hypnotism is just as much hypnotism when it appears as good as when it appears as evil. When you come into a state of life, however, where you can look at the harmonious human appearance and recognize it as hypnotism or appearance or suggestion, and when you can look at the inharmonious or discordant human picture and recognize it as the product of the same hypnotism, as appearance or suggestion, then you have arrived at a point in consciousness in which you will not try to improve, heal, or correct the erroneous picture, nor experience undue satisfaction over the harmonious picture. That is because you will know through your spiritual sense that, regardless of the picture or the nature of its appearance, right there is spiritual reality and harmony, right there eternal and immortal being is. So you will make no mental effort to correct, heal, or improve it. And with that ability to refrain from all attempts to heal, correct, or improve, you will have demonstrated the consciousness of God's allness.

If you can know that the harmonious human appearances are no more real than the inharmonious or discordant ones and if you can know that inharmonious, discordant, sick, sinful, dying human appearances are no more real than harmonious or healthful appearances, then you have arrived at a state of consciousness that spiritually discerns harmony right where any form or human appearance may be.

When you have become accustomed to the idea of observing the harmonious human appearances and the inharmonious human appearances with the same degree of unconcern, you will know that you have arrived at a state of spiritual consciousness in which you see that which is invisible, hear that which is inaudible, and know that which is unknowable. This is Christ-consciousness.

ACROSS THE DECK

In March, we traveled to California, and in May we start on another trip through the United States and Europe. Again we will experience the joy of meeting with those who have dedicated themselves to God.

We are ever-mindful of the many revelators of spiritual wisdom whose lives have been consecrated to God's purpose, and of those who have devoted themselves to carrying on their work. Even to think of Zarathustra, Lao-tze, Buddha, Jesus the Christ, and

Shankara is to find oneself on holy ground. There are many others, too, to inspire us because we witness the nature of their consecration.

There is another form of dedication which we meet in the lives of those who have surrendered their personal sense of life to give themselves, yes, dedicate themselves, to the cause of freedom, and this is a consecration to loving one's neighbor as himself. These unselfed Souls brought forth the freedom of England, France, Holland, Switzerland, countries in North and South America, as well as others throughout the world.

Many now are devoting themselves to worthy causes in different parts of the world. Some have given themselves to youth in the work of the YMCA and the YWCA, the Boy Scouts and Girl Scouts, to the poor through their work in the Salvation Army, and to the suffering by carrying food and clothing to friendly and enemy countries. Such movements as Care and the Peace Corps demonstrate love in concrete form.

This dedication to God, expressed as consecration to our neighbors' needs ennobles the lives of those who are called and furnishes inspiration to the rest of us so that we, too, may rise above the deadness and dullness of human living. Real living begins only when inspiration enters. Self-completeness is attained only in giving and serving. Freedom is attained in consecration, and peace is found in dedication.

When the Spirit of God touches us, there follows an unrest, a disquiet, a lack of satisfaction with ordinary human experience, and this persists until we find ourselves serving God in our neighbor and resting in Him.

Living the Principle of Impersonalization

———•———

To different people, and for many different reasons, travel is a stimulating and fascinating activity, but in my experience the main function of travel has been to meet people. My interest has always been in people. I have seen all the scenery, sometimes once and sometimes many times and I have seen the art galleries, too. But I like people, and I do not go around the world over and over again to see more scenery or even to see more art galleries, but to meet people. Life is for living, and the living cannot be done except it is done with others. No one can live a life unto himself and be fulfilled, and no nation, race, or creed can live unto itself and become anything but ingrown.

The more traveling there is, the more opportunity there is for a meeting of minds and for a greater understanding of others, even on the human level. Think what it would mean to the world if, in our contact with other people, we could attain the awareness that everyone is the temple of the living God, if we were no longer to ascribe evil to one another, no longer believe that evil is a component part of this or that race, of this or that nation, but were to learn to impersonalize. Think of the kind of relationships that could exist in the world if we were to embody these spiritual principles. Think of the invisible bond that would be established among all peoples of the world through such spiritual illumination.

These principles will never become effective on a world-wide scale, however, unless you and I begin applying them where we are in our home, here and now. Let us assume that there is a member of your family who is not living up to the highest standards of humanhood, much less of his spiritual identity, a person who is unruly, disobedient, dishonest, untruthful, untrustworthy, unfaithful, or one who is not measuring up to the standard of normal health, physically or mentally.

Surely, it must be clear to you that you have a responsibility in your own home. True, you are not necessarily responsible for the purity of everyone in your home, nor is it your responsibility that everyone there conform to your standards of life, since one of the privileges of living in a free country is that each person is an individual and has the right to live his own life.

This is true, however, only up to a certain point. Each and every person is entitled to liberty, but not to license. There are things that no one should tolerate in his home. Remember that your home is your domain, and you should permit nothing to enter that home "that defileth . . . or maketh a lie."[1] Therefore, it is your function to prevent the entrance of whatever may disturb your household, or to eliminate it after it is there, in other words, to bring about a change in the situation.

Changing the Atmosphere of Your Home

To each one of us, then, comes this question: "How can I change the atmosphere of my home? How can I improve it? And, even if

[1] Revelation 21:27.

it is humanly good, how can I lift it above human goodness into the demonstration of spiritual harmony, spiritual health, spiritual purity, spiritual abundance?"

It is at this point that you bring the three basic principles of The Infinite Way into operation. First of all, you must realize that it makes no difference whether at the moment you are looking at a person in sin, disease, or nearing death. The truth is that God constitutes individual being. God is the quality, God is the quantity, God is the essence, and God is the law unto every person in your household. God constitutes his being; and therefore, his nature is pure, godly, good.

With that thoroughly established in your consciousness, you can turn to the second step, which is the most important principle of all, impersonalization. Whether a member of your family is suffering from sickness, sin, false appetite, unemployment, lack, bad disposition, hate, envy, jealousy, or malice, the all-important step is to impersonalize the error. *You must impersonalize.* You must be able to look at that individual, realizing that the only nature there is, is godly. This sin, this disease, this whatever it may be is not of a person. It has its source in the carnal mind. This of which he is a victim, this which is manifesting itself in him, on him, through him, or as him, this actually is an activity or substance of the carnal mind or devil.

Does that not contradict much of what you have been thinking about this person? Perhaps, because of your previous metaphysical background, you have been probing into his consciousness, seeking to find the error so that you could remove it. You may have been blaming his religious beliefs, or his lack of them, or in some way or other you may have been attempting to eradicate the error from him. By now you must understand that it is impossible to do that because the error is not, and never was, a part of his being. God constitutes his being, and God has constituted his being from everlasting to everlasting.

Let me remind you again that it is for this reason that you must never use the name of a person in treatment, nor must you ever name the disease or the problem because you are then personalizing it and fastening it to the very individual you would like to see free. It is vitally important for you to understand that this trait or quality of character, this apparently evil nature, this false appetite, or this diseased condition is an activity of the carnal mind.

Therefore, when you have impersonalized whatever the problem may be to the extent that you really have released the individual and can feel that this is something that does not belong to him, but something that exists only in the carnal mind, you then take the third and final step and realize:

> *There is only one mind, the mind that is the instrument of God. Therefore, there is no carnal mind or mortal mind. That which has been termed carnal mind is not a mind at all: it is a belief in two powers. When there is no belief in two powers, there is no carnal mind.*

In other words, if you could wholly remove from yourself the belief in two powers, as far as you are concerned, there would be no human beings left to be healed or improved. There would be only children of God, or Adam and Eve in the Garden of Eden before they ate of the fruit. All there is to humanhood is a belief in two powers. Without that belief, there is no human race any more: there is only immortal being.

Loving Your Neighbor by Living the Principles

After you have practiced these three principles in your home and have begun to see some changes, you broaden your horizon by practicing them when you go to market, to your business office or factory, or when you are driving an automobile or riding in a bus.

The moment you leave your home, you are faced with countless pictures of carnal mind: drunkenness, obscenity, vice, mean disposition, poverty, deformity. You cannot pass by on the other side of the road. You have to be the one who ministers to those persons so afflicted—only in order to do this you do not have to leave whatever it is you are doing. All you have to do is to recognize:

> *God constitutes all being; therefore, the nature of man is godly. Even the body is the temple of the living God. Body, mind, Soul, and Spirit—these are the temple of the living God, and this that I am seeing or hearing is carnal mind, the "arm of flesh,"[2] nothingness. It is a belief in two powers.*
>
> *Thank You, Father, that I know enough to know that there is only one power, one mind, one life, one law; and that power, mind, life, and law are spiritual.*

In this meditation or treatment, you have not treated any person; you have not used anyone's name or identified his fault; you have not directed a treatment to him. All this was a truth realized within you *about the appearance.* It does not matter who the appearance is or what the appearance is: it is nothing but an appearance, and you are recognizing it as the carnal mind, the "arm of flesh," or nothingness—and you can rest in that word.

Secrecy

It will not take long for you to discover that you are having experiences different from any you have ever had before, and that a change is taking place within you. But here I must caution you about something both in your home and outside of it. Be sure that all this is taking place in secret. Never voice this to anyone. No one must ever be told; no one must ever know that you are knowing the truth.

The day does come, however, when someone in your family says, "You have changed," or "You know something," and then, if you find that he is really serious in wanting to know what has brought about the change in you, you can begin to impart what you have learned. But you have to be very, very sure that he really

²II Chronicles 32:8.

wants to know, that he is not going to let you unburden yourself and then ridicule it, and thereby probably deprive you of your "pearl." Be very sure that you treat this truth as the "pearl of great price."[3] If anyone comes to you for it, be sure that he is coming to you in humility and in earnestness, that he is coming to you really and truly seeking, and not just out of curiosity.

Until a person is well grounded in these principles, it does not take much for him to lose what little awareness he has gained and the benefit of it. When people mock, scorn, or deride his study or beliefs, it begins to undermine his faith, and unless he has beheld its activity and witnessed its fruits time and time again he can be made to waver. Many persons have. Like Lot's wife, they sometimes look back if they do not know the principles thoroughly, and if they have not seen them work so often that nothing, not even crucifixion, could make them change their minds.

Evil Is Impersonal

Always remember that, whatever belief you or I may be suffering from, it is not your belief or mine: it is a universal belief which we have temporarily picked up, accepted, or to which we have yielded. Never blame anyone and never try to make anyone better than he is. You will not succeed, and you will only give yourself heartaches. It is useless to tell a person to be more loving, more generous, or more forgiving because he cannot be anything more than he is, until a change of consciousness takes place through the realization that any undesirable qualities he seems to possess never were of him. They are of the carnal mind: they are not, and never were, power; and they operate only because of the universal belief in two powers.

If you see a man stealing, do not call him a thief. Realize instantly, "This is a belief in two powers operating, but it cannot

[3]Matthew 13:46.

operate because there are not two powers." If you do this, you will not only heal yourself, but you will be loving your neighbor as yourself—and that is important. If for any reason you might be tempted to steal, and someone should see you, surely the one thing you would most appreciate would be for that person to know that you are not a thief, that you were but responding to an impersonal impulse, and that is not power. If such truth were known for you when assailed by temptation, probably you would stop right in the midst of the act.

When we live in this higher consciousness, we are living in an entirely different atmosphere, in a world where we are not conscious of the evil traits in people, or even the erroneous ones. We are far more aware of the good qualities that are being expressed. This is in no wise a Pollyanna attitude because when we are in the consciousness of God as the only Being, then the evil that may be presented to us as a person dissolves, and we bring to that person a higher and richer experience than he knew before— especially if he is at all receptive to the spiritual way of life.

This has been proved to a large degree in the work that I have carried on in prisons. It was while I was working with the inmates in a prison that I first became aware of the principle that there is no evil, as such, in people, not even in those who are in prison.

Several years ago, I was invited to speak to a group of prisoners who had found a couple of Infinite Way pamphlets through one of the teachers working in the prison. Evidently these pamphlets had been circulated rather widely because I found a good-sized group of men waiting to hear me. Before I went into the room where the men were assembled, the man in charge of such activities called me aside and said, "You're in trouble, and I'm going to get you out of it. There are sixty-six men in there waiting for you, but I've read *The Infinite Way*, so I can tell you that they don't want anything you've got. I have an idea you will be able to hold them for about ten minutes, so when you find yourself slipping, just look at me and give me a wink, and I will call for a smoking recess, and then I'll have someone else take over."

"All right," I replied. "I'll be on the alert."

One hour passed, and there was not a sound in that room. By then, the man in charge was beginning to wonder what it was all about and called a recess for smoking, but the men said, "Can't we smoke and have you go on with your talk?" Two hours passed, and then he announced that the time was up. He told me afterward that he was astounded that these prisoners had displayed such a deep interest in, and could be so attentive to, a talk of this nature.

Actually, the secret was what I had learned in my first experience in prison work, and that was that there are no sinful men. There is no such thing as evil in the mind of man. Evil is absolutely impersonal. Man, himself, is an incarnation of God. God is the very fiber and fabric of man's being, and everything else is superimposed upon that perfect expression. It is not any more a part of man's spiritual identity than dirt is a part of the water in a pail. Even after the dirt gets into the water, it can always be removed because it never becomes water.

Evil never becomes man, nor does it become a part of man. Whatever appears to be there can be removed by anyone who realizes the impersonal nature of the appearance. That has been the secret of The Infinite Way in working with every form of sin, false appetite, disease, and all the other inharmonies that come into human experience.

There is not one of us who has a fault—and we all have them—who would not be grateful if the members of our family who know our faults, instead of blaming us or trying to reform us, would silently, secretly, and sacredly know this truth, "This is an impersonal belief in two powers, just an impersonal claim of a power apart from God. There is no mind but that mind which is the instrument of God; therefore, carnal mind is not enmity against God. It is nothing. Carnal mind is a belief in two powers, a universal belief. It is not my belief. It has no person in whom, on whom, or through whom to operate."

Practice, practice, practice, until you can look at the saint or the sinner and know that the saint never could be a saint any more than the sinner could be a sinner. Do not make the mistake of saying that there is no evil, but that all is good. Good and evil are just two ends of the same stick. "Why callest thou me good?"[4] Do not call anyone good. Do not forget that there are no saints. God alone is good.

When a person is showing forth any measure of goodness, be assured that it is only God expressing through him. The part for which a person deserves credit is that he is willing to be a transparency, and thereby he plays his role in this work. No individual can be good: God alone is good, but that goodness must find expression as individual being. once you perceive that, you will find it very easy never to judge, criticize, or condemn an individual because you will know that whatever evil is present is nothing more nor less than a universal belief in good and evil. If that individual does not know enough to annihilate that belief, you can help to do it for him, more especially if he is reaching out for help.

The Significance of Ananias and Sapphira

Any person who lives and moves and has his being in the realization of God's presence as Omnipotence is living in one power, and there is no secondary power that can touch him. Whether that power is in the form of a mental projection, a germ, a hereditary condition, infection or contagion, age, or what not, rest assured that no individual who is living in the life of Oneness—one power, one law, one being, one cause—can be the victim of malpractice.

Many persons misunderstand the meaning of the term "malpractice." They believe that if someone hates, dislikes, or mistrusts them or if a person is directing evil thoughts toward them, his hatred, dislike, mistrust, or evil thought acts as a form of malpractice, and may have a harmful effect upon them. Un-

[4]Matthew 19:17.

doubtedly, this does operate wherever there is a belief in two powers, but be assured that the only power it has is the power they give it. To the person who knows that there is no one to malpractice or be malpracticed, and who thereby impersonalizes it, any evil that comes knocking at his door will not touch him: it will only backfire to the one who sent it.

That is really the significance of the story of Ananias and Sapphira. After the Crucifixion, the disciples were so persecuted that they were forced to go underground. They were unable to earn a livelihood, so they banded together and agreed to put into one fund all that they owned, thereby helping to support one another out of this common fund until the period of persecution passed. This they all did and gave the fund over to the care of Peter for safekeeping. Sapphira and her husband, however, decided to hold out a little of what they had, a deception which Peter was quick to discern. When he rebuked them, "Thou hast not lied unto men, but unto God,"[5] what he really was saying was that there is no man, but only God-Selfhood, and that their act of deception was unto God, the consequences of which were so great that both Sapphira and her husband dropped dead.

The very moment they consciously wronged God, the evil whanged back on them and destroyed them. God did not cause this; God did not do this: the evil that they committed against that little band of disciples hit up against the Selfhood of God which is invisible and incorporeal. There was nothing there and nobody to receive it, so it had to boomerang right back to the senders. Thus it is that the evil that is directed against man is really being directed against God. But when there is nothing in man but the Christ-Spirit, there is nothing for evil to strike at, and it boomerangs and destroys the sender.

In thinking of the episode of Sapphira and her husband, it is important to remember that it was not really Sapphira and her husband who held out their savings from God. It was the carnal mind. So, too, with us: it is not we who are evil. It is the carnal

[5]Acts 5:4.

mind operating through us, and inasmuch as this carnal mind is not a person and has no person in whom, through whom, or upon whom to operate, it becomes a nothingness. When we impersonalize it and begin to understand that no person has done any evil unto us because there is no "us" separate from God—we have no Selfhood but the capital "S" Selfhood—and therefore no one has wronged or injured us, no one has aimed any evil at us, but at God, we will find that we have so impersonalized our own self and all others that any human error that is directed toward us will not strike us.

Then if we remember, also, that those who aim evil in our direction are not really aiming it at all, but that they are merely instruments through which the carnal mind is operating, we shall more than likely release them from their sin and bring about their forgiveness. In other words, if we impersonalize evil and recognize that it has not been done unto us, it may turn around and strike back at the sender. If it did, it would probably be his fault in the sense of permitting himself to be used.

We want to go higher, however, than being avenged or wreaking vengeance upon someone: we want to see those who do evil to us forgiven and released from whatever evil is holding them in its grasp.

If there is any ingratitude directed toward us, or any lack of mercy or justice, we realize first of all our capital "S" Self and then realize that, because of that, this is not aimed at us at all: it is aimed at God. Furthermore, by realizing that it is never a person who is aiming evil in our direction, but that he is merely the innocent victim of the carnal mind, a victim of ignorance, we can truthfully repeat, "Father, forgive him, for he knows not what he does." and then we can realize that this carnal mind is a nothingness. Thus we nullify it, and we shall then discover how quickly we come into our freedom. There is a joyous freedom when we are living in a world where no one has anything against us, and if there does seem to be anyone, we have now recognized that it is not person, but an impersonal source which is really not power.

This act of impersonalization is a conscious one. Eventually, it will make clear to us why we could sit around from now until doomsday praying to God for something, and it will not come. We could pray for justice or cooperation or gratitude from now to the end of time and not get it. In other words, good can come into our experience only through an act of our own consciousness. There is no God outside our being to see that we get mercy, justice, or kindness.

The Universality of the Divine Selfhood

In our meditations, let us impersonalize the evils of this world and begin to know that we are not the source of evil to anyone because God constitutes the selfhood of our being. Moreover, no person is the avenue or channel of evil toward us, for God constitutes his selfhood, and any evil apparent in our world is a product of the universal carnal mind which, in and of itself, is nothing until we accept a person as an outlet for its activity. The responsibility is ours The Master said, "Ye shall know the truth, and the truth shall make you free,"[6] but he did not say that the truth would make us free without our *knowing* the truth.

As we sow, so shall we reap. All harmony and success in life are up to the individual, and to sow to the Spirit means to impersonalize to the extent that we realize God as the true identity, not only of every human being, but of every animal and every plant.

God is the life of all of us, and that Life does not begin or end with a human being. The life of God is infinite; the life of God is the life of you and of me, of animals, vegetables, and minerals. Even the rocks and the stones are living things; they are not inanimate as they appear to be, but they live and breathe, and God is the life and breath of their being.

[6]John 8:32.

This, too, is impersonalizing. It is making God the divine Self, the Self of you and the Self of me and the Self of all living things in the universe. For most of us, it will be necessary to meditate on this day in and day out until its truth begins to unfold from within ourselves, until we gain the conviction of it and something wells up within us and says, "This really is true. This is the truth of being. God does constitute my Selfhood, and therefore my Selfhood is not subject to hate, envy, jealousy, or wrong thinking. My Selfhood is intact in God. My Selfhood is divine, immortal being."

As you meditate upon this, it will not be too long before you will begin to see fruitage appear. Remember, the promise is that you are to bear fruit richly because of your identification with God, your Father within you.

Once this has been established in you, you now have to begin secretly, silently, and very sacredly to look around at the members of your household and at your friends and begin to change your concepts of them so that you realize that all this that you have been declaring of yourself is likewise true of them. They, too, are one with this divine Selfhood. The fact that at the moment they do not know it is not your concern. You are not dealing with their demonstration but with your own, and you will not have any kind of demonstration unless you begin to perceive that this truth that you have declared and realized about yourself must be a universal truth.

All Malpractice Is Self-Malpractice

Regardless of any person's lack of demonstration, regardless of his unwillingness even to want to learn about his true identity, you are secretly and silently knowing the truth. You are knowing the true identity of your employers, employees, your customers or clients, and the officials of the government. It makes no difference what these persons may seem to be or may seem to be doing. You are now realizing their oneness with their Source. This is not for the purpose of giving them a treatment, but just to save yourself from being a malpractitioner because unless you are seeing people as they really are, you are malpracticing them, and your malpractice eventually comes home to roost. Your malpractice of other persons never harms them, and their malpractice of you never harms you.

Any malpractice acts as a boomerang: it goes out from us and eventually hits nothing because it is aimed only at our *concept* of a person—not at the person—and therefore it turns around and returns and cuts our heads off. It never strikes those at whom it is aimed. It always turns around and reacts upon the sender.

Not all malpractice is malicious; not all malpractice is intended to harm someone; but unless you are seeing everybody, even your enemies—and this is the meaning of praying for your enemies— as one with God, unless you are seeing that Self with a capital "S" as the true identity of everyone, you are malpracticing. Unless you can do this, you are setting up a special hierarchy consisting of your friends and you, all of whom are perfect in your eyes, and all the rest of the people in the world are not. This is not true.

The truth is that we are all one in Christ Jesus; we are all the offspring of God. None of us has a human father. There is but one Father in this universe, and that is God. All of us are offspring of that one creative Principle, and we are malpracticing when we do not live this truth. To recognize the truth of oneness is to impersonalize our sense of self as applied to yourself and myself and as applied to all the people of this world, including our enemies.

What happens when you have sufficiently meditated on this truth so that you do not recognize any selfhood apart from God? Could you possibly suffer loss or destruction from another? Could you ever be the victim of injustice, inequality, or any evil if there is no selfhood other than God?

This principle of oneness can be applied in cases at law where individuals are seeking justice. Unless the person involved in litigation is seeing God as his Selfhood and as the Selfhood of judge, jury, and attorneys, how can he possibly expect justice? Can justice, equity, or mercy come from "man, whose breath is in his nostrils"?[7] Anyone who looks for it in that quarter is likely to be very much disappointed. In all our relationships in life, unless we are looking to the divine Self of all being for our good, we are looking amiss and we may not find it.

Meditation on this subject will eventually bring a person the conscious awareness that God constitutes the Selfhood of every individual. So, whether he is seeking justice in court, from his employer, or from a labor union, he must be sure that he is expecting that justice from the divine Selfhood of individual being and that he is recognizing God as that Selfhood. When he does that, he will have impersonalized the good he hopes for and the evil he fears.

Whenever we have a grievance against anyone, we are faced with the belief of injustice from that person or a lack of mercy or cooperation; and in accepting that, we are pinning the evil on him. Our solution to this problem consists of our ability to impersonalize, and that means that regardless of who it may be that we think is ungrateful, unjust, immoral, or neglectful of us, this must be reversed instantly in the realization that to identify error with a person is to be guilty of malpractice, because it is seeing God's child as a sinner, as ungrateful, unlawful, unmerciful, instead of realizing God as the Selfhood of individual being, and thereby impersonalizing any erroneous appearance.

Eventually we include the entire world in our realization of God as individual being. We do not pin error on to any individual—not even ourselves. We do not claim that our jealousy, envy, greed, or lust is responsible for our ills because we do not have any such qualities. If temporarily those qualities may be expressing themselves through us, they must be recognized as having their source in the impersonal carnal mind, and as long as they are out there, they are nothingness. This principle of impersonalization is one of the most important in our work, and

[7]Isaiah 2:22.

we must make every effort to embody it in our consciousness because we will not find it expressed in our experience until we make it our own.

Watch what this secret of impersonalization does for you; watch what it does in the experience of those around you; and you will understand why the Master could say, "Love thy neighbor as thyself."[8]

ACROSS THE DESK

Please use the following as a meditation so frequently that never again will you forget it:

> *Regardless of what I think or believe, this does not change That which is. Regardless of what I may have faith in, this faith carries no power since the power is That which is, whether or not I have faith in It. There is really no power in my beliefs or my faith, since power exists whether or not I believe or have faith.*

To know that there is sky, earth, and sea requires no belief or faith. To know that apples come from apple trees or peaches from peach trees requires neither belief nor faith. To know that fish are in the sea, birds in the air, and that rain is wet requires neither belief nor faith.

Suppose that we do not believe these things or have faith in them, does that change anything? Does our lack of belief or lack of faith prevent the operation of nature's laws? So, no more does our lack of belief or lack of faith prevent the operation of God's laws. To know that God is, is spiritual attainment. Not to know does not change the Is-ness of God.

Since God does not function in the human scene, no belief or faith in God will make It function there. For this reason, millions are praying to God, believing in God, and having faith in God, and receiving no answers to their prayers. God is not in the human scene. To bring God into our life and activity, it is

[8]Matthew 19:19.

necessary to *experience* God, and the knowing of the truth, becoming actually conscious of truth, and meditation—these help us to attain the experience of God.

Let us assume that we are faced with human problems that seem insurmountable. *There is a way out!* Relax. Rest. Let *My* Spirit be upon you. Let *My* peace be established within you. Let *My* grace take over the situation. There is an invisible Presence within you which will go before you as you withdraw thought and emotion and let the inner Invisible live and work through you.

When there are no problems, set aside time for daily meditations so that the weapons of the world do not prosper. Clothe yourself in *My* invisible robe. Let *My* light flow through you to human consciousness everywhere: friend and foe, near and far. Live *consciously* in *My* presence through *My* grace, and you will always experience *My* peace.

IS THE INFINITE WAY TRUTH?

It is inevitable that occasions will arise which may cause you to question whether The Infinite Way is really truth. Many questioned the truth of Christianity even while the Master walked among them. Did not the disciples fall away at times? Lao-tze became so discouraged by the lack of recognition and acceptance that he just walked away from it all and disappeared.

This is to assure you that The Infinite Way *is* truth, but students—even practitioners or teachers—may at times fail. It is not the teaching that is power, but the measure of the student's *attainment* of the consciousness of Infinite Way truth. Only in proportion to our *attained* consciousness of truth are we the light that dispels the appearance of darkness. The principles of The Infinite Way will develop that consciousness in proportion to our study and meditation.

The Infinite Way is truth, and it cannot fail. our devotion to the study and practice of its principles will enable us to attain the consciousness of truth, which reveals divine harmony where material evil or good appeared.

The object of The Infinite Way is not overcoming or destroying or rising above evil, but rather attaining that mind that was in Christ Jesus, or the Buddha-mind, which reveals the spiritual man and universe where evil or good humanhood has claimed existence.

Let us for a while forget about "doing good" or "saving the world" or "helping our fellow man" and give our entire attention to our own spiritual enlightenment until we are sought out. Be assured that as we attain a measure of realized Christhood the world will beat a pathway to us. Actually, we can benefit others only in proportion as we attain some measure of spiritual realization.

The multitudes came to the Master—he did not have to seek them. The multitudes still seek the Master. Be That, even in a degree, and the multitudes will seek you for the Light.

From

BEYOND WORDS
AND THOUGHTS

Building a Consciousness of Grace

---•---

It is not possible to reach God or to embrace truth through the human mind, although it is possible for truth to impart itself to us. It is unlikely, however, that the fullness of truth will be revealed to any one of us because, as human beings, we do not have the capacity to receive truth in its fullness. Instead, we receive certain facets, realizations, and principles of truth, which are continually flowing in proportion to our receptivity and openness.

Nothing that can be known with the mind is absolute truth; and therefore, we cannot depend on any statement of truth we know. In any and every experience, we must open our consciousness and be receptive to whatever may be imparted to us.

For this reason, we can never live on yesterday's manna, nor depend on anything we knew yesterday. In other words, if we are in meditation, we are not in meditation for the purpose of remembering something we have read in books: we are in meditation for the purpose of receiving an impartation from the Father within. That impartation may come to us in the form of a passage we have heretofore known in Scripture or in spiritual writings; but when it comes in the silence of meditation, it comes to us as an impartation from the Spirit, not as an activity of memory.

A KNOWLEDGE OF TRUTH DEVELOPS CONSCIOUSNESS

The activity of the human mind is not power in the sense of spiritual power, and not all the knowledge that can be embraced in the human mind—even all the knowledge of truth—is spiritual power. Knowledge of truth acts to remove from us our ignorance of the nature of Spirit and Its activities and operations.

An example of this is that when we first come to the study of truth we believe that if we can just reach God, we are going to have the power that will destroy all earthly errors; but, as our understanding of the principles grows, this ignorance is chipped away, and we stop looking to God with the expectation that He will remove the evils of "this world." [1] Similarly, as we learn through reading, listening, and study that there is but one power, we stop trying to use that one power to do something to another power called evil, sin, disease, or death. With this knowledge of truth, we are given the Grace to cease the mental activity involved in attempting to get God to overcome our enemies, and we are thereby enabled to relax inwardly and await the realization of Grace, which is the non-power.

These principles of truth that we learn through study and practice develop our consciousness to the place where we "resist not evil," [2] where we can put up the "sword," [3] where we can retire within ourselves in an inner peace, and in that descent of peace become aware of Grace. That Grace is not a power: It is a presence, and in the presence of Grace there is no need for any power because nothing of an erroneous nature is there.

The Scriptural statement, "In thy presence is fulness of joy," [4] is a clear promise that in God's presence there is no sin, disease, death, lack, or limitation because otherwise there could be no fullness of joy. So, in "thy presence," evil of any name or nature cannot function, for it has no existence. The study in which we engage leads us to a place in consciousness where

[1] John 18:36.
[2] Matthew 5:39.
[3] Matthew 26:52.
[4] Psalm 16:11.

we can relax, rest in a state of receptivity, and then eventually hear or feel something that would indicate, "Fear not, it is *I*.[5] 'It is I; be not afraid.' [6] Nothing shall in any wise come nigh thy dwelling place."

This must inevitably bring us to a place of resting from taking thought, realizing, "I cannot use Truth, but if I relax, Truth can use me, and It can function in my life. 'I live; yet not I, but Christ liveth in me.' [7]" But, if Christ is living our life, if Christ is functioning through us and as us, we are not taking thought or doing, and it is as if we were standing to one side, being a beholder of Christ, Truth, living our life.

As you are reading this, at the same time, be relaxing: let go of any and every thought. Release the belief that there is anything that you can do about anything. Relax; be still. Be still and *let* God be God. Recognize that you could not possibly embrace God in your mind. Let your remembrance be: "Christ liveth my life. God functions as my being." Let the whole earth be still, and above all let your mind be still.

As you relax in this surrender, letting the mind that was in Christ Jesus be your mind, Grace will begin to function. Grace will function as wisdom; Grace will function as harmony and peace; Grace will function as health, wholeness, completeness, inspiration, and as the source of all knowledge, and It will flow through you, in you, and as you.

Those who have been working with Infinite Way principles are now approaching the state and stage of consciousness that lives by Grace—not by physical might, not by mental power, not by knowledge, but by Grace. The knowledge of truth always serves a function in your experience in that such knowledge helps you to settle back into an attitude of expectancy. That is the only purpose that a knowledge of truth is serving at this stage of your unfoldment because now you should be rising

[5] The word "*I*," italicized, refers to God.
[6] Mark 6:50.
[7] Galatians 2:20.

above the letter of truth into the Spirit, into that area of consciousness where you live without words and without thoughts, above the law.

There are physical laws that operate on the physical plane and mental laws that operate on the mental plane, and in your humanhood you live by these laws. In your spiritual attainment, however, at first you live less by physical laws and more by mental laws, and then eventually less and less by mental laws and more and more through Grace without any physical or mental laws operating because Grace transcends all law.

For example, the law of self-preservation keeps birds as far away from human beings as possible, and it is not often that you find birds making friends of human beings. Yet, there is the example of St. Francis, who proved that even this law can be transcended and that it is possible to live in such an atmosphere of Grace that birds will come to you and rest on your shoulders, your head, or on your hands.

Certainly, for the most part, human beings want to stay as far away from wild beasts as they can, yet there have been states of Grace where wild beasts could be faced without fear. Daniel demonstrated this, and many today have been able to prove that wild beasts do not always act like wild beasts. This would be true, however, only where an individual is living above the law and is under Grace, that Grace which is the absence of any power.

Once you realize that you cannot use spiritual power and you no longer rely on physical or mental powers, you then reach that attitude and altitude of consciousness which is a state of Grace, a state of nonpower, and you discover that what heretofore has operated as power is no longer power in your individual experience. That it will probably be a long time before the Grace-consciousness is demonstrated in its fullest degree is evidenced by the fact that after the Master's resurrection he was still full of nail wounds and knife wounds. To that degree, he was still under physical law.

The point is not whether you can, at this moment, walk on the water; the point is not whether you can deliberately swallow a bottle of poison and survive. That is not the point. The point is that from the moment you begin to function under Grace, physical and mental laws have less and less power over you. When you function under Grace, you may be called to those who have swallowed poison or to those who have been seriously injured, and by your realization of nonpower, you can bring them through it and lift them above whatever law they may have come under.

You must remember that to some extent, almost from the beginning of your experience in The Infinite Way, you have been under Grace. Every healing that you have witnessed has been a proof of Grace because the law involved has been overcome. If you have had a spiritual healing of a cold, the flu, pneumonia, or any of the diseases that are presumably caused by germs, it was Grace that proved that the material law was of noneffect. The law of germs, infection, or contagion could not operate where the consciousness of Grace is.

So it is that any healing—physical, mental, moral, or financial—is a proof that material law cannot function in the presence of spiritual consciousness. It is not that your developed consciousness of truth is a power over the law: it is a proof that the law is not a power in the presence of your consciousness of Grace.

THE REBORN CONSCIOUSNESS

What constitutes your consciousness of Grace and how is it developed? It can be attained only by working consciously and conscientiously with the principles of one power, reading about it on every page of The Infinite Way books, and hearing about it on every Infinite Way tape recording. Through that, gradually your consciousness comes to accept the truth that there is but one power, and it is spiritual; there is but one law, and it is spiritual law. As your consciousness accepts this truth, material or mental law hits up against that developed consciousness, and like darkness, it is not there any more. That is how spiritual consciousness operates.

At first, spiritual consciousness is formed by an intellectual awareness of these principles. You come to accept God as your consciousness, as the only power. Over and over again The Infinite Way books hammer away at the theme that God is individual consciousness, your consciousness and mine. If God is your consciousness, what chance would anything have of operating for evil in that consciousness? Nothing shall "enter . . . that defileth . . . or maketh a lie." [8] Enter what? Enter God-consciousness, enter your consciousness because your consciousness is God-consciousness.

As you work with the Writings and are filled with the principle that God constitutes your consciousness and that your consciousness is the one and only power, you are building a consciousness of Grace. There is no power external to you. All power functions from within you, and it is only of a spiritual nature; therefore, it does not govern anyone, control anyone, or dominate anyone, but is a spiritual law of freedom unto everyone.

Then, lo and behold, when something claiming to be a law comes to your attention—something of your own, of your family, your patient, or your student—and it touches your consciousness, which is no longer your consciousness, but God-consciousness functioning as your consciousness, the one and the only power, and therefore the light of the world, what happens? Exactly what happens to darkness when the light shines. It disappears! You have not used a power; you have not even used the power of Truth: *you have been the power of Truth.* You have not used It: if anything, It has used you.

As you continue to abide in the principles that have been

given to you in this Message, every principle that becomes a part of your consciousness constitutes the reborn consciousness, and the "old man," [9] or the old consciousness that believed in or feared two powers, that used one power over another power, is "dying." The old consciousness is being educated out of itself. As this "old man" with his belief in two powers and his subservience to the law "dies," this new consciousness is born, and eventually you rise above the law into a consciousness of Grace in which you are not thinking in terms of overcoming or of power. You are not thinking in terms of words or thoughts: you are living; you are being; and you are letting the divine Consciousness flow through you, animate, and live your life for you.

THE GRACE-CONSCIOUSNESS LIVES AS A BEHOLDER

As a way station to this consciousness, you have had the Ten Commandments to tell you what to do and what not to do, and up to a certain extent you must have succeeded in attaining at least a goodly measure of obedience to them. Then, with the Sermon on the Mount, you went a step further. But in all of this, you were still living your life: you were trying to love your neighbor as yourself; you were trying to be philanthropic; you were trying to forgive your enemies; you were trying to improve yourself. All this is commendable and highly desirable, but it is not the ultimate goal of spiritual living.

When the new consciousness is attained, you have risen above trying to do or to be something of yourself: you are living by Grace, and it is the grace of God that functions through you as benevolence, purity, kindliness, and integrity, and you are now enabled to say with the Master: " 'Why callest thou me good?' [10] Why callest thou me spiritual?"

It is a state of Grace that is functioning in your life. You

[9] Ephesians 4:22.
[10] Matthew 19:17.

have no power to be either good or bad; you have no power to be spiritual or unspiritual; you have no power to be charitable or uncharitable. Whatever it is that is functioning through you, that is what you must be, and it is not your little self being it.

Your personal sense of "I" has moved over to where it is now only a beholder of life. It is always beholding and marveling at what things the Father is doing, but it is not participating —just beholding, beholding, and beholding.

It beholds sometimes with sadness. Can you not hear the pathos and the sorrow of the Master, "O Jerusalem, . . . how often would I have gathered thy children together, even as a hen gathereth her chickens under her wings, and ye would not!" [11] And with that same poignancy, the beholder sees this world and mournfully cries out, "Oh, it would be so easy to have world peace; it would be so easy with all of God's wealth that is in this world to have abundance for everybody, but 'ye would not.' " So he stands by, praying that consciousness be opened to receive Grace, to rise above this law of power.

NO POWER IS NECESSARY
IN A STATE OF GRACE

It is that word "power" that is a stumbling block. Man is always seeking a power, a power to overcome something or destroy something; and therefore he is not living in the awareness of God, because in the realization of the presence of God there is no power needed to overcome, to destroy, or to do anything.

Some people act as if God-power were necessary to increase the supply of this world. The supply of this world—and I am speaking of material supply—is already infinite. There is already more of whatever is necessary for food, clothing, and housing than the entire world could consume, and these forms of good are being renewed faster than they are being used. There is no need to turn to God for greater supply: there is

[11] Matthew 23:37.

need only for us to be willing to share the supply we already have.

The world prays to God for peace. God has no peace to give! God is not withholding peace. God's peace is already established, but peace must be established in the consciousness of the individual. If you and I are not at peace with each other, God can do nothing about it: it lies within you and me to decide what it is that will establish peace.

Peace is a state of Grace, and it functions in that moment when you are demanding nothing of another, when you are realizing that God's grace is your sufficiency in all things and that there is a sufficiency of God's grace omnipresent to meet the need of this and of every moment. In that realization, you free every person, and he can feel that you have freed him. He is at peace with you because the only reason for a lack of peace is fear, the fear of what the other person may want of you. Individually and collectively, nationally and internationally, that is the one fear, and the only antidote is the realization:

> *I have a hidden manna. I have a hidden source of supply that*
> *is not dependent on "man, whose breath is in his nostrils."* [12] *It*
> *is not dependent on anyone's good will.*[13]

NEW LIGHT ON FORGIVENESS

People are at war within their own families—not over money particularly or over land, but because there is nearly always something that one is demanding of another that is causing a breach. The healing can take place only in release, and you can

---

[12] Isaiah 2:22.
[13] The italicized portions of this book are spontaneous meditations which have come to the author during periods of uplifted consciousness and are not in any sense intended to be used as affirmations, denials, or formulas. They have been inserted in this book from time to time to serve as examples of the free flowing of the Spirit. As the reader practices the Presence, he, too, in his exalted moments, will receive ever new and fresh inspiration as the outpouring of the Spirit.

release every person only when that state of Grace has come to you and you realize that you no longer need power. Your oneness with God is your assurance of Omniscience, Omnipotence, and Omnipresence, and because of that you can release anybody and everybody.

This might be called forgiving, but it is a far better way of dealing with the whole subject of forgiveness than the traditional approach. To forgive is difficult because forgiveness has always implied the forgiving of an actual wrong done, which in some way one is supposed to forget. This is rather difficult to do. It is far easier to forgive if you can see that the reason that you think a wrong has been done to you is because you were expecting something from someone, and you had no right to expect anything from anybody. So in the beginning it was your fault; you brought it on yourself. You expected something of someone; therefore, that person did to you what you are having a hard time forgiving. If you had not expected anything of him, however, you would have nothing now to forgive, and you and he would be at peace.

GRACE BRINGS FREEDOM FROM KARMIC LAW

So it is that under the law of self-preservation you can see how we injure one another, all because we are trying to protect ourselves, or to save ourselves at somebody else's expense. Also, you can see how we have been taught to consider certain things as law which were not law at all, and we then have come under the belief of that law. For example, the Hebrews once taught that the sins of the fathers would be visited on the children unto the third and fourth generations, yet later this law was rescinded by the Hebrews themselves.

The truth is that you are under the penalty of your own thoughts and deeds, and under no other penalty. No longer can the thoughts and deeds of another operate against you. Now you are released from the sins of your parents and your grandparents. Now you turn within and realize what Paul said, "For he that soweth to his flesh shall of the flesh reap corruption; but he that soweth to the Spirit shall of the Spirit reap life everlasting." [14] So it is *your* sowing that determines your life. You are not under the law of domination; you are not under the law of anyone else's mental powers, sins, or fears. You have the choice to live either under the law or under Grace.

Man is a prisoner of mind-created laws which sooner or later will be revealed as not being law at all. This may take centuries, but today we are becoming aware of the fact that material and mental laws are law only while they are accepted in mind as law, whether it is the law of heredity, the law of racial belief, or the law of karma.

If the law of as-ye-sow-so-shall-ye-reap, the karmic law, is valid, think what penalty the United States has stored up for itself because of its dropping of atomic bombs. Try to think what degree of karmic law it has brought itself under, and if you are the kind of American who approves of this type of wholesale slaughter, you also are under that law. But that is law only to those who accept it as law, to those who accept the fanatical patriotism of "our country, right or wrong." [15] Actually, karmic law of any kind does not operate except for those who are prisoners of the mind and who, therefore, accept that law.

If you are abiding in Grace, there is no law. The law is the law to those who are still prisoners of the mind and live by it, but the law is not law to those who are abiding above the letter of truth, without words and without thoughts, above the law, abiding morning to night, night to morning in the realization:

> *"I and my Father are one."* [16] *What can touch that oneness? Is there a law of matter or of mind that can touch God? If I and the Father are one, then I am that One, and that is the One who is not man, not a human being, but spiritual being.*

[14] Galatians 6:8.
[15] Stephen Decatur.

I am not man; I do not have to be forgiven. I and the Father are one, and that One is Spirit. That One is life eternal, the spiritual Self which I am.

You will not become that Christ-Self by reading books. The reading of the books will tell you of your *I Am-ness,* but then you must turn from the books to meditation and attain the realization of *I AM.* Your study of the letter of truth is primarily to lead you back into the kingdom of God within yourself where you tabernacle with your inner Self and receive therefrom the assurance, "Be not afraid, it is *I.* Thou art *I*; *I* am thou."

Then you are under Grace—not under the law, but under Grace—and there is no law touching the Grace that you are under that does not dissolve. You thereby arrive at a place above words and thoughts, above using any truth, to an abiding in stillness, in quietness, in peace, and if there are any words or thoughts to come, let them come from the divine Grace, from the Father within, from the Source.

When the Master said, "I have overcome the world," [17] did he not really mean that the law could not function? Did he not mean that he was living in a state of Grace where there are no laws? The law can operate only in the minds of those who are accepting law. "Know ye not, that to whom ye yield yourselves servants to obey, his servants ye are to whom ye obey?" [18] Will you yield yourself to the law or to Grace? Will you serve God or mammon? The question is whether you are letting the world of effect be the law unto you or whether you are living by Grace. Is money going to be your God? Is the law of health going to be your God? Is anything in the realm of effect going to be power? Or are you realizing that there are no powers?

[16] John 10:30.
[17] John 16:33.
[18] Romans 6:16.

PRISONERS OF THE MIND

Through this, eventually you will be able to look down into the universal mind, which is the mind of mankind, and you will see how enslaved it is and how that entire slavery is within itself. For instance, one man may have to pass through a barroom, and he almost has to run through it, he is in such fear of those bottles there and of what is in them, a fear that he may pick one up and drink from it. Any power the bottle might have is in his mind: it is not in the bottle, because you and I can walk right through that same room, and we do not even see the bottles that are there because they are not in our minds as a power. You can observe what it is in this person's mind or that person's mind that is making him a prisoner of the mind, holding him in fear and in bondage to something that has only the substance of a mental image.

With another person, it may be gambling. He cannot rest while he has a dollar in his pocket. He must gamble it away! Why? The attraction is not out there at the gaming table, because it does not attract most of the people in the world: it attracts only the few who are prisoners of that particular form of bondage. Or it may be the person who gambles on the stock market on Wall Street. He is just as much a victim of gambling as the one at the ten-cent dice table, and if you could look into his mind, you would see what is animating him and pushing him. He is not aware of it: he is a victim of it.

You learn never to condemn, never, because the person who is afflicted with the two-dollar race track or the hundred-thousand-dollar Wall Street betting mania, the one with the alcohol or drug habit, or the sex problem is a victim. He is not a sinner: he is a victim; and he is a prisoner of his own mind. You can free him only when he is ready to be freed, when he appeals for help, when he asks for it; and you can free him only by being free yourself, recognizing Grace and not law. Then, you sit in a complete silence, without any thoughts.

RESTORING THE MIND TO ITS PROPER FUNCTION

Always remember in your treatment work not to be concerned if thoughts do not come. Do not be concerned if no truth comes to you. You are not the actor; you are not the healer; the concern is not yours. You are relaxing yourself into Grace, and Grace is going to do the work: you are merely going to be the instrument of Grace. Therefore, whether the problem is physical, mental, moral, financial, or one of human relationships, do not struggle to know any truth, do not strive to give advice. Be still! *I* within you am God, so just be still and let *I* be God, and relax in the Grace that realizes law is not power. The law of the mind is not power; the law of beliefs is not power. *Grace reveals nonpower!* The presence of Grace reveals the non-presence of power, of law.

So, as long as you can abide in an inner stillness, do not be concerned whether you have words or thoughts because it might well be that you have gone beyond that place of needing words and thoughts. Words and thoughts are part of the activity of the mind, and what we are trying to do is to rise above the activity of the mind into Grace.

In quietness and in stillness is the presence of Grace. In God's presence of stillness, quietness, and peace is fulfillment, divine harmony. You are at the place now of not overcoming, not destroying, not removing. All of us in The Infinite Way should move out of the state of mind that is overcoming, rising above, and destroying, into the realization of Grace which is the light that reveals no darkness. It does not remove it, it does not send it any place: it reveals its nonpresence.

Do not try to do something to or for those who come to you with sin, disease, and lack. Be that state of Grace which reveals their nonpresence! Where they went, or how, or when, you have no idea, and do not try because you will be trying to use your mind again.

Do not think for a minute that this will destroy your mind, because your mind will always have its function as an avenue of awareness. All that you are doing is stopping the false activity of making a power out of your mind, which it was never meant to be in the beginning. "Take no thought for your life, what ye shall eat, or what ye shall drink; nor yet for your body, what ye shall put on.[19] . . . The Son of man cometh at an hour when ye think not." [20] You are not to destroy your mind; you are not to give it up; you are not to surrender it: you are to allow it to settle into its normal function as an avenue of awareness.

Truth is infinite. How terrible it would be to try to grasp Truth! If the thought came to you, or if someone asked you, "What is Truth?" and if you could smile at the idea that anybody could know what Truth is and, like the Master, turn on your heel and walk away, think how much you would be proving. Who can know what Truth is? "I am . . . the truth." [21] Try to define what or who *I AM*. Impossible!

So, the closer you get to that place where your mind is not busy seeking for some truth, the sooner you will see that Truth keeps pouring Itself through you from the Source—not a made-up truth, not a formula—Truth, not a truth that somebody wrote. But it is the truth that you know that helps build your consciousness to the point where you receive Truth Itself, and then the Grace which is your sufficiency is flowing in full measure.

[19] Matthew 6:25.
[20] Luke 12:40.
[21] John 14:6.

Rising to Mystical Consciousness
in Prayer and Treatment

In the spiritual life, you must never forget that you are not living your own life and that you have no right whatsoever to consider what you would like to do, when you would like to do it, or how. Always in the back of your mind is the reminder that it is God's life that is being lived, and it is your privilege to be at that state of consciousness where you can watch God live your life without interposing a wish, a will, or a desire of your own.

The average truth student is not at the stage of development where he can do this because he has duties to his family or his business, and until such time as the Spirit Itself says, "Leave all for *Me*," [1] or "Leave your nets," no student should ever forget his responsibility to his family, his associates, and to his work. Rather should his study and his meditations become the foundation for the more harmonious functioning of these facets of his life.

It is only to the few that the call to leave their "nets" eventually comes, and when it does come, it is unmistakable, and it compels obedience. After that, the nature of one's life changes. This change does not permit the neglect or desertion of one's business or family obligations, but it does make it possible to provide for their independent care so that one may be set free for whatever demands the call may make. Let no Infinite Way student believe, however, that the call to leave his "nets" is an excuse to desert or neglect his human duties or obligations.

[1] The word "Me," capitalized, refers to God.

Those who enter the spiritual ministry because of a human desire to do good, or before they have heard the spiritual call, make little or no progress. This is because they have not yet learned to rest on the Infinite Invisible. They do not have the spiritual vision that makes it possible for them to know the Unknowable.

The message of The Infinite Way did not come through the human mind, nor can it be imparted by or to the human mind. To the human mind, this message is as nonsensical as was the Master's command to his disciples to go "without purse, and scrip." [2] A human being would have to know how he could afford to get to his destination, but not so with the spiritual disciple. The spiritual disciple would not stop to question how, when, or where: he would just start traveling. This he could do, however, only if this call came as a true spiritual impulse and out of a developed spiritual consciousness.

THE LIVING OF THE SPIRITUAL LIFE IS WHAT ATTRACTS

Through the message of The Infinite Way, it is revealed that God is individual consciousness, our own consciousness, not our human awareness, but a deeper level of awareness than the human. Because this consciousness is spiritual, we can go within —meditate, commune, seek the kingdom of God that is within us, seek spiritual wisdom—and then all the "things" [3] of the world, including whatever is required to perform any spiritual activity given to us or even such things as what to eat, what to drink, and wherewithal to be clothed, will be added to us.

I dare not teach anything as transcendental as that, and I dare not write a book about it until the realization of it is so strong in me that I can turn within, in silence and in secrecy, seeking only the spiritual grace of God, desiring to know only the things of God and letting the Spirit of God bear witness with my spirit in silence. Then I discover that I have better

[2] Luke 22:35.
[3] Luke 12:31.

health, greater happiness, or a sufficiency of supply. When that happens, someone or other is bound to say to me, "Will you teach me?" or "Will you reveal to me what you have discovered?" and eventually a book is written, classes come forth, and then more books. But first of all there has to be the discovery and the demonstration of a principle.

The point is that if I wish to impart anything to anyone that I expect him to believe and to follow, I must have attained some measure of success in the living of it, so that a person who reads and studies my writings has a feeling of rightness about them and a desire to follow this teaching.

If you attain some measure of demonstrable good in your own experience, it is inevitable that sooner or later those associated with you will want to go and do likewise. Eventually, others will learn about it and will want you to share with them what you have discovered that is proving to be good in your life. But it must be understood that you have nothing to impart until you have attained such a consciousness of it that you yourself are showing it forth.

Unlike other religious teachings, the message of The Infinite Way is imparted only through the fourth-dimensional consciousness, or a measure of attained Christ-consciousness. Therefore, the teacher must lift students up to the point where they are able to perceive spiritually because, as human beings, students do not have that capacity. One Infinite Way teacher, lifted to that fourth-dimensional consciousness and thus spiritually endowed, can handle, not only a tremendous ministry, but one which grows until it seems to be almost beyond handling.

GOD'S HOLY TEMPLES REVEALED IN MEDITATION

The principle is that God is Spirit, and that Spirit is your Spirit. God is infinite consciousness and constitutes your consciousness; therefore, your consciousness is infinite. Knowing this, you must, in a sense, forget the world. In other words, you must not go out into the world seeking your good, but at least for a period, you must refrain from asking or expecting anything, and go within to seek the Kingdom.

In this state of consciousness, it is further revealed that since the kingdom of God is Spirit, that which It has to impart is spiritual. Therefore, to go to It for money, houses, employment, marriages, divorces, or happiness in the human realm is utter nonsense because Spirit knows no such things. God knows only a spiritual universe. So your inner life becomes one of seeking more and more the experience of this inner Grace without trying to translate It into terms of physical health or material wealth, or even human peace on earth. The whole approach is summed up in such questions as: What is the spiritual kingdom? What are the spiritual children of God like? What is the nature of the spiritual temple of God? What is the spiritual household of God? What is spiritual health? What is spiritual prosperity?

The human mind is full of concepts. Its concept of health is that of a painless body, and a heart, liver, and lungs functioning normally. Its concept of supply is that supply consists of money, income, property, or investments. The human mind has many different concepts of home and church. But this will not do. God is Spirit. "Know ye not that ye are the temple of God?" [4] What is the spiritual temple of God? "Know ye not that your body is the temple of the Holy Ghost?" [5]

"Ah, no," you say, "I have seen too many physical bodies in sickness, sin, disease, age, disintegration, and deterioration. Do not tell me that they are temples of God!"

What then is the temple of God? How are you going to find out? Ask "man, whose breath is in his nostrils" [6]? Ask a spiritual teacher? How could he tell you? He knows only what his vision is and what God has revealed to him. But how can he impart that to you? No, it is folly to ask a spiritual teacher what spiritual creation is like. It cannot be told: it can only be experienced. It can be imparted in meditation, but it cannot be

[4] I Corinthians 3:16.
[5] I Corinthians 6:19.
[6] Isaiah 2:22.

expressed in words. Therefore, you must go within; you must go to that which the Master called the "Father." [7] You must go there and, if necessary, plead: "Reveal Thyself. Reveal Thy temple to me, the temple which I am, the temple which my body is, the temple which my family is, the temple which my health is. Reveal these to me. Reveal spiritual Reality."

As long as you have only a human mind with which to receive, you will not get the answers, because "the natural man," [8] the human mind, cannot receive or know the things of God. Therefore, you must keep seeking, not in the world of men or in the world of books, but in the inner temple of your own being, in that sanctuary where Jesus told us we must go to pray, that inner sanctuary of your own consciousness. You must seek until the activity of the mind is stilled, and the mind settles into peacefulness and quietness, so that in that quietness and confidence you can be still.

When you have attained a state of stillness, something within reveals, "*I* am Spirit," and then you know that you have attained some measure of spiritual discernment, enough of Christ-consciousness so that you can keep on listening for the rest of the message. Eventually, God will reveal Himself, His kingdom, His laws, His temples: temples of health, temples of wealth, temples of love, temples of family, temples of all good, each of which is a temple in the consciousness of God. In fact, each one of these is the consciousness of God formed as a temple.

MY PEACE BRINGS FREEDOM FROM CONCERN

In seeking spiritual truth, you are seeking only His grace, His love, His life, and eventually that is what you will receive. You will receive His Spirit, which translates Itself as "My peace," [9] not worldly things, but "*My* peace."

[7] Matthew 5:48.
[8] I Corinthians 2:14.
[9] John 14:27.

This peace is a freedom from concern, from anxiety, and from fear. You may not recognize it at first, but all of a sudden you realize that you have no more fear, no further concern, no more doubts. "*My* peace," the Christ-peace, has given you a new-found freedom. Now you can be in the world, but not of it. You have none of its fears, none of its doubts, none of its worries. Death is no longer an enemy, since in the realization that God is your life, you can never be separated from life even in death. If God's love is governing you, you cannot be separated from God's love in death, so even the last enemy has been overcome.

Then you recognize that a miracle has taken place: you are no longer just a human being. There is a spiritual Presence within you, a spiritual Companion, a spiritual Gift, a spiritual Grace, a spiritual Peace. There is much more to you now than appears outwardly. To you, this spiritual Presence is the miracle, but strangely enough, the world does not see this as a miracle because it does not even know that it has happened. What the world begins to say is, "Oh, you seem to have better health," or "You have greater supply," or "You have more success in business," or "You have better judgment in investments." To the world, that is the miracle, but to you that is not the miracle: that is the fruitage of the miracle.

THE REAL MIRACLE

The miracle is Grace; the miracle is a spiritual inner life that has come to your awareness, that which the Master recognized as "the Father that dwelleth" [10] in him, and which Paul recognized as the "Christ which strengtheneth" [11] him. So the miracle is the attainment of the Christ, but the world does not see this. It says, "What a miracle has happened to you! You have health, wealth, and happiness." And the reason it says this? Because

[10] John 14:10.
[11] Philippians 4:13.

the world is seeking health, wealth, and happiness: it is not seeking the Christ.

You are not of the world if you have sufficiently grasped the principles of The Infinite Way so that you are no longer seeking the health, wealth, or happiness that the world can give you, but are seeking the miracle of inner Grace. Many, at first, do not know that that is what they are seeking, but sooner or later they must learn that they will attain those things they long for only when they stop seeking for them and seek *Me,* the Spirit, the Father within. When they learn that they must turn from seeking the things of the world to seeking the kingdom of God, many of them fall by the wayside. That is why the Master said, "Few there be that find it.[12] . . . Ye seek me, not because ye saw the miracles, but because ye did eat of the loaves, and were filled." [13] Because their whole concern was on the "loaves and fishes," they did not find *Me,* and they dropped away. Only the remnant remained. The remnant remained to say, "To whom shall we go? thou hast the words of eternal life." [14]

You Infinite Way students who through the years have been seeking the one great miracle, seeking with every means that The Infinite Way has offered, you who have left your "nets," [15] left the seeking of "loaves and fishes"—and by this I do not mean that you have given up your employment or your profession, but that you who have reserved an area of your consciousness for seeking God, even while fishing, making tents, or whatever your outer life may be—you, then, are the ones who must eventually discover this Kingdom within, this inner Grace, this *My* peace.

SHARE WITH THOSE IN THE WORLD
AT THE LEVEL OF THEIR RECEPTIVITY

Be still about this great gift of Grace that has been given you;

[12] Matthew 7:14.
[13] John 6:26.
[14] John 6:68.
[15] Matthew 4:20.

be secretive about it. Do not think that you are called upon to share this Grace with those outside, for you are not to do this until they come seeking It, and then only as you realize that they are seeking It, not the "loaves and fishes." You will never be called upon to go out into the world to proselyte, to save it, or to tell what you know.

I have never been called to that purpose. I have been called only to those who were seeking this Path. They have sent for me, and I have gone. Never yet have I gone to the world; never yet have I gone to the public; never have I been called there. My call has been only to those of my own household, those who were seeking that which I had found.

It is because I have not tried to convince the world that it was wrong or tell it that I had discovered something that is right that I have found no antagonism in the world and no persecution there. What I have discovered is not for the world, until the world realizes that it is a prodigal and that it must seek the Father's house.

Be wise. Learn to live within the sanctuary of your own being and stay there until someone comes to your doorstep; then share with that one to the extent of his capacity to receive, and no further. In proportion as you continue to receive an inner Grace which will be made manifest in a peaceful and happier life, more and more seekers will be led to your state of consciousness to be fed.

This consciousness which you have attained, this state of peace which you have, this inner Grace, which is your meat, your wine, and your water, is also that of those who recognize it and seek it. It is not for the neighbor; it is not even for those members of your family who cannot recognize it. Therefore, it is not offered to them. Love is offered them at their level of receptivity, but not beyond that. Love, charity, and benevolence are offered to your neighbors, and if their level of receptivity is a check, books, or last year's clothing, then that is the level of love and benevolence you must share with them. But you must not expect that attempting to give them the real meat, the real wine, and the real water which you have discovered will feed them.

Even the same material food that we eat would not really feed people of other nations. Their systems could not take it! Their bodies are not conditioned to it. There are some people who thrive on rice, poi, or fish, but if we tried to give them Napoleons, ice cream, or other delicacies characteristic of the diet of most Westerners, they might not be able to assimilate them. So it is that there is a part of this world that can accept our money, our clothing, and other comforts that we can give them, but they cannot accept the word of God.

LET YOUR CONSCIOUSNESS BE PREPARED
TO FEED A HUNGRY WORLD

Once you recognize God as your consciousness and as the substance of your life, you will be wise to let It feed and prosper you, let It appear outwardly as whatever form It may, and then share It with those who seek It, but share the twelve baskets full that are left over with the others.

If you leave the world alone, it will awaken to what you have and want it; but if you try to force truth on the world, you may prevent the world from ever being receptive to it. Such is the nature of the human mind. It rejects that which it does not seek. I am not criticizing or judging anyone or anything: I was in the same boat. I was invited to the "feast" [16] a long, long time before I came. I found my feast in a different direction with a different kind of food, and I had to hunger and thirst until I myself sought the meat that does not perish.

It is inevitable that the world will soon realize that it is the Prodigal, that it is not going to be saved by the tens of thousands of bombs stored away, that it is not going to be fed substantially by the food laid up in storehouses and barns and not available to anybody. The world is even going to recognize that it is not going to be supported by all the gold in Fort Knox, or even by

[16] Luke 14:15-24.

all the gold that is not there. It is going to realize some day that it is not going to be saved by these bombs, nor fed by the reserves of food that never come out of storage until they rot or are burned up.

But do not ever think for a moment that this world right now is not famished. It is famished for that food that is stored where no one can get at it, and it is famished for a sense of safety and security and peace. It is hungering for these things. It is inevitable that just as we have hungered for, and finally found, the Spirit, so the people of the world in their hungering will find it, and fortunate it is—no, not fortunate, because this is the way God operates: "before they call, I will answer." [17] Before they are ready for it, the "banquet" has been arranged, the "feast" has been planned, the "food" has been prepared and set out.

I am sure that never has there been a bit of food created that there was not somebody also created to consume it. So, too, the spiritual feast that is set before the world now will find "banqueters" and "feasters." But all the books of spiritual wisdom in themselves are not sufficient. In the background there must be the "ten" [18] righteous men waiting, tabernacling within their own inner sanctuary, enriching their own consciousness, storing up spiritual treasures, so that when those hungering and thirsting come, there will be those ready to say, "Yes, come and eat. We have storehouses filled, filled and ready, storehouses of Grace."

Then, just as everyone who has come to the message of The Infinite Way has witnessed some measure of fruitage in my life, in my family's life, in our teachers' and practitioners' lives, and in many of our students' lives, so, too, will they come seeking it, the people of this world, and you must be prepared. The real preparation will come forth from the degree of silence and secrecy in which you maintain yourself, because then you will not be wasting your substance on the air, or wasting it by

[17] Isaiah 65:24.
[18] Genesis 18:32.

letting it hit up against the human mind that would like to dispute it, argue with you, and discuss it. You will be storing it up, and those who come to you, even though you do not feel led to say a word to them, will feel that inner peace, that inner Grace, and will be fed by it. Even if you say only one word to them, if you give them but one quotation, one passage of Scripture, it will be a whole meal because it will carry with it spiritual consciousness.

When I started in the practice, I gave one hour to every patient who came to me, and at that time it probably took an hour for me to give a patient enough spiritual substance to meet his need; but later, five minutes would do, and still later three minutes. Why? Because it was not the words feeding him: it was the consciousness. As you work in this ministry through the years, your consciousness deepens, and then one word, one quotation, sometimes just a look, a smile, and it is done. Without that consciousness, it may take a whole hour of words.

God is infinite consciousness; God is individual consciousness: yours. God is Spirit; therefore, turn within to your God-consciousness and seek the peace that passes understanding. Seek God's grace which is your sufficiency in all things. Seek His love, and whatever else you may seek, be certain that it is something spiritual. Abide in this Word; abide in this Grace; abide in this peace, never looking to the outside world to see what is going to happen or how it is going to manifest.

LIFTING UP THE SON OF GOD

As long as you live and move and have your being within the spiritual temple of your consciousness, realizing only the presence of spiritual Grace, you are living in and through God, and God is really living as you: you in the Father, and the Father in you—one. You are relaxing your own sense of life that the divine life may take over. This you do silently and secretly, and that which God sees in secret is shouted from the housetops. Not by you—no, by God! It appears outwardly as the forms that the people of the world recognize as good, and this draws them to you, just as the masses were drawn to the Master for loaves and fishes, but ultimately came that they might find His peace, His grace.

In practical experience, this means that when someone comes to you and asks for help for supply, you answer, "No, I cannot work for your supply because you already have an infinity. You think money is supply, but money is not supply. God's grace is supply. Let me give you help to realize that Grace and that peace. Let me give you help to realize the Christ. Let the supply be added, but let us not go to God for supply. Let us go to God for God."

How does one say that to a person? All the money in the world cannot be used as food; even gold mines cannot be eaten. Money is not supply except in the human three-dimensional world, and even then it is here today and gone tomorrow. We are not dealing with money as supply: we are dealing with consciousness as supply; we are dealing with love, gratitude, and benevolence as supply.

When a request comes from someone for help on supply, Infinite Way teachers or practitioners should answer, "Are you referring to money, employment, or property? Please realize that I cannot give you these. I can give you help to lift you higher in consciousness, and if you attain that higher conscious-ness, you will find the omnipresence of supply in your con-sciousness, as long as you do not think of supply as money."

In the same way, as patients or students continue to say, "It is my right knee that hurts," or "It is my left ear that aches," the teacher or practitioner should reply, "I understand that, but please remember that spiritual help does not touch the physical body at all. Our work is helping you attain that mind which was in Christ Jesus, in which there is no sin, disease, lack, or death."

Mercifully and gently, not unkindly, turn the patient away from the thought of the health problem to the idea of going within to seek God's peace, "Let us seek spiritual health. Let us seek the temple of God which is your real body."

When someone comes with a tale of unhappy family life, it is so real to him that all he wants is to change his unhappiness to happiness; but as gently as possible, make it very clear, "I cannot give you that without the presence of the Christ, because I do not know how. It is the presence of the Christ that can establish harmony between you and your family. Humanly, I would not know how to do this for you or tell you what to do. In fact, you could give your family all your money, and you would not be at peace with them. You could give them your land, and you might not be at peace with them. You could give in to your wife; your wife could give in to you; and you still would not have peace. But let us go within and tabernacle with God; let us bring God into your family life, and let the Spirit make the adjustment, 'for we know not what we should pray for.' [19] Let the divine Spirit bear witness with our spirit and see if It will not bring peace between thee and thy household."

Persons may keep coming seeking a demonstration of employment, but you have no employment to give. So, for the moment, forget employment, and see if you can receive a message from the Father, because "Man shall not live by bread alone, but by every word that proceedeth out of the mouth of God." [20] Therefore, man shall not live by employment: man shall live by the word of God. Let your work be to bring forth the word of God. Then he will eat and drink and be satisfied, and maybe employed too.

In this way, you will be hastening the day when Infinite Way students will know that the teacher or practitioner is not another branch of *materia medica,* a vice-president of a neighborhood bank, or even a marriage counselor, but that his function is to lift up the son of God in those who turn to him for help.

[19] Romans 8:26.
[20] Matthew 4:4.

THE ONLY GOAL MUST BE
ATTAINING CHRIST-CONSCIOUSNESS

There are many more individuals seeking a spiritual solution to life than there are persons prepared to help them find that way. Even today in The Infinite Way, we are unable to take care of the many demands that come in asking for spiritual help. It would be sad if the world turned to us now, and we had to say, "We are sorry. We know this truth is the answer, but our students have not attained a high enough state of consciousness to give that spiritual help."

After seventeen years? How long does it take? How long does it take a student to attain spiritual consciousness? I can give you half the answer. A student cannot even begin to attain that consciousness until his goal is no longer that of meeting his personal problems of health, supply, or happiness. He must no longer be preoccupied with personal gain. The search for God-awareness must become the primary motive of study. When that is true, then the spiritual student is halfway "home." He must decide that the attainment of Christ-consciousness is his only goal and that having help for his other problems is of secondary importance. I am not saying that anyone should neglect human situations or obligations, but these should be secondary. It then might not take a student too long.

Attaining that mind "which was also in Christ Jesus" [21] should be the primary purpose in life. It is an interesting thing for me to watch this work and see some students who are attaining it beautifully, and then watch those who are seeking a healing for a minor physical claim and complaining because they have not yet attained heaven. In other words, such students are still living for themselves and are making themselves the goal rather than having as their goal the attaining of heaven.

Our concern must be to lift the world into the higher dimension of consciousness where all the "things" of the world are added. "I, if I be lifted up from the earth, will draw all men

[21] Philippians 2:5.

unto me." [22] Let us hurry about this business of being lifted up, so we can lift others into the higher consciousness. Then all problems will solve themselves.

FROM METAPHYSICS TO MYSTICISM

The Infinite Way is embarking on the attaining of a higher realm of consciousness in its presentation and demonstration. It is taking the students above the metaphysical and into the mystical, but it is asking them not only to come up out of the metaphysical into the mystical, but also not to burn down the metaphysical temple behind them, any more than they would want to burn down their schoolhouses just because they do not need schools for themselves.

For your own demonstration of spiritual attainment, seek to live "by every word that proceedeth out of the mouth of God." That means to live by turning within to your consciousness and letting your consciousness speak to you, letting the activity of the Christ be your demonstration, rather than the demonstration of employment, supply, happiness, or health.

Those of the present generation have been led up through the metaphysical, where it was legitimate to call for help when their child had a 103 degree fever, and then call up to express gratitude when it when down to 101 degrees, as if we were practitioners of *materia medica*. Or it was legitimate when someone called up and wanted increased supply, and then reported, "Oh, my salary has been doubled!" to consider that a demonstration.

But in the mystical realm, this is not demonstration. The demonstration is the realization of the presence and the activity of the Christ: that is the demonstration. The demonstration is hearing the word of God, because it is This that we live by. The demonstration is the attainment of the meat the world knows not of. The demonstration is the attainment of *My* peace.

[22] John 12:32.

This is the point in mysticism at which we have arrived; this is the standpoint from which The Infinite Way has been practiced by those who have recognized this principle. But now it is necessary that every student recognize it, because the world is not going to be saved merely by multiplying the food that is in storehouses and barns, by multiplying the gold in Fort Knox, or by the signing of a peace treaty.

THE DEMONSTRATION OF THE CHRIST

The world will be saved only by the demonstration of the Christ. It may call it "the second coming of the Christ"; but actually the Christ never came and never went, so there is no first or second about it. The Christ has always been present, since God and the son of God have always been one; therefore, the demonstration is not really the second coming of the Christ: the demonstration is our recognition of the *omnipresence* of the Christ. This is the demonstration, our recognition of that which eternally is, eternally has been, and eternally will be.

God is the same forever, from everlasting to everlasting. He changes not; therefore, there has never been a going or a coming. The Christ has always been omnipresent, awaiting recognition, and there have always been individuals to recognize and demonstrate the Christ. But now the Prodigal is no longer an individual; now the Prodigal is the whole of the human world, and today it is the entire human world that thirsts and hungers to get back to the Father's house.

Only through meditation can you go deep down inside your Self, inside your own consciousness, the temple that is within, be at peace, and draw forth the word of God. Otherwise the mind is living out here in the world and is of it, but in meditation it can be in the world but not of it. If, however, you permit your students, your patients, and your friends to believe that you are going to go within for them and draw out a new house, a new automobile, or new employment, you will keep on deceiving them and preventing your own higher unfoldment.

Your higher attainment is really dependent on your not permitting those who come to you to believe that you are going to demonstrate a material universe for them, not even a healthy, wealthy one. It is dependent on the degree in which you can turn them gently away from trying to improve appearances to seeing what the kingdom of God has for them, to what the indwelling Christ has for them, to what manner of temple It can bring forth, and to what happens when the Word is spoken through you.

So, also, the degree of your attainment is dependent on how little you can say to those who come to you, and to what degree you can listen within and let the Voice do the saying—not how much truth you can speak to your friends, students, or patients, but to what degree you can become aware of the Word and let It perform Its work.

We used to think that if we sat with a patient or student and talked with him for a half hour or an hour, we were doing great things for him, and not one second did we let the voice of God come forth, and yet it is the voice of God that really does away with this material world. It is the word of God that we must live by, and all we did was talk to our students and rehash statements of truth, forgetting that it is the word of God that does the miracles, not we, and not any passages we have memorized.

Your own heights of spiritual awareness will depend on your ability to speak to those who come to you for help for five or ten minutes and bring peace to them, and then go within and let the Word come forth, because the more the Word utters Itself within you, the higher your attainment, until ultimately you will not have a voice of your own any more: it will be Its voice, it will be It speaking through you always. This is the mystical height.

From

GOD, THE SUBSTANCE
OF ALL FORM

Building the New Consciousness

———•———

Many aspirants on the spiritual path experience inner unfoldment or revelation when they begin to gain some understanding of what meditation is. Meditation is our method of building a consciousness of truth, a new consciousness. Meditation is our mode of prayer. First, however, it must be understood that prayer is not what we say to God, but rather what God says to us. Because of the noise of the world, we do not hear the still small voice or receive the benefit of the Presence, and therefore, we must learn to be silent and receptive.

Learning to Meditate[1]

The purpose of meditation is to gain a conscious awareness of the presence of God—such a conscious awareness of our oneness with

[1]Since *God the Substance* was first written, two books of instruction in meditation by the author have been published: *The Art of Meditation* (New York: Harper and

God that we may come into an actual realization of the truth of being. Although successful meditation requires silence and receptivity, never try to still the human mind; never try to stop thinking or attempt to blank out your thoughts. It cannot be done. When you begin to meditate and thoughts of an unruly nature come, let them come; do not be disturbed by them. They are world-thoughts, not yours. Take the attitude of sitting back and watching them. See them impersonally. Soon they will no longer disturb you, and you will be able to sit down and be at peace.

There are many schools of thought as to the proper method of approaching meditation, and for the beginner there probably should be some procedure or method outlined. If it is remembered that in meditation our whole attention is to be focused upon God and the things of God, it will readily be seen that in sitting down to meditate, it is wise for the body to be in a comfortable position so that the attention is not unconsciously drawn to the body. Always remember, though, that the posture assumed is not important, nor the method used. Any procedure adopted is only for the purpose of making it easier to hold the attention on God and to become consciously receptive to the infinite power of your own consciousness.

Be very patient in meditation and try to conquer any sense of unrest. No truth is going to be given you from without which you do not already know, but the light presented on that truth from within your own Soul makes it applicable in your experience. Truth which seems to come from without is a ray of truth, but that ray imbued with your own consciousness becomes the "light of the world" to you and to all who come within range of it. "And I, if I be lifted up from the earth, will draw all men unto me."[1] Meditation, being a consciousness of the presence of God, can draw you and lift you to that place where you can apprehend the

Brothers, 1956; London: George Allen and Unwin, Ltd., 1957) and *Practicing the Presence* (New York: Harper and Brothers, 1958; London: L. N. Fowler & Co., Ltd., 1956).
[1]John 12:32.

word of Truth in its inner significance. Be not impatient with your progress. You are learning a new mode of life and developing a whole new consciousness of existence.

A Conscious Experience

Meditation is a conscious experience. Those who have difficulty in meditating and sometimes fall asleep are not making it a conscious experience. Do not try to stop the thinking process in meditation. There is nothing wrong with thinking. As a matter of fact, it is a great help to begin meditation with some question or with some specific idea on which you wish light, and then, when you go into meditation, you could not possibly fall asleep. It may be that you are going into meditation to receive guidance for the day. In that case, you would take that question into your meditation, and whether you voice it or whether you think it, you would be consciously aware of the fact that you are in meditation for guidance and direction. You cannot go to sleep with a mind open and waiting for instruction.

In the same way, if your business or your husband's business has been uppermost in your mind before going into meditation, you will not go to sleep. You will be going into meditation with the idea of receiving an unfoldment from God, an unfoldment from the inner Wisdom locked within you. That Wisdom may give you a comforting sense of protection, or it may give your husband, your father, or your child an all-embracing protection.

You will not be sleepy or drowsy while meditating, if you realize that meditation is a conscious activity of your mind and Soul. It is not a lazy sitting-back and saying, "All right, God, go ahead." And that is what much of the meditation amounts to in which there is the temptation to go to sleep .The student drifts off into sleep while he is in meditation only because he does not realize that he should constantly be alert for some inner guidance, alert to hear the voice of God. He should go to his inner Self with attention focused on some specific truth and then wait for God to reveal Himself: "Here I am, Father, alert and awake for Thy guidance."

Sleep as a Resting in Consciousness

In this work, I have found that the closer we come to the spiritual sense of existence, the less sleep we need. Speaking not only from my own experience but also from the experience of others working for any length of time on this path, it has been found almost an impossibility to sleep continuously for eight hours. It may be that we will sleep eight hours out of the twenty-four if we have the opportunity, but seldom is it possible to sleep for eight consecutive hours. After two or three hours, we awaken and are awake for a period in which some unfoldment comes, or a sense of peace or harmony, depending on how the period of wakefulness is treated. If this waking period is fought, however, and the effort is made to go back to sleep, it cannot be of much benefit; but if this wakefulness is accepted as an activity of divine Wisdom and there is a willingness and sufficient patience to let that Wisdom disclose and reveal Itself, it will be found that the waking hours in the middle of the night are the most beneficial ones of the entire twenty-four.

An interesting thing about this, too, is that when our waking in the middle of the night is the result of spiritual activity in consciousness, even though it leaves us with less sleep than we have been accustomed to having, it results in no tiredness the following day. I have watched this for many years and, from my own experience, as well as that of businessmen and women, housewives, and people from all walks of life, I know that as soon as this spiritual activity begins to result in wakeful periods at night, which are accepted joyfully as opportunities for the unfoldment of peace and harmony, the following day is filled with an awareness of the divine Spirit rather than with any sense of weariness.

Those who are on this path need very little sleep for any activity required of them. This is because it is possible to derive all the benefits of sleep while still awake. Sleep is really but a mild form of death, or unconsciousness; it is a loss of consciousness, and that is next door to death, itself, or at least only one step removed.

Sleep, however, from the standpoint of Spirit, is not a state of unconsciousness, but is a resting *in* consciousness. Thought is filled with Spirit, with spiritual awareness, with an actual sense of the Spirit of the Christ, and this causes a person to be wide awake, vital, alive, almost electric. You see, what we are doing in this work is actually contacting the Spirit of the Christ, the Spirit which is God, and that makes a person vital and dynamic. Sleep has nothing to do with that aliveness, but rest—resting *in* consciousness—has a great deal to do with it. And that is how we can receive the full inflow of rest while we are awake.

Birth of the Christ in Individual Consciousness

Through the practice of meditation, we open our consciousness to the flow of Truth and we become the transparency for infinite good to the world. We lose the sense that we, as persons, can do anything, and we gain the understanding that the Christ, or Spirit of God, which lives as us does all things. It is the Spirit which produces, causes, animates, and permeates all form, all formation, and all creation. Spirit is the law unto all effect.

With us, then, it becomes necessary to gain the conscious awareness of the presence and power of God, acting and appearing as our individual consciousness, and to know that this consciousness is the law, substance, and reality of our universe, whether appearing as our body, our business, or our home.

Where we have failed is in our lack of recognition of this truth, and our lack of recognition is because the human mind rebels at this truth which annihilates the supposititious power which the mind as assumed.

From the standpoint that Christ is the revelation of the oneness of God and His creation, let us ponder the spiritual meaning of the scriptural record of the birth of Jesus. Jesus was born in a manger, probably the lowliest place on earth at that time. This manger can be interpreted as symbolic of the human mind, the lowest place in which the Christ can be born. When human thought is awakened to seek light, it is then that the reaching out is greatest, and it is probably then that the Christ is born in this "stable" of the human mind.

The babe, Jesus, was wrapped in swaddling clothes, and so it is with us, when the Christ is first born in the human mind. It is wrapped in the gentlest of truths; It is clothed in the simplest of thoughts upon which we can feed for our growth and unfoldment, until the danger of the "Herods" that would come and destroy It is past—until we have grown in understanding so that the questions and doubts of the world cannot overwhelm us. Always the human thought will endeavour to destroy the Christ.

Joseph and Mary carried their small son down into Egypt, where they kept him hidden until the danger that would destroy him was past. There is a great lesson of wisdom for us in this. We, too, must hide this gentle Truth, not showing it forth in words but only in effect. We must not go around voicing it, but rather let it appear as it appeared to Jesus at the age of twelve, when he astounded the rabbis in the temple with his wisdom. It was not until twelve years after the birth of Jesus that the Christ became manifest in the child.

So, also, it was nine years after Paul's illumination before he went out to preach and teach. The newborn Christ must not be carried out into the highways and byways, but must be permitted to develop and "wax strong" in our consciousness, and then we shall see that it is unnecessary to proselyte. The world will always resist the teaching of oneness, omnipresence, and omnipotence, but when the presence of the Christ has been felt, we can then speak of It without fear of losing It.

It is better to keep this truth within our own being and let it become visible to the world through the results rather than to go out and preach it. It is surprising how the world senses what is going on without our speaking about it. The very Christ, the very Spirit of God, is manifest as the peace of our being, as the prosperity of our purse, and as the joy in our faces. It is then that the world recognizes that we have something, and it is then that the healing work takes place without "taking thought"—"not by might, nor by power, but by my spirit,"[1] through the peace of mind that we have found.

It is through meditation that we develop a conscious awareness of the presence and power of God, and we feel that Presence with us all through our days and nights, guiding and protecting. The object of our work is the realization that "I and my Father are one,"[2] and that where I am, God is. When this realization is attained, it makes no difference what picture is presented:

> *There is a Presence and a Power instantly available to me. Where I am, God is; and therefore, the place whereon I stand is holy ground. "Whither shall I go from thy spirit? or whither shall I flee from thy presence? If I ascend up into heaven, thou art there: if I make my bed in hell, behold, thou art there."[3] Even though I make my bed in hell, this Presence is there. It may be trouble, sin, disease, lack or limitation. The nature of the picture makes no difference because my remembrance always is, "Thou art here," and consequently this is holy ground. Whither shall I flee from Thy presence since that I is God?*

[1]Zechariah 4:6.
[2]John 10:30.
[3]Psalms 139:7,8.

Individual Consciousness as Law

———•———

Thus saith the Lord, Let not the wise man glory in his wisdom, neither let the mighty man glory in his might, let not the rich man glory in his riches:

But let him that glorieth glory in this, that he understandeth and knoweth me, that I am the Lord which exercise lovingkindness, judgment, and righteousness, in the earth.

JEREMIAH 9:23,24

This statement from Jeremiah can be carried out in practical experience. We are not to glory in the world of effect, whether that effect appears as person, place, circumstance, condition, or thing, because the substance, the reality, does not lie in any effect. The power and the glory, the substance and the reality, the cause and the law lie in the Spirit which produces all that appears to us as form, circumstance, or condition. We can enjoy and use the things of this world, but our faith and confidence must not be centered in the world or in the things of the world. Our faith and confidence must be in the Spirit which produces, forms, and animates all that exists.

No Power Acts upon Us

The Infinite Way teaches that man is consciousness and that that very consciousness is the cause of body, business, and home. Many people believe that a discordant body, business, or home is due to a power outside of themselves, acting upon them. As long as we accept the belief that there is a power outside of us, just that long will we be seeking to get in touch with a good power to do something for us. If the belief is accepted that a law of time is acting upon our bodies and mentalities, our experience will be on that level. There is no power operating in our experience separate from our own consciousness, but as long as we believe that there is such a power and as long as we are trying to get in touch with it, we shall never contact it.

The world has been praying to God for things. It is no more sensible to pray to God for things than it is to pray to the principle of electricity to light your house. Rejoice not in the "things," but rejoice that you understand and know *Me*, the reality of being, your being and mine, and that you understand that Being to be God. Then you will see the uselessness of praying to that which forms your own body, your own business, your own home. This is brought out in your experience, however, only in proportion to your recognition and realization that your own consciousness is the law and that there is no other reality outside of you:

> *I am life eternal. "I am the way, the truth, and the life*[1] *. . . I and my Father are one."*[2] *All that the Father has is mine, since I am an heir of God and joint-heir with Christ. I and the Father are one, and that oneness*

[1] John 14:6.
[2] John 10:30.

*constitutes the immortality, harmony, grace, joy, and abundance of my
body and my Soul.*

"Before Abraham was, I am.[3] *. . . lo, I am with you always, even unto
the end of the world."*[4] *The divine Consciousness of my being formed me
before I was born. It knew me before I was conceived. The reign of God, of
Consciousness—that Consciousness which is my individual consciousness—
is going on in my body and in my affairs now.*

The higher you go in the understanding of Consciousness as
God, the greater transparency you are for the reign of God in
your affairs. God is omnipresent, but it requires our conscious
feeling of it to make it effective. Mere affirmations are useless
because in them you are declaring a God separate and apart from
yourself. You are seeing God as being "out there," instead of
understanding life, truth, and love as the consciousness and law
of your own being. Jesus referred to your Father and my Father:

> We have one Father, even God.[1] . . . Have I been so long time with
> you, and yet hast thou not known me, Philip? he that hath seen me
> hath seen the Father. . .[2] The kingdom of God is within
> you.[3] . . . Greater works than these shall he do.[4]

How could anyone do those "greater works" if the same Presence
and Power were not manifested as his being?

No Power Separate from Consciousness

Spiritual healing is accomplished through divine silence, not
through conscious thought-taking. When you are confronted with
sin, disease, lack, or limitation, watch to see if you immediately

[3]John 8:58.
[4]Matthew 28:20.
[1]John 8:41.
[2]John 14:9.
[3]Luke 17:21.
[4]John 14:12.

begin to refute it mentally. If you do, your very denying of it is proof that in some way you believe it is true, and in the degree that you believe in it, you are the victim of it. When you really know the nature of error, it is not necessary to protest too much about it. We are too apt to go around declaring, "I am not sick." A rich man does not say, "I am not poor." When anyone goes around declaring that he is not sick, you can well believe that he is not feeling any too healthy and thinks to be made whole by his declarations. In the same way, when you speak to someone about not feeling well and he responds with the cliché, "It is not true," he really does not have an inner awareness that it is not true, or he would not have to voice it. Error, being only a universal belief, is unreal in any form, and it is dispelled by the power of silence.

Denials and affirmations serve for a time until we can become receptive to the truth of being, but we should give up their use in our recognition that there cannot be God and error, and we are not going to be fooled by appearances. If we are to show forth Principle as substance, law, and cause, we must not accept the belief that there is a condition apart from God or an activity other than God's government of the universe. The right attitude is the realization of the impossibility of such a thing and the "Thank you, Father," that you do know the unreality of such a claim. The state of consciousness which does not hate or fear any appearance is the healing consciousness, and only such a consciousness can say, "What hinders you? Rise up and walk. There is no power apart from the consciousness of your own being."

At the pool of Bethesda, the crippled and diseased were waiting for a power separate and apart from themselves to come and act upon them, but had they realized that all power is within their own being, they would have turned within to the power of their own consciousness, and with that realization they would have had no need of the pool. While we are believing that there is any power that is going to act on us separate from the power of our own consciousness, we, too, are at the pool of Bethesda, "waiting for the moving of the water," and we might also have to wait thirty-eight years, as some did, before one of enlightened consciousness comes along to bring us out of it.

It is not necessary to wait for complete liberation. It is necessary and important for us to get up and do all that is possible for us to do, even though it seems to be very little at the moment. We should continue striving to gain dominion, and thus gradually the shell of human belief will be broken—the belief that there is a power of evil somewhere that can act upon us. The only action there is, is mind-action. If, at the moment, we can only move a finger, then let us move that finger, realizing that the dominion and power are always in the Spirit of God, in Consciousness, never in effect. Maintaining this attitude of only one Power and that One not something separate from our own consciousness, we gradually come into this awareness: "I am the life, I am the truth, I am the power, itself."

Idolatry is the belief that there is power in effect; it is a faith in that which has form, a faith that that which appears as an external thing has power of itself. The most important thing for you to know is that you are cause and not effect, that all of the Godhead appears *as* you. It is true that, in a material sense, you cannot have forty billion "alls," but in a spiritual sense, Allness can be multiplied throughout infinity. For example, an individual can be wholly honest and yet not deprive his neighbor of honesty. Anyone can be one hundred percent loyal, faithful, and true, and yet not deprive his neighbor of any part of these qualities. The allness of God is appearing individually as you and me—all the health, all the wealth, all the peace, all the dominion. What is true of you and me must be true of everyone. To be true, truth must be universal. Therefore, since life is God and God is your life and my life, it must be the life of all. The joys and fruits of this great truth, however, are brought into individual experience only in proportion to one's conscious realization of it, as the inner awareness of God, Life ever present, is developed.

No Power in Effect

As infinite individual consciousness, each one of us is a world unto himself, and each one has to find himself to be the law of life unto his own being—the kingdom of his own being. Nothing exists separate from consciousness. The power is in the consciousness that produces the effect and not in the effect itself. It is only while we believe that the power is in the effect that we continue seeking the demonstration of things.

In 1948, a call came for me to go to Hawaii. The call for help was the apparent reason for making the trip, but as it developed that was but a decoy, because the help given was only a small part of the outcome. Among other things, the opportunity came to meet one of the Hawaiian chiefs, who told me about the difficulties his people experienced during the depression and how they met together to try to rediscover the principle underlying the demonstrations made by the early tribes.

One day when he was pondering this question, it unfolded to him that if he were in the water drowning and could reach up and catch hold of a raft, it would save him. Then he thought, "Suppose I reached up and caught hold of only a handful of leaves instead of a raft?" With that idea came the realization that the same Spirit which was in the raft was also in the leaves, and that the sustaining Spirit which would hold him up was neither the raft nor the leaves, but the Spirit, Itself.

If you understand this point, you will see that the power, the substance, and the life are never in the effect as such, but always in the Spirit, Itself, the law which produces the effect. This is true of every effect. Once you see that supply is not in any effect, but is in the Spirit, you will have the secret of Jesus' multiplying of the loaves and fishes. Then you will see that the same sustaining Spirit is as much in the dollar bill as it is in the thousand dollar bill.

When John the Baptist was in prison, he began to wonder if the Master really were the Christ, and he sent to Jesus and asked him, "Art thou he that should come?"[1] to which Jesus replied:

Go and shew John again those things which ye do hear and see:

[1]Matthew 11:3.

The blind receive their sight, and the lame walk, the lepers are cleansed, and the deaf hear, and dead are raised up, and the poor have the gospel preached to them.
And blessed is he, whosoever shall not be offended in me.

MATTHEW 11:4-6

If the principle that performs the miracles is not perceived, the real truth is lost, and if you do not perceive the principle that performs your healings, you will receive nothing but temporary relief. You must understand that it is not the "raft" which supports you, but it is the Spirit of God appearing *as* the raft.

Spirit Underlies All Effect

Eddie Rickenbacker proved this principle when he was able to sit quietly, without even telling his friends in the boat with him what he knew, and have his food fly to him, fish jump into the raft, and rain fall from a cloudless sky. He demonstrated that it was not the food or the water, but the Spirit of God—Omnipresence, Omnipotence, Omniscience—which appeared to him *as* bird, fish, and water, the Spirit of God appearing as the thing needed at the moment. Never again look out at the world, at "things," and think that any thing is your need. It is the omnipresent Spirit of God which fills the need, and if It must appear as money, It will; or if It must appear as food, health, home, or companionship, It will. It makes no difference what the form is, as long as there is the awareness that the substance of the form is Spirit. The substance of all form is Spirit, and Spirit is omnipresent as each one of you, only awaiting your recognition. God is omnipresent, but God must be recognized because it is the conscious recognition of the Spirit of God that makes It become manifest as the form necessary at the moment.

Once we gain the realization that God, Spirit, is the consciousness of individual being and that nothing exists separate from this consciousness, we shall begin to see that it is the Spirit of God in the "leaves" or in the "raft" that would support us, that it is the Spirit of God in the ten-cent piece that would pay our way to any place in the world, that it is the Spirit of God in the few loaves and fishes that would feed five thousand. We shall begin to see that supply is not in the dollar bill, but in the Spirit of God that produces it. Let us never forget that. Let us not place our dependence upon a dollar bill or a bond, but upon the Spirit of God, that brings them to us. If we were to lose all that we have at one blow, that same Spirit could produce it for us again. Until we become so at-one with the Spirit of God appearing as effect that we are never tempted to believe that power is in effect, we shall find that the Spirit of God does not operate in our experience, and we shall be on the fluctuating human plane of having much today and nothing tomorrow.

Until there is an awareness and recognition of the Spirit of God as the substance, power, and law of all effect, it is as if there were no Spirit of God. There is only one way to experience the presence and power of God, and that is through the recognition and realization of Spirit as the reality of all that appears, but always with the understanding that the appearance itself is not the reality. Concern for the effect persists only as long as there is the belief that the power, law, or reality is in the effect. The moment there is a realization that consciousness, the Spirit of God, appears *as* effect, there will no longer be concern for the effect.

Let this be our theme: *Recognize Spirit as underlying all effect.* Have no dependence on persons or things, but place all dependence on Spirit. Behold Spirit, Consciousness, appearing as effect—your consciousness appearing as form.

From

LIVING NOW

Living Now

———•———

Above all things, the message of The Infinite Way emphasizes the dignity and infinite nature of individual man, revealing that we are always in control of our own destiny because of our oneness with our Source. To accept this spiritual status means also to accept the responsibility to let the divine Spirit live our life

EDITOR'S NOTE: The material in *Living Now* first appeared in 1963 in the form of letters sent to students of The Infinite Way throughout the world in the hope that they would aid in the revelation and unfoldment of the transcendental Consciousness through a deeper understanding of Scripture and the practice of meditation.

The italicized portions are spontaneous meditations that came to the author during periods of uplifted consciousness and are not in any sense intended to be used as affirmations, denials, or formulas. They have been inserted in this book from time to time to serve as examples of the free flowing of the Spirit. As the reader practices the Presence, he, too, in his exalted moments, will receive ever new and fresh inspiration as the outpouring of the Spirit.

and not permit it to be lived for us by the universal beliefs of this world—economic, medical, or theological—but rather to live a life governed by the truth.

The thesis laid down by the Master was: "Ye shall know the truth, and the truth shall make you free" [1]; and inasmuch as we accept the guidance of Christ Jesus, who laid out the Way for us, the truth that we must know is the truth that he has given us:

> "I and my Father are one.[2] . . . Son, thou art ever with me, and all that I have is thine.[3] . . . I am the way"—not the conditions outside, and not the people outside. "I am the way, the truth, and the life.[4] . . . I am come that they might have life, and that they might have it more abundantly" [5]—healthfully, joyously, freely, intelligently. "I will never leave thee, nor forsake thee.[6] . . . I am with you alway, even unto the end of the world." [7]

The truth that we must know is that from the beginning of time God has planted in the midst of us that which is to be our saviour, our power, and our dominion, dominion over everything in the earth and above the earth and beneath the earth. Although we have gradually let this dominion slip away from us, by knowing the truth we can recapture it and once again live freely, sharing that life of abundance and joy with all who are receptive and responsive to it.

Every Day Is a Day of Decision

In the first few days of a New Year, it is customary to greet one another many, many times with "Happy New Year," but in the

[1] John 8:32.
[2] John 10:30.
[3] Luke 15:31.
[4] John 14:6.
[5] John 10:10.
[6] Hebrews 13:5.
[7] Matthew 28:20.

very act of saying and hearing "Happy New Year" so often, let us be ever mindful that a happy New Year cannot come to us. There is nothing in the atmosphere that can act upon us to give us a happy New Year, and, unless we permit it, there is nothing in the atmosphere to give us an unhappy one.

Who is there who is concerned whether we have a happy or an unhappy year? We may search far and wide before we find any such person. No, every year will be the result of what we make it, the result of something that we put into operation this minute. It will not do to wait until midnight tonight; it will not do to wait until tomorrow. The kind of year that we are to experience must be started now, in this moment, by an act of decision, and each one must make that decision for himself.

This moment we must choose whether we will serve God or man. Are we to be God-governed or man-governed this year? If we are true to God, we need have no fear that we will be untrue to man, to our government, or to any government that stands for individual freedom, liberty, justice, and for the integrity of individual being. Therefore, we take our stand for government under God.

But what does government under God mean? First of all, it means that we must acknowledge that God has given to us His only begotten Son, and the function of this Presence that has been planted in the midst of us is to go before us to "make the crooked places straight." [8] It is to go before us to prepare mansions for us.

Now Is the Power and the Dominion

In making this acknowledgment, we are at the same time forsaking our dependence on "man, whose breath is in his nostrils." [9]

[8] Isaiah 45:2.
[9] Isaiah 2:22.

We will not seek the favor of "princes": we will understand that this son of God in us is there for the specific purpose of doing the will of God in us; and this will of God, as demonstrated in the ministry of the Master, is that we might have life, health, and joy, and that we might have all these more abundantly.

If we are to have dominion, we must acknowledge that there are no powers antagonistic to the son of God in us, for the power of God is infinite, and besides this spiritual power there is no power. Every day of every year we will be faced with the temptation to accept material, mental, and legal powers; but at this moment we must embrace in our acknowledgment the great truth that God is Spirit, that the law of God is spiritual, and being spiritual, it is infinite; and being infinite, there is no power in any law other than the spiritual law which is embodied within us.

This son of God, the *I* [10] that I am, is our food, shelter, protection, fortress, hiding place, and our abiding place, embodying all the good necessary to our experience throughout the years. At this very moment, we possess all that will unfold as our experience for all the days to come: it is embodied and embraced within our consciousness, and day by day it will unfold and appear as necessary in our human experience. All that God has is ours now.

Our Consciousness of Today Molds Our Tomorrows

Every new minute is a continuation of this present minute, and what we put into this minute is what is going to be a continuing experience for us throughout eternity. All that is embraced in our consciousness now will continue to unfold unto eternity because there is no future time. Now, in the present, is the substance of that which unfolds to us as time, and it includes that

[10] The word *"I,"* italicized, refers to God.

which we are placing in it at this moment. What we embody in our consciousness now unfolds as the next minute, the next hour, the next day, the next year. The truth that we embody in consciousness at this moment will be the continuing, unfolding truth throughout all time. What we do not embrace in our consciousness now cannot appear tomorrow.

"For he that hath, to him shall be given: and he that hath not, from him shall be taken even that which he hath." [11] Therefore, we must make certain that now, in this instant, we claim for ourselves all that the Father has, and that not by might, not by power, but by the grace of God, as heirs, as joint-heirs to all that God has. But if we do not consciously claim it now, we will not have it tomorrow. We will have tomorrow only what we claim today, now, in this moment.

Do we have the life of God? Then we have immortal, eternal life. Do we have the Spirit of God? Then we have the spirit of freedom, for "where the Spirit of the Lord is, there is liberty." [12] Only under the grace of God and His law can man be free. What we have in our consciousness of God-realization this moment will continue to flow day by day, and in ever greater measure as we renew ourselves many times a day by turning within to the Source of our good, thereby releasing the kingdom of God that is within.

The Inseparability of God and Man

Let us see how we can make this more practical in our experience, and why it is that no person or circumstance can deprive us of health, wealth, harmony, joy, and freedom. Let us rise, right now, to the realization that will forever set us free. You can do this by asking yourself two questions: Who am I? What am

[11] Mark 4:25.
[12] II Corinthians 3:17.

I? With your eyes closed, and in complete silence, say the word "I" within yourself, following it by your own name, whatever it may be. Then, with your eyes still closed, ask yourself: Am I in my feet? Am I in my stomach? Am I in my brain? You know that you are not. You know that the *I* of you cannot be found any place between your head and your feet.

I am God-created, and since God is Spirit, I must be spiritual. God is invisible, and therefore, I must be invisible: I can never be seen by anyone. I am as invisible, as spiritual, and as incorporeal as God, for this I that I am is the offspring of God, made of the life, substance, and being of God.

It is for this reason that even when we lay aside our earthly form, *I,* in Its full identity, will continue. Being one with God, *I* is inseparable and indivisible from God, and not even death can remove us from the life of God or the love of God, for our life and God-life are one.

God-life and my life are one, inseparable, indivisible, and incorporeal, not at the mercy of "man, whose breath is in his nostrils," not at the mercy of "princes," but a divine life lived under God.

"I and my Father are one," [13] *incorporeal and invisible. I live, and move, and have my being in God; I live and have my being in Spirit, in the Soul of God, in the Spirit of God. I am hid with Christ in God: this is my fortress; this is my dwelling place—to live, move, and have my being in Spirit, under spiritual government.*

To acknowledge the life of God as our life reveals our life as immortal and eternal. To acknowledge God as the substance, even of our body, makes our body indestructible, not subject to age or change, to sin, disease, or fear.

[13] John 10:30.

Consciousness Is I

As we silently repeat *I,* together with our name, we may begin to wonder about the nature of this *I* that we are, and soon the one thing we can be sure of is that we are a state of awareness or consciousness. In other words, we are conscious of living, of thinking, of moving about; we are conscious of the world in which we live; and through what we have read, heard, or studied, we are conscious of other worlds, other countries, other nationalities, and other languages. Therefore, we are consciousness.

Sight is one of the avenues of consciousness. Because we are consciousness, we are conscious of things by seeing them. We are also conscious of things by hearing; and hearing, therefore, is an extension or an activity of consciousness. It is consciousness that is conscious, but it is consciously aware through the activities or instruments of our consciousness: sight, hearing, taste, touch, and smell. These five senses, plus our capacity to think, are extensions, or outer activities, of the consciousness which we are.

Is it not clear that this *I* that we have declared ourselves to be is really consciousness? *I* is consciousness, or consciousness constitutes the *I* that we are. Therefore, what we are as consciousness is what becomes our experience. If we are conscious of the truth that there is only one infinite Consciousness, by virtue of our relationship of oneness with God, that infinite Consciousness, God, must be our individual consciousness; and that makes us as infinite as God, as immortal and as eternal.

God As Individual Consciousness

There is not an infinite Consciousness and your and my consciousness, otherwise there would be Infinity plus something, which cannot be. Therefore, the infinite Consciousness which is God is the consciousness which we are. Because of our oneness with God, we, individually, have access to the infinite nature of God's being, to the infinite, eternal life of God. God is consciousness; we are that Consciousness individualized; but that Consciousness is one consciousness, indivisible, indestructible, immortal, eternal, and above all things, omnipresent, here where we are, and It [14] is omnipotent.

Because God is our Selfhood, God is the measure of our capacity. Infinite Being is the nature of our being; infinite Being is the capacity of our being; and now, in this moment, we must recognize, acknowledge, and submit ourselves to It. As we remind ourselves of this each day, then this particular moment of our life, which we are now making happy, joyous, and prosperous, becomes the continuing moment of every day of every year. This no man can take from us. Even we ourselves will not be able to limit it to one day or to one year. It will be the joy and prosperity of all the years to come on this side of the veil or the other, for neither life nor death can separate us from the love of God, the life and the consciousness of God, the awareness which is now our being.

God is consciousness, therefore, there can be but one Consciousness, and the fact that we are conscious is proof that the Consciousness which is God is our individual consciousness.

---

[14] In the spiritual literature of the world, the varying concepts of God are indicated by the use of such words as "Father," "Mother," "Soul," "Spirit," "Principle," "Love," "Life." Therefore, in this book the author has used the pronouns "He" and "It," or "Himself" and "Itself" interchangeably in referring to God.

We, therefore, have access to unlimited wisdom, power, dominion, and law. Since God is the life of all this universe—and no one as yet has discovered a form of life separate and apart from the universal Life which is God—this Life then is our life. Our life and the Father's life are one. The Life which is God is the Life which is man: one Life, eternal, immortal, spiritual. God is the lawgiver. Then there can be only one law, and that is the law of God, and if we come in contact with material law, legal or economic law, it is our responsibility to realize that it has no power except as it is of the law of God: spiritual, harmonious, abundant, and infinite.

Daily Sowing and Reaping

"I"—the Spirit of God—"am come that they might have life, and that they might have it more abundantly." [15] That abundant life is ours when we live, and move, and have our being hid with Christ in God, where the universal beliefs of "this world" cannot intrude, nor enter to defile or to make a lie.

When we know the truth, then the truth can operate and make us free, and the truth that we are to know is that *I*, the presence of God, the consciousness of God, the life of God, is come in the midst of us that we might have life, and that we might have it more abundantly, freely, and joyously, and that we might share it with all those who are in spiritual darkness. It is not ours to keep; it is not ours to hide in a mountaintop or in some remote ashrama or temple. We may retire to such a place for a week or for forty days of inner contemplation, but we must come down to the plains, down to the seashore, yes, down even to the valley to share with the people of this world who are not yet enlightened and who, therefore, are not yet aware of their destiny of freedom under God. With those whom we find receptive and

[15] John 10:10.

responsive, we must share this great secret of the oneness of our individual being, and theirs, with the infinite and eternal Source.

> Let us pour out our gifts of the Spirit to the multitudes; but let us never seek the multitudes. We do not go up and down the highways and byways, even of our family, trying to find somebody upon whom to force this gift; because if we squander the gift of the Spirit on the unprepared thought, we shall find ourselves depleted. We wait for the multitudes to come to us. Should the multitudes consist of only one person, we wait for that one to come to us. We sit quietly at home, or in our shop or office, with our finger on our lips, keeping our treasure hidden from the world. Those who are receptive respond to the light within us, and recognize the glint in our eyes, or the smile on our face. As they come, one by one, let us accept each one as the multitude. They come to us for bread, which we give them, and cold water and warm water, too. We give them what they are seeking. We give it to them gently; we give it to them gradually; we give it to them with love, with joy, and with the power of authority. We can draw upon the infinity of our being, and anything will flow: words of truth, compassion, love, healing, grace, finances, food, water, drink, protection, care, companionship—all these will flow forth from the Christ within us.[16]

"Whatsoever a man soweth, that shall he also reap." [17] As we sow now to the Spirit, so will we reap life everlasting. If we waste our time in sowing to the flesh, we will reap corruption. But now, in this moment, which is to be the continuing moment of the year to come, we are sowing to the Spirit, sowing to the truth, sowing to life eternal, sowing to spiritual freedom under God's grace. Then will come the reaping and the sharing.

Let us daily remember the spiritual nature of our being, and at least once every day close our eyes and silently repeat to ourselves that word *I,* followed by our name, and then pause to realize the incorporeal, indestructible nature of our being. The incorporeal, invisible nature of the Father is the incorporeal, in-

16 From the author's *The Art of Meditation* (New York: Harper and Brothers, 1956), pp. 90, 91.
17 Galatians 6:7.

visible nature of the *I* that we are, and all that the Father has is ours unto eternity. Neither life nor death can separate us from the allness of God.

Living Love Is Living the God-Life

To pray for our enemies, our friends, and for our relatives is to know the truth. This truth that we have been knowing is the universal truth about all God's creation. It is not the truth about mortal man because mortal man is living in defiance of the laws of God. It is true only of that *I* that is living in conscious one-ness with God, and we are living in that conscious oneness only when we are living the life of love, loving our neighbor as our-selves, loving our fellow man, forgiving even our persecutors and enemies.

The mortal life is not of God: it is destructible. The life that is lived in the belief in good and evil is not under the law of God, and only when we live forgiveness, live in sharing and giving, are we living the God-life, that incorporeal, spiritual life that is in-destructible, the life that not even flames can destroy or swords pierce.

This life which we bring to our remembrance when we realize the true meaning of *I* is our God-given, immortal life, and we live it through love, and only through love. When selfishness, greed, lust, animality, hate, envy, and jealousy are permitted en-trance into our consciousness, we are living a life apart from God, a life which has no support from God, and therefore a life which must come to an end.

We can reject that human sense of life by renouncing the per-sonal sense of self which is characterized by a lack of love, a lack of justice, or a lack of benevolence; and we can accept the *I* that is one with God, the *I* that is the Spirit of God that has come as our individual being that we might have life, and that we might share this life through love and forgiveness, by releasing everyone from all obligations to us, through praying for others, and through knowing the truth.

"Owe no man any thing, but to love one another: for he that loveth another hath fulfilled the law.[18] . . . This is my commandment, That ye love one another, as I have loved you." [19] Love—this is the heritage, this is the nature of the *I* that we are.

Since "I and my Father are one," my whole reliance is on Him, on the I *that I am, the Consciousness that I am, the Consciousness that embraces within Itself infinity.*

I am conscious through sight, through hearing, through taste, touch, and smell. I am conscious through thinking: I am consciousness itself.

In the consciousness that I am are embraced the whole universe and all the worlds to come, for the consciousness which I am and the Consciousness which God is are one and the same consciousness. All that the Father has is mine; all that God is as Consciousness, I am as consciousness, for I am that I AM.

"He that hath seen me hath seen the Father." [20] If we can see the *I* of individual being—Consciousness, incorporeal, spiritual Being—we are seeing God, that *I* that is one with the Father. Let us remember always that when we are outwardly and openly saying, "Good morning," or wishing anyone a happy New Year, inwardly we are adding:

I, *the Father within you, give unto you a good morning or a happy New Year.* I, *in the midst of you, give unto you* My *peace.* *God's morning, God's New Year, give* I *unto you.*

ACROSS THE DESK

Everyone is surrounded to some extent by human love, care, consideration, and resources, but until we think about it, we

[18] Romans 13:8.
[19] John 15:12.
[20] John 14:9.

may not fully appreciate how much human good we are enjoying. What we receive from parents, husband, wife, children, and friends, we usually take for granted, or we tend to dwell so much on our nagging lacks that we do not fully realize the gifts, inheritances, and blessings we are continually receiving.

At some time or other on his spiritual journey, this is brought to the attention of the spiritual seeker. It is often when his human resources fail him that the budding mystic is born because now he must turn his attention to spiritual resources, to the Kingdom within himself.

There are those who under the stress and strain of a period of barrenness fall away and are lost for this lifetime at least. Others can go through the period of human desertion and material lack and gradually shift the base of their dependence from the outer to the inner realm of consciousness. These are the ones in whom that Something within has been awakened; these are the budding mystics who know that He "hangeth the earth upon nothing," [21] that He that is within them is greater than he that is in the world. These are the few who finally reach the realization that "I have meat to eat that ye know not of." [22]

With this understanding, the transition from the man of earth to that man who has his being in Christ begins to be made. "The natural man receiveth not the things of the Spirit of God," [23] and as long as man lives secure in, and content with, his human relationships and material resources he is "not subject to the law of God, neither indeed can be." [24]

When, however, he becomes aware of the clinging to, and dependence on, "man, whose breath is in his nostrils," [25] and begins consciously to change his base of reliance to the Nothingness which constitutes spiritual Presence and Power, he begins to bud spiritually and eventually must bear fruit richly.

[21] Job 26:7.
[22] John 4:32.
[23] I Corinthians 2:14.
[24] Romans 8:7.
[25] Isaiah 2:22.

A mystic lives in something like a shell of Nothingness: he feels no dependence on outer circumstance, person, or condition; he feels no fear of external powers, whether appearing as person or condition. He lives in a sense of Self-completeness, sustained first by the realization that "I have meat to eat that ye know not of" [26] and finally by the conscious awareness that "I am the way, the truth, and the life.[27] . . . I am the resurrection." [28]

The mystic, having attained spiritual Grace, finds himself well endowed materially and mentally as well as spiritually, and therefore has "twelve baskets full" to share.

[26] John 4:32.
[27] John 14:6.
[28] John 11:25.

Barriers to Spiritual Attainment

———•———

As human beings we all want or need something, and it is the desire for that something that blocks our spiritual development. It is the desire or need for something apart from God that sets up within us a sense of separation from Him, or leads us to believe that we could be satisfied with something other than the presence and power of God.

The very desire for something good, something as good as to be of service, is a barrier to spiritual development for we have no right to want anything, even to want to do good. We have only one right: to want to know God. Then, if God places us in some form of service—teaching, healing, nursing, painting, writing plays or books, or whatever it may be—we perform our work with joy and gladness because we are permitting ourselves to be transparencies through which God can shine. But for us to desire to do any of these things would be to glorify ourselves, and that is wrong.

It is difficult to live the spiritual life because in the human picture we are continuously desiring something—to be something, to do something, to benefit or to bless someone—and that is the barrier to spiritual development. The dissolving of the barrier comes with the relinquishment of our desires, wants, wishes, or outlining, so that we can go to God pure, not asking for supply, companionship, or to be of service, but asking only that God's grace be established in us, that God envelop and permeate us, that we may come to know Him aright, realize our oneness with Him, and thereby become consciously one with the creative Principle of our being. That is all. We, then, have no further needs, no further wants, no further desires.

The Fruitage of Conscious Oneness with God

To live in conscious union with God draws to us all that is necessary to fulfill our experience as long as we do not outline what that experience is to be or desire it to unfold in some particular way. That union with God, acting through us, forces us into the particular activity that will be of the greatest service to others and brings the greatest fulfillment to us.

Our conscious oneness with God constitutes our oneness with every spiritual idea and with every form of life.[1] Behind every form of nature, there is spiritual life, and when we are consciously one with God, we are consciously and instantaneously one with the life of every plant and animal—not with their physical life, but with their spiritual life. As long as they are a part of our consciousness, they will partake of our consciousness, and

[1] For a further exposition of this subject, see the author's *Conscious Union With God* (New York: Julian Press, 1962).

our consciousness of truth will be their resurrected and renewed life.

Our consciousness of God becomes the consciousness of our patients and students. As long as they are in our consciousness, they are partaking of our understanding; they are eating of the bread, meat, wine, and water which is our realized consciousness of truth, and our consciousness of our oneness with God becomes a law of harmony unto them.

Being Single-Minded

Thousands of students all over the world who maintain contact with The Infinite Way consciousness, either through the monthly *Letter,* reading the books, hearing the tapes, or attending Infinite Way meetings where there is an uplifted consciousness, find that they go through years and years with little or no disease or discord. For long periods of time, they have few problems of a serious nature, and those that do arise dissolve more readily.

This is not always true in the first, second, or third year of study because beginning students have not yet learned how to make contact with the higher Consciousness, and they are still engrossed in living their own lives. They have not accepted themselves as a part of The Infinite Way consciousness, and they are, therefore, living part of their life following The Infinite Way and part of it with some other form of metaphysics or sometimes with six different forms. Such students do not wholeheartedly embrace the principles of any particular teaching, and consequently their consciousness is united with nothing.

From the moment a student realizes that The Infinite Way is his way of life and has united himself with it, he begins to find that The Infinite Way consciousness itself maintains his freedom for him. "And I, if I be lifted up from the earth, will draw all men unto me:" [2] I, if I be lifted into God-consciousness, will lift those who come to me to that same state of consciousness, and they will then partake of its fruitage.

The Master placed a condition on the continuous enjoyment of that fruitage when he said, "Behold, thou art made whole: sin no more, lest a worse thing come unto thee." [3] In other words, we must not go back to the state of consciousness in which we originally were, because it can bear only the same kind of fruit. Now that we have been lifted into a higher consciousness, we must be sure that we continue acting out from that consciousness. Before we knew the truth, we could do many things that brought no penalty upon us because we had not touched the higher, more rarified consciousness.

But now we cannot afford to be untrue to our highest sense of integrity or to violate the least important spiritual law—not even to accept appearances at face value—without paying a penalty for it. In the degree that we come down from that high sense in the slightest measure, we suffer. That is because we have become so sensitive and so attuned to the Spirit that coarse or evil thoughts or actions react very quickly upon us.

Give Up Seeking Forms of Good

To sow to the flesh has a far deeper meaning than the usual meaning the world has given it. If in any way we put our faith in form rather than in the essence or substance of the form, in that degree are we going to bear only material fruitage, which is corruption.

No matter what we achieve or possess humanly—whether a fortune, a marriage, or a healthy physical body—it is subject to deterioration and death; in fact, it is dying from the time of birth. Anything that is acquired humanly has only the substance

[2] John 12:32.
[3] John 5:14.

of itself and is bound by its own limitations. If, through our conscious oneness with God, however, some good comes into our experience—money, home, marriage, companionship, employment, or service—it is an until-death-do-us-part relationship, an eternal relationship. We can never be separated from any good that comes to us through our conscious oneness with God.

If we can go through lack of any nature and are able to stand fast, not seeking to demonstrate persons, things, or conditions, but seeking only to demonstrate conscious union with God, the substance of all form, then the supply of whatever is lacking will unfold.

Some students who experience a temporary sense of economic lack are unable to rest in a complete reliance on the Spirit when their situation becomes acute, and they resort to human manipulation and conniving, thereby losing their whole demonstration of spiritual living. Other students to whom economic abundance comes very soon after they have entered the spiritual path become so fascinated with the money that is accumulated or with the things that money can buy that they also lose their demonstration. It is not money that makes or loses the demonstration, nor is it a lack of money. Nothing in the outer form is the determining factor: what counts is conscious union with God.

Many a person has had to come to death's door before he found God, and he could not find God until he reached that point. Why? He was trying to find health, and as long as a person is trying to find health, he will not find God. He must give up the search for forms and realize that health is not all-important, and that if he had all the health there is in the world today, it could turn into sickness tomorrow.

As a matter of fact, what difference does it make how healthy, youthful, beautiful, or handsome we are as long as the passage of time will inevitably change this so that the picture is completely reversed? What point is there, then, in taking pride in youth, health, or wealth? They are all fleeting.

But if we make God our goal, realizing that nothing is going to satisfy us except conscious union with God, there will never be such things as age, lack, loneliness, or emptiness in our experience. In God's presence is the fulfillment of life, and there is no other way to attain real fulfillment. In the presence of God, there is joy: freedom from every form of lack.

The Continuity of Life Is Not Dependent on Processes

Another step forward in our spiritual development is taken when we come to the place where we are not demanding that life fulfill itself on this side of the grave, because now we are not desiring this or that side, but only fulfillment. If the Spirit of God dwell in us, then do we have the capacity to release our desires, even the desire for human life, as we realize: "What possible difference can it make whether I am looking at life from this side or that? As far as God is concerned, does it matter on which side of the border life is being lived? Life is eternal: it cannot be otherwise. It is going on continuously and fulfilling itself without end."

> *Nothing do I seek—nothing. The realization of my conscious oneness with God is enough. In my oneness with God, I am one with all spiritual life everywhere: on this side of the grave, the other side, and the side of life that has not yet come into manifestation in this world.*

All space is filled with the life of God, all space and all time—past, present, and future—and we are one with that life, even one with that which is unborn. Life exists before birth, and life exists during and after birth, and life exists after death because God is life and God is the only life.

There is no power that can prevent the life of God from expressing. The life of God lives to express itself. We can hold it back, however, by the belief that it is dependent on physical organs or functions. But the life of God is Spirit, and that needs no material aids to sustain it. Therefore, the life of God can express itself whithersoever it will, and it does. But it is up to us to remove the barriers that would claim that it is dependent upon a process, dependent on an organ or on a function. Life is dependent on God's grace, and on God's grace alone. When God's grace wants the life of God to appear, it appears.

Conscious Oneness with God Brings Fulfillment

To be consciously one with God is to be consciously one with the spiritual life of all being and all form; therefore, whatever is necessary to our fulfillment will come into our experience. If it is patients to be healed or students to be taught, they will find us; if it is pictures to be painted, or books to be written, if it is marriage, family, or business, it will all flow out into expression. Nothing can stop God from fulfilling Itself, once we have made contact with God. If we do not make contact with God, God is still fulfilling Itself—but not in our experience.

Harmonious and successful living depends on one demonstration alone: the demonstration of conscious oneness with God. If a person comes to us with a problem and if we can become consciously one with God, that oneness with God appears in his life as the experience he needs, even though we may not know what that need is, and he, himself, may not know what it is. All he knows is the lack he feels, but we do not know, nor can we know, the way fulfillment will appear in any particular situation.

In The Infinite Way, it makes no difference what the nature of the problem is. One person may have a fever, another one chills; one may have a growth, and another a lack of substance. All we have to do to help him is to become consciously one with God, and whatever the nature of his need is, it is met. If fulfillment must come in less flesh or more flesh, it will; if it has to demonstrate itself in more companionship or less companionship, it will.

Letting the Divine Intelligence Operate in Human Relationships

Whatever the form of the need, divine Intelligence takes care of the whole matter without our interposing our beliefs. This underscores the point that a practitioner should never give human advice when he is called upon for help. For example, in marital affairs, he should never advise separation, divorce, or a continuation of the marriage. He must have no opinion about it at all: he must make conscious contact with God, and let God do to the life of that couple what It will. If their life will best be fulfilled together, all the obstacles to that togetherness will be removed. If, on the other hand, it is necessary for them to be separated to find individual fulfillment, this consciously realized Spirit will bring about the separation quickly and painlessly without loss to either one. If the practitioner enters such a case with a preconceived notion of what the demonstration should be, he is operating on the level of a marriage counselor or a psychological adviser, and that is not spiritual healing.

A practitioner's function is not to determine whether a person should be married, single, or divorced, whether he should live in this city or that city, or in this country or that country. The practitioner's function is to go to God, make conscious union with God, and then let the presence of God do what It will.

The Realization of God's Presence, the One Essential

The principle of attaining conscious oneness with God is effective in every activity of life. When I am giving a lecture or conducting a class, I never go to God for a message. When I meditate, it is for the realization of God's presence, and when I attain that, God's presence provides the message. If I should go to God for a message, I would be going for an effect or for a form, and I would lose the essence. As long as I do not seek for a message, but desire only the presence of God, it is the presence of God that will speak and give the message that is to come through me.

Much of what is in my books, I myself did not know until it came flowing out, and I was taught at the same time the students were. I have no way of gaining knowledge except as it comes through inspiration. So, from experience, I have learned not to want messages, not to want patients, and not to want students.

One thing alone do I want and need: the feeling and the awareness of God's presence, the consciousness of my oneness with God. Let me feel that God is living my life, and I will trust myself to go around the world without purse or scrip, or into any class without a message. Just let me feel that God is holding my hand, that the presence of God is with me, and, like Daniel, I will not fear lions either—but I would want to be sure that I had God right there beside me, or I could be very much frightened by a harmless little pussy-cat.

If we make our conscious contact with God, our life will be fulfilled according to God's plan, not according to our outline of what it should be, and God's plan usually turns out to be much better than anything we could have planned.

There is no such thing as personal power, and those who believe there is sooner or later find a power greater than themselves and are sometimes broken by it. Even leaning on God for something can be dangerous because, too many times, it is not God on whom we are leaning but on an idea in our mind, a belief, or a concept of God, and we cannot afford to lean on that. The only thing we can lean on is Nothingness: nothing we know, nothing we can see, hear, taste, touch, or smell. On That we can lean. And we will not really have to lean: we will be resting in the Is-ness of God.

"For my thoughts are not your thoughts, neither are your ways my ways.[4] . . . My peace I give unto you: not as the world giveth, give I unto you." [5] God's thoughts and God's peace transcend human understanding, but they come only to the person who has made conscious union with God. In that union, all things appear in the outer world.

Losing Fear of Effects

The correct letter of truth, taken into our consciousness, thought about, pondered and meditated upon, lived with, and practiced, develops a spiritual state of consciousness. We can see how this practice becomes realized consciousness if we take the basic premise that there is no power in form or effect and work with it.

This principle might be tested by placing money in front of us and then watching to see whether there is any power in it. Immediately, we observe that it stays where we put it, and there it will stay forever and forever and forever—just dead. It has no power; it cannot go out and buy even a cup of coffee; it cannot draw interest; it cannot multiply itself. It cannot come to me, and it cannot go to you. The minute this is perceived, we can relax and give up the struggle for it. Is something as dead as this piece of metal or paper in front of us worth struggling for?

[4] Isaiah 55:8.
[5] John 14:27.

Power is not in money: the power is in supply, the invisible Spirit of God, the Intelligence or Love that is within us. That Spirit of God draws the form of supply to us. It will maintain it, and the Spirit of God within us will intelligently and lovingly make use of it. Now we can use money as a tool or an instrument because the Intelligence that brought it to us is the Intelligence that knows what to do with it and can spend or invest it. It is not money that is worth struggling about: it is the spiritual wisdom that brings it to us that is worth achieving.

Money is an instrument or form of supply; it is the outer expression of supply, but it is not supply. Every time any thought of needing money, food, clothing, or housing comes to us, we should remember: "That is not supply. That is the form of supply, but supply itself is infinite and omnipresent, because God is supply. God is infinite, God is omnipresent, and wherever I am, God is; therefore, I have an infinity of supply."

Repeating this or reading it will not make it come to pass. It will become realized consciousness only if we ponder it, think about it, if each day we continue to remind ourselves that we have supply, and if each day the idea that money is power becomes deader and deader to us. We do not even have to pray for supply. The whole kingdom of God is established in us, and even God cannot withhold or take it from us because infinity is the measure of our supply.

Gradually our consciousness changes from one that places reliance on money to one that has an understanding of the omnipresence of supply, and thereby we develop the spiritual consciousness of supply. It may take a week, a month, or a year before this is completely attained. It will not take that long, however, to make a beginning. Within a short time, we shall find that we are losing our fear of lack. Our fear and our love of money are diminishing, because now we are beginning to see that, in and of itself, money is dead, just a form to be used. That changes our consciousness.

Losing the Material Sense of Body

In the area of health, also, harmony depends on our demonstration of God. There are persons suffering with diseases, and behind that suffering is the belief that harmony is dependent on some function or organ of the body. All human life is built on that premise. If anything happens to the heart, we die; if anything happens to the digestion or elimination, we become sick. We have to reverse that. Life is God, so life is not dependent on heart, liver, or lungs. Heart, liver, and lungs are dependent on life. It is life that beats the heart. It is life that activates the liver, the digestion, the elimination, and the muscles. It is not the body that moves life: it is life that moves the body, and life we are.

As long as we can say, "I am," we exist, we have life, and that life governs the body. As we maintain that, we lose the materialistic consciousness of body as governing life, and we attain the spiritual awareness of life governing the body.

"Man shall not live by bread alone." [6] Man shall not live by form or effect, whether it is baker's bread or butcher's meat, or the form that we call heart, liver, or lungs. Man shall not live by effect, but "by every word that proceedeth out of the mouth of God." [7] When we realize that the word of God is our life, the life of our being and of our body, our whole consciousness begins to change, and we stop fearing the organs and functions of the body. Through this practice, a new consciousness is being developed.

[6] Matthew 4:4.
[7] *Ibid.*

Releasing Desire

The barriers to our spiritual progress are our hopes, ambitions, and desires, even when they are good. Some of us cannot release the quest for health, and others cannot release the seeking for rent, food, clothing, or companionship. Always one of these lacks or desires is the thing that we feel must be solved first. We believe that if we could just be rid of our pain, then we could seek God; or if we could demonstrate more supply, then we could think of God. No, it works in reverse: if we think of God first, we will have all these other things. "Man, whose breath is in his nostrils" [8] must always want things, conditions, or persons, and therefore he is never free to seek the kingdom of God and His righteousness.

We may want to be given a thought with which to do healing work, but that is an effect. We may want to be given a truth about supply or companionship, but that, too, is an effect. Even desiring good thoughts is desiring effects. We do not desire good thoughts: .we desire only one thing: peace, peace, peace.

Desire is always the barrier to our progress, and certainly a barrier to the attainment of meditation. When we reach a point where there is nothing we want to gain from meditation, where we are not going into meditation for any purpose, but just turning within to be still, meditation is easy to attain. It is only when we take into our meditation our desire for some thing, and such a desire is a desire for an effect, that that inner stillness and peace of meditation elude us.

Working with the principles that constitute the letter of truth develops the spirit or consciousness of truth. Eventually we are living in Christ-consciousness where it is very easy to meditate because we have neither hate, fear, nor love of anything in the external realm. Even our love for friends and family takes on a

[8] Isaiah 2:22.

spiritual nature, which brings about in them a change toward us so that they do not cling to us as they once did, or depend or rely upon us.

The realization that God is the fulfillment of our being sets them and us free to love because we are free to give and receive without any clinging or attachment. We can love our families without believing they owe us anything and without feeling we owe them anything but to love them. They have the same God we have, and now we are united in a closer bond than we ever were before: we are united in that bond of love which can freely give and freely receive, and never feel that in giving we have deprived ourselves of anything or that in receiving we have deprived anyone else of anything.

To come to the realization of our oneness with God is the most freeing experience in the world. But we come to it by practicing and practicing and practicing, and by holding to this truth until gradually our whole consciousness changes. When it does, and this world becomes "dead" to us, we have won the whole world: it is all ours then, every single bit of it. It was only the desire for it that kept it away. There is now nothing to be achieved, nothing to be gained, nothing to be won. All already is. The Lord already is our shepherd, not because we earn or deserve it, or are worthy, not because we are going to do anything, but just because the Lord is our shepherd, and we shall not want.

Gain the conscious realization of the presence and power of God within your own being. Regardless of the name or nature of the problem or need, do not try to solve it on the level of the problem. Do not try to solve supply as supply; do not try to solve family relationships as family relationships. Drop all thought of these things. Go within until you actually find that place within your being which gives you the God-response. Then your problems will be solved. Once you have touched the Christ within your own being, you have touched the wellspring of life more abundant.

Conscious oneness with God! This constitutes conscious one-ness with all spiritual being and with every spiritual idea.[9]

ACROSS THE DESK

It was in 1947 that the first edition of *The Infinite Way* was published. Today it is in its eleventh edition, and it and the many other Infinite Way writings since then have traveled the world in American and British editions, and some in German, Dutch, French, and Japanese. Fifteen years ago, I was the only Infinite Way student in the world, and now see what God hath wrought around the globe! Only God could produce such a miracle.

It is becoming increasingly clear to me that God is permeating human consciousness with His presence and His grace. Each one of us as an Infinite Way student is His love and His life in action: "I live; yet not I, but Christ liveth in me." [10] Each one of us must realize that Truth is living in us for Its purpose.

"Ye have not chosen me, but I have chosen you." [11] Neither you nor I chose this Way, but we have been chosen that God's grace may be made visible on earth through us. Through us, God's plan is being revealed, and His will is being done on earth as it is in heaven.

Just as God has always chosen as His temples, teachers, disciples, apostles, and students, so today, God has chosen those men and women dedicated to conscious union with Him to appear as the temple of Truth evidenced all over the world. Those who abide in meditation experience His presence and thereby release into consciousness His grace and peace. "I can of mine own self do nothing," [12] but "I can do all things through Christ

[9] By the author. *Conscious Union With God* (New York: Julian Press, 1962). pp. 252-253.
[10] Galatians 2:20.
[11] John 15:16.
[12] John 5:30.

which strengtheneth me." [13] Except we be chosen of God, we cannot fulfill His mission, and we are chosen when we feel His Spirit within us.

"But the natural man receiveth not the things of the Spirit of God" [14]—only those in whom His Spirit consciously dwells. "Ye shall know them by their fruits," [15] and hereby do we know if His Spirit dwells in us: if we bring His grace and His peace with us in whatever place in life we walk. We need not leave our homes or our business, but we must carry into these His comfort, healing, and peace.

Let us always be recognized by our awareness that the joy and peace we bring are His. "If I bear witness of myself, my witness is not true":[16] it is the Father's will that comforts, heals, blesses, and multiplies. By His grace are we the light that His will may be done, not man's will or man's thought.

Looking out at the world, we see His light shining in the face of man. Looking at the events of the world, we witness more and more of His will and His grace. The Infinite Way again reveals the kingdom of God on earth, the will of God in man, and the grace of God come as peace in the heart of man.

We have not chosen this or done this, but the Father has chosen the time and the way.

[13] Philippians 4:13.
[14] I Corinthians 2:14.
[15] Matthew 7:16.
[16] John 5:31.

An Idea Whose Time Has Come

———•———

Truth received and embodied in consciousness eventually becomes known throughout the world without any human effort or human striving. By abiding with truth within oneself, it has a way of establishing itself. This does not always happen as quickly as you might like to have it happen, but you must learn that in the realm of truth "a thousand years in thy sight are but as yesterday when it is past," [1] and one day as a thousand years. There will be periods of thousands of years when little progress seems to be made. Then suddenly more progress is made in one day than in the preceding thousand years.

[1] Psalm 90:4.

An Idea in Consciousness Must Manifest Itself

The process of consciousness coming into expression in changing and better forms is a painfully slow one, and in religion the world has been more backward than in almost any other area of human experience. Until after the middle of the nineteenth century, religion in the Western World was a total state of darkness and ignorance, almost without even the tiniest bit of light. But in the middle of the nineteenth century, some of the Oriental Scriptures were translated into English and German and later into French, although it was in England and in Germany that they took root and the first spiritual light began to dawn. Then, in the United States, there was the period of the Transcendentalists in New England and the founding of Christian Science and Unity. All these were the light casting its shadow into visibility and prophesying things to come.

"Nothing is so powerful as an idea whose time has come," [2] and the idea of freedom, liberty, justice, and equality is an idea whose time has come in this age. Colonialism, the holding in bondage of one people over another, has to go. Nothing today can stop the breaking down of racial, religious, and nationalistic prejudice. Unfortunately, the world, not knowing how to achieve this by spiritual means, has had recourse only to the human means of force. To go out and fight for what it wanted is all the world has known.

Any idea or principle, real and true, revealed in consciousness, will manifest itself in human experience. Had more persons been sufficiently aware of the operation of this principle when the idea of freedom entered human consciousness and became tangible as form in ancient Greece, I believe that worldwide freedom would have been attained long ago. Instead, today

[2] Victor Hugo.

there are large segments of the population of the world where there is not a semblance of freedom.

In its widest sense, freedom includes religious, economic, political, and racial freedom—yes, even physical and mental freedom. Man cannot create freedom: freedom is of God. It is a divine impartation that comes to the consciousness of those who are receptive to that idea. Freedom must be received in consciousness because the only way God functions is as consciousness. Freedom is not to be begged for or fought for: freedom is to be recognized. Freedom in whatever form is God's gift to God's kingdom, God's activity operating in God's kingdom, God's grace appearing as liberty, justice, and equality, all of which are qualities of divine Consciousness, omnipresent where we are.

God's Instruments

In every generation there are certain persons born unselfed, with a love in their hearts that is not entirely self-love, a love that looks across the visible horizon and wonders, "What can I do to help?" To such persons, divine impartations are revealed. Florence Nightingale was one of the unselfed persons of the world, and certainly Christopher Columbus played a part in freeing the world of its bondage to time and space.

Freedom is "a many splendored thing" and has many facets. So it is that, here and there, individuals receive impartations from the infinite Source which is divine Consciousness, and these individuals draw others unto themselves. In this way, then, the ideals of political, economic, racial, and religious freedom are spread over the earth. There will always be instruments of God on earth because in every age there are persons born who are attuned with their Source, but of themselves, men and women are nothing.

The age of material power is a thing of the past. We are now living in the age when spiritual power is beginning to be understood, and spiritual power means nonpower. It means to "resist not evil," [3] to abide in the Word, and let the Word abide in you: " 'It is I; be not afraid.' [4] *I* in the midst of you is mighty. Put up your sword."

All power is in the hands of the Infinite, the Eternal, and it operates through Grace. How do you make this come true? By knowing it. This truth cannot make you free without your knowing it. You have to ponder truth, meditate upon it in your innermost secret sanctuary, and it will establish itself externally in miraculous ways.

Every time that you entertain a spiritual truth, you are in some measure attaining freedom, or life by Grace, but because there is only one infinite, unconditioned Consciousness, you are doing more than this. Somewhere in the world there are those attuned, and every time you individually receive an impartation of truth in your consciousness, it is being received in the consciousness of those who are similarly attuned. In other words, all over the world at this minute, there are persons longing with all their hearts and souls and minds and bodies for freedom. There are persons who are turning to their Withinness, sometimes in prison and sometimes because they have no one or nothing to turn to. In this way they are making themselves receptive to truth. They have created a vacuum, and they are thereby attuned to the unconditioned Consciousness.

The greater the degree of your spiritual freedom, the more widespread is the freedom that you can give. Through your study and meditation, you may attain such a degree of spiritual freedom that you will be a blessing to members of your family and to your immediate neighbors. You may attain such a great degree of freedom that you may become a healer on a wide scale: city-wide, state-wide, nation-wide, or world-wide. It may

[3] Matthew 5:39.
[4] Matthew 14:27.

give birth in you to some idea of commercial or political freedom and so be a freeing influence for thousands of persons. Or, you may go so high in consciousness that you bring about a new world-wide religion. Who knows? But if you do, please do not organize it.

The Infinite Way Ideal of Freedom

Always remember that the freedom you crave in your heart everyone else is also craving, but do not believe that anyone can ever be free through binding another. When you set a person free, remember that you must set him free to have any religion he may choose or to have none at all. Set everyone free, and you yourself will be free to a greater extent.

The Infinite Way ideal of freedom has always been that of a spiritual bond uniting individuals in an eternal relationship of love, sharing, and good will. As one of its foundational points, The Infinite Way has no memberships and no dues; there is no binding of anyone to itself. It not only sets all free but maintains their freedom.

Freedom Has Been Loosed in Consciousness

This spiritual idea of freedom has no limits or boundaries, and if you look beyond the visible horizon, you will see how it is functioning in one group and in one country after another. History records events, but seldom records the causes underlying or leading up to those events.

For example, a cursory knowledge of the War between the States might lead one to believe that this war was fought because some persons so loved the Negroes that they were willing to die to free them, or because of the commercial rivalry between the northern and the southern states. Such a conclusion would ignore the fact that the idea of freedom, liberty, equality, and justice had been infiltrating consciousness as far back as ancient Greece, on down to the period when the Magna Carta took form in England, and on through the American, French, and South American revolutions. All these events were but the outpicturing of a changed state of consciousness, which culminated in more and more freedom for the people.

This idea of freedom is now spreading into the area of religion: Bishop Pike of the Episcopal Church is setting many of his people free of their superstition and ignorance, and the late Pope John endorsed the idea of universal and complete religious liberty for all persons. Pope Paul VI, upon his election to the pontificate, announced that he favored the aims of the late Pope John, stating that the Roman Catholic church should continue along the course indicated by his predecessor. A high churchman of England, the Bishop of Woolwich, has written to the effect that prayer is not asking anything of God, that prayer is listening, and that we must give up concepts of God to attain the God-experience. These advances are the fruitage of the truth that has been imparted to human consciousness from the infinite divine Consciousness.

A truth that is given to one individual in consciousness, and which he holds sacred within him and imparts only to those who are responsive so that it makes a circle or flow between them, must eventually be established for all men on earth. The divine Presence has within Itself the power to establish Itself, if It is remembered and held to sacredly.

We must reach the place where we can dedicate ourselves to something higher than our own interests. We must rise above self to the place where we consecrate some portion of our time to the cause of establishing God's kingdom on earth, holding to the vision that has already entered human consciousenss, remembering silently and sacredly that all freedom is a quality and activity of God as much on earth as in heaven, and then let this divine Principle open up human consciousness, first in one place and then in another. When an idea's "time has come," it always finds a way to establish itself on earth.

When one individual receives a principle in consciousness, it has at that moment entered human consciousness. The principles of electricity, for example, discovered and received through one individual, became available to everyone else in the world, and impossible as it may seem, when the idea of a horseless carriage was born in the consciousness of a gas-meter reader just barely able to care for his family, he received all the support necessary to found the Ford Motor Company. So it is with any idea. If it is born ahead of its time, it dies. If it is born at the right time, it carries with it all that is necessary for its fulfillment.

Establish Truth in Consciousness
by Living the Contemplative Life

So it is, also, with a spiritual truth that is received in the consciousness of an individual. Recognize that the truth which is within you is greater than all that is in the outer world, rendering null and void the weapons of this world. This principle will establish individual freedom at every level of human life through an inner communion with the Spirit. These ideas established in consciousness—pondered, meditated upon, communed with inwardly—will establish themselves outwardly. Men here and there will voice these truths and, because they are authorities in their fields, they will be believed. Then we can take the greater step of establishing the kingdom of God on earth by living the contemplative life.

The life we live as Infinite Way students is really not a religious life, as religion is usually thought of. It is a contemplative

life, the life in which we ponder, meditate, and cogitate upon
Reality. It is a life in which we commune with our inner or spiritual Self. It is a life which, by means of receptivity, makes us
responsive to impartations from the Infinite to the individual. It
is a life in which we look to the divine Source for our good, a life
in which we are not enslaved by words. Too often a word gets a
grip on us, and then we are the victims of that word, such words
as "he," "she," and "it." The devil usually takes the form of
"he," "she," or "it." In fact, all evil is bound up in these words.
But what we must do is to look beyond every "he," "she," and
"it" in the world and realize:

> *God is the source of my good. God is the source of my supply.*
> *God is the cement of my relationships.*

In such moments, we will be looking over the heads of those
who are venal in their conduct, those who are merely selfish, and
those who are neither venal nor selfish but who are ignorant, and
thanking God that freedom is not at the mercy of any of these,
that freedom is the gift of God, and it is God who establishes
freedom on earth as it is in heaven. Then, instead of becoming
angry at some "he," "she," or "it," any sense of anger is directed
at ourselves for being enslaved by the "he," "she," or "it."

If we look to friends, relatives, patients, or students, we are
looking amiss, and will some day be disappointed. But if we
keep our vision above their heads, not looking to "man, whose
breath is in his nostrils," [5] if we keep our vision on the divine
Source of our being, then "no weapon that is formed against
[us] shall prosper." [6] We can share with every "he," "she," and
"it," but leave each one free to do his own degree of sharing or not
sharing. Sometimes living this way results in persons being taken
out of our lives. At other times, this does not happen, and they
remain with us. That is when we have to rise higher and higher

---

[5] Isaiah 2:22.
[6] Isaiah 54:17.

and be indifferent to their conduct. We must rise to where we can realize:

> *None of this moves me. I am looking to the Kingdom within me, to my Source. My conscious oneness with God constitutes my oneness with all spiritual being and idea.*
>
> *God is my freedom; God is my life, the Source of all I am and can ever hope to be. This was true before I was born, and it will be true after I leave visibility.*

Only a few are born with the spiritual instinct of wanting to give, and inasmuch as giving does not come naturally to most persons, every child should be taught not only the Ten Commandments, but that it is more blessed to give than to receive. Being obedient to the Ten Commandments, however, is in no wise living the spiritual life. The righteousness of the spiritual student must exceed that of the scribes and the Pharisees. It must go beyond a literal obedience to the law; it must be an inner realization.

Live As Guests of Life

One of the most releasing experiences that can come to a person is when he can grasp the meaning of "the earth is the Lord's, and the fulness thereof." [7] An understanding of this truth would eliminate the widespread misconception there is in regard to the subject of tithing. Since those who tithe seldom know lack or limitation, it has been believed that if people could be taught this principle they would always be prosperous. This is not true. Tithing is a practice that can take place only when individuals inwardly receive the realization of what great gifts of God they have received, and in gratitude decide to share some part of these. This sharing is done with the idea of thankfulness for the realization of God's grace, and it is for this reason that those

[7] Psalm 24:1.

who spontaneously practice tithing are always generously and abundantly provided for.

How foolish it is to believe that we of ourselves possess something and that it is ours, or even that we have earned or deserved it! We are guests of Life, and Life has provided us with everything necessary to our fulfillment.

Freedom is ours as a spiritual inheritance. So freedom is a quality and an activity given to us as guests of Life, and we need take no thought for what we shall eat, what we shall drink, or wherewithal we shall be clothed. This does not place us in the position of parasites who take all, nor does it grant to a person the right to do anything he wants to do. We must realize that with this privilege goes also a great responsibility. Whatever we receive is for sharing, not for storing up "where moth and rust doth corrupt."[8] . . . Freely ye have received, freely give." [9]

We are guests of Life. This world was here before we were born, and we came into it as a guest of a world that had already been established. Food was in the larder; clothing was in manufacture. There was wood for building, and iron and steel; and there were diamonds, rubies, and pearls for adornment. Everything was put here for our use.

If we can understand that we are guests of Life, it is then not too difficult to see the debt we owe one another. We know that if we were guests in someone's home, a return would be expected of us. We would never have the feeling that we possessed anything in the home in which we were guests, but that it was all there for our enjoyment and use, and all without any monetary consideration. To the host, the hostess, and the guests of that household, we would owe gratitude, helpfulness, courtesy, cooperation, and sharing, giving and receiving joyously.

Individually, we must come to the realization that our purpose on earth is to dwell harmoniously in this spiritual household, this kingdom of God which is on earth, conducting our-

[8] Matthew 6:19.
[9] Matthew 10:8.

selves as intelligent guests conduct themselves. As we are able to do this, our entire attitude toward one another will change, but only after the Experience has taken place within. It is like an alcoholic who wants to be free of alcoholism, but cannot be free until a certain moment when something takes place in his consciousness. Then suddenly he is free because now he has no power to be anything else.

Only a Change of Consciousness Can Bring Improved Conditions

We understand that improved humanhood will not bring lasting harmony any more than a change in the political party in power will bring a radical change in our living conditions. Putting politicians out of office is not the answer. There must first be a change of consciousness, and if there is a change of consciousness in the man on the street, this will change the nature of politicians. The answer is to rise above the belief of good and bad humanhood to the realization of spiritual identity. We will then have a different type of candidate, and we will have a higher quality of leadership because of our inner realization.

The entire world does not have to be transformed. The history of the world can be changed by "ten righteous men" here and there. The illumined consciousness of one pope can change the attitude and altitude of large segments of the world. One pope here, a bishop there, a minister here, a priest there, a rabbi there, one man in the business world—all with the idea of freedom attained individually by spiritual means—can work miracles. So it is not a matter of transforming the world but of bringing to the surface one here and one there to be lights in their communities. Then those few will raise up others with them.

The primary object of this work is not trying to improve ourselves humanly. Our goal is God-realization, and when that is attained we automatically become children of God, children of that one spiritual household. It is the experience of God in us that sets us free, but when we attain our freedom, that attained state of consciousness blesses those in our household or community who are receptive and responsive, and in some measure sets them free.

What you and I are receiving as benefits from our study and practice of The Infinite Way is of far less importance than what the Message is doing in the raising up of the entire world. It must be remembered that there is no Infinite Way separate and apart from your consciousness and mine. There is no Infinite Way hanging in space. Whatever Infinite Way there is on earth is what is active in consciousness, and unless Infinite Way principles find activity and expression in individual consciousness they will not be expressed in the world. Therefore, each of us has the responsibility to live these principles.

Liberty is not gained by fighting or by crusading for it, but by keeping it sacred and secret within our own consciousness, living it and granting it to others, and thereby watching it spread to the world. Crusades do not change anything because they do not change the consciousness of the individual. Attaining spiritual, economic, or political freedom is not accomplished by the outward attempts people make to gain these ends. Consciousness must be lifted out of its humanhood, out of its belief that self-preservation is the first law of human nature, into the Master's idea of loving another as we love ourselves, and more especially must it accept the revelation that no man on earth is our Father. There is one Father and one great brotherhood.

Perceive the larger vision. Place the freedom of the world in the hands of the Infinite. Take it out of the hands of man and realize that this world is not at the mercy of sin or stupidity. If we return the authority to the divine Consciousness, then this freedom, this idea whose "time has come," will express itself.

If freedom is to be attained and maintained in the world, therefore, it will have to be brought about by replacing self-preservation as the guide to conduct with a love for our neighbor. This requires an unselfedness. The average human being lives primarily for himself and his family. There is seldom any vision higher than that. Very few can go even so far as to give away the unused clothing hanging in the closet or send out extra food to the poor. Almost all human experience is a living for the individual or his family, with only a tiny scrap left over for others. Therefore, it is meaningless for anyone to think in terms of freedom for his country or for the world until he is ready to dedicate himself to the task of bringing it into expression in his own experience.

We must reach the point where we are Self-complete in God. Because "I and my Father are one," [10] the place whereon I stand is holy ground. This is the spiritual liberty in which man is wholly dependent on God's grace. Only then has he attained freedom. He has to know that even if all his earthly good were taken from him, he still stands on holy ground, and the lost years of the locust will be restored. Look over the heads of people, and see the spiritual Grace that is Omnipresence, that is the Source of all human harmony.

Try to vision this larger canvas of life so that you do not measure your spiritual life by what it is doing to you and yours and for you and yours alone. Rather, see how the measure of spiritual freedom that you attain is the measure of spiritual freedom that you are giving back to the world, hastening the day of freedom for all.

As guests of Life, we are really only temporary visitors to earth. It is not given to us to possess anything here permanently because we can take nothing with us when we leave except the spiritual treasures we have laid up. But remember that every spiritual treasure that we will carry into the next plane of existence is a spiritual treasure that we will also leave behind. It is not finite: it is Omnipresence Itself.

[10] John 10:30.

Once we have acquired the realization of a spiritual truth, it is ours throughout all eternity, but it is also one that will remain behind in the consciousness of mankind to multiply itself. This is spiritual law.

ACROSS THE DESK

When we first come to a spiritual study, most of us are thinking in terms of the benefit that we hope to receive from it. In one way or another the object in seeking any kind of a teaching is self-benefit or some form of self-improvement. It would be very unusual for anyone to go out and look for a teaching that would benefit the world because until consciousness has been spiritualized a person's interests are concerned primarily with himself and his family.

It is surprising how many persons, hearing of this work, write and ask for help for a member of their family who has a handicap of some nature: physical, mental, or moral. But when they are told that there must be some cooperation and study on their part, nothing further is heard from them. Apparently their interest does not go even that far beyond themselves, and while it is true that this does not happen in every case, most persons are to a greater or lesser degree seeking only to benefit themselves.

But this should not ever be true of Infinite Way students because almost from the very beginning, as part of The Infinite Way message, students have been instructed to carry on world work. As a result, groups have been formed all over the world, working secretly and sacredly to bring to light the spiritual age. The very fact that today we have an Infinite Way must indicate that the time has come on earth for such a transition in consciousness, a change that takes place when our consciousness is open purely to receive the awareness of the indwelling Christ, without any reason for doing so. As long as we are living by the Ten Commandments and the Sermon on the Mount alone, we are still living by the letter of truth. But we can move from the letter of truth at any moment that our meditations contain no thought of self-improvement or self-betterment.

In the early 1900s, the electrical wizard Steinmetz said that the secret of spiritual power would be revealed in this century. His prediction is about to be realized because the age now drawing to a close has not only given the world great scientific discoveries and inventions, but it has also given it the letter of truth. The letter of truth includes those principles with which most of us are familiar, and which are hidden in the Ten Commandments and the Sermon on the Mount.

Human beings are so completely centered in, and circumscribed by, themselves, however, that honesty and integrity are not natural to them. Self-preservation, rather than honesty and integrity, is usually accepted as the first law of human nature. It was even thought necessary to command us to love our fathers and mothers—even that is not natural to human beings, and so it has had to be drilled into them.

There is an entirely different attitude, however, among those persons who follow the Christ-way of life. To them it is normal and natural to love their neighbors as themselves, for they have evolved out of the self-preservation state of consciousness. They have come to a place in their development that can be described as Christ-consciousness. This is the consciousness that normally and naturally prays for the enemy and forgives seventy times seven. This consciousness has no trace of revenge or punishment, of an eye for an eye and a tooth for a tooth.

If at any time we turn to God to fulfill a desire, even a good one, we have not yet spiritualized our consciousness because spiritual consciousness is a consciousness that gives no power to anything or anybody. It does not need a God-power. This is not doing away with God: it is a recognition that God is; it is a complete relaxing in God.

The consciousness that does not fear external powers is the God-presence and the God-power, and this is spiritual power. A complete relaxing from power, from desiring power, or from trying to contact power leaves us in a state of *is,* and this is spiritual power *released.*

As long as there are persons fighting evil conditions, there will be evil conditions to fight because the mind that believes in two powers is still creating conditions of good and evil. Only when we withdraw power from them, when we cease fighting them, will these evil powers cease to be.

The world work in which Infinite Way students engage is not fighting evil persons or evil conditions: it is withdrawing power from them, and the students becoming such clear transparencies that the Christ can flow through their consciousness and dissolve the pictures of sense. Infinite Way students do not pray for peace or temporary good. Their prayer for the world is the realization of the nonpower of the carnal mind and the nature of God as individual consciousness.

Universal human consciousness is what constitutes the belief in two powers, and thereby creates the conditions of this world; but it is the individual's recognition of the nonpower of this universal carnal mind with its pictures that releases the Christ into human experience. Every time that we have an experience that proves the nonpower of anything to which the world gives power, we are not only lessening the universal belief, but we are making it possible for somebody, somewhere, to pick up what we have loosed into consciousness.

The fifty or sixty thousand of us who are studying The Infinite Way and who in some degree are impersonalizing good and evil are responsible for others picking up that very principle because there is only one Consciousness. This is a principle of life not yet known to the world at large, but understood by students of The Infinite Way through their study of its teaching. The effects of this principle have been felt throughout all known time, but the principle itself had not been revealed.

The Infinite Way is one of the first of the purely mystical teachings of modern days. It is enlightened consciousness appearing in human experience as the consciousness of those individuals ready for it. But an activity of God, Truth revealing Itself in human consciousness, could not be limited to the few who write or read its message. Actually, we are but transparencies through which this message must reach the entire world.

You can witness that this is what is happening. Everywhere individuals are receiving these impartations, and books are being written setting forth ideas new to those who are not Infinite Way students. These are now reaching human consciousness on a world-wide basis.

What you are reading about in the newspapers is just the product of the good and bad karmic influences of past generations. What is happening in the world everywhere is of a freeing nature, and while the world is not aware of the significance of events taking place now, twenty or thirty years from now it will be seeing their significance as people read accounts of these events in their history books.

There is ample proof that the principle of impersonalization is being loosed in consciousness and, as we continue our work, it is inevitable that this principle will show up in one place and then in another. The late Pope John made innovations which, if understood, would startle the world, and they are an indication of the degree to which he was responsive to whatever spiritual truth is active in consciousness. That this is true is evident from a quotation from a newspaper article by Walter Lippmann:

> In reaching out beyond the clergy and the faithful of his own church to all men of good will, including the declared enemies of his church, the Pope has based the argument of his message not on revelation and the inspired teachings of the church, but *upon a philosophical principle.*
>
> "One must never," says the Pope, "confuse error and a person who errs. . . . The person who errs is always and above all a human being, and he retains in every case his dignity as a human person, and he must be always regarded and treated in accordance with that lofty dignity.
>
> "Besides, in every human being there is a need that is con-

genital to his nature and never becomes extinguished, compelling him to break through the web of error and open his mind to the knowledge of truth."

The Pope's encyclical seems to have been timed after deciding that the "moment has arrived . . . when it is honorable and useful" to restate the old philosophy for the modern age.[11]

Here is the principle of the divinity of man even when he is a sinner, and here is the principle of impersonalization, which, to my knowledge, has not been incorporated in any religious teaching since the Master's day. The Master used the principle of impersonalization in all his teaching when he said, "Who made me a judge . . . over you? [12] . . . Neither do I condemn thee.[13] . . . Father, forgive them; for they know not what they do." [14]

Can it be merely coincidence that the Pope's Easter message was given approximately in the same month in which Bishop Robinson's paperback edition of *Honest to God* was released? Is it merely coincidental that spiritual healing is becoming such an important subject in the churches today? Or, is all this the result of the world work which has been carried on over a period of years?

The children of future generations will probably wonder how anyone could have indulged in such a relic of the Dark Ages as personalization, and, surprisingly enough, they will undoubtedly benefit more from this teaching than those of the present generation. This is because coming generations will be born into a higher spiritual level of consciousness than that into which we were born. Those who are born into that higher consciousness will not be brought up, as we have been, with the idea of self-benefit.

Once we perceive that the only power there is, is the power of our own consciousness, how then would it be possible to fear

[11] Reprinted by permission of the Los Angeles Times Syndicate.
[12] Luke 12:14.
[13] John 8:11.
[14] Luke 23:34.

what mortal man can do to us? How can we speak of omnipotent Omnipresence and, at the same time, be subject to universal beliefs?

The only reason we suffer from anything is because of a universal malpractice, arising out of the carnal mind which is comprised of all the theories and beliefs of a mental or material nature. All evil is the projection of the carnal mind, the belief in two powers. The antidote is the recognition of nonpower, and the degree of awareness of this nonpower is the measure of our progress into spiritual consciousness.

These truths are stated clearly in the Writings, but when it comes to living them, we have not even begun to scratch the surface. The development of spiritual consciousness begins when we release all concepts of God in the recognition that the *I* that is seeking God is God. Then, when we sit down in meditation, we take no thought for any condition of the world or any person of the world, and become a state of receptivity so as to hear the still small voice: "Who convinceth me of sin? Who convinceth me of any presence or power but the One which I am?"

Watch that you do not have that One separate and apart from *I AM,* or you are then out of focus. Watch that you do not have concepts of God, because this is a projection of an image, and that is idolatry.

The more these Infinite Way principles are recognized by persons outside The Infinite Way, the more you will know that this work is permeating human consciousness. Probably all the people in the churches who are engaged in world-wide prayer activity are praying for peace on earth. But peace can never come to earth as long as man's consciousness remains what it is today. What good would peace be as long as consciousness remains at the human level? It would mean only an interval between wars. First, man's consciousness must change.

So, when we are doing our world work, let us hold to our two major principles that God constitutes individual consciousness, and that the carnal mind is not power but is the "arm of flesh" or nothingness. Then we shall witness a change in individual consciousness, and future generations will be born into that higher state of consciousness.

Spiritual consciousness, then, is one that is not warring with evil, nor is it believing that spiritual power can be used. It is recognizing spiritual power as divine Grace. Think a great deal on the term "spiritual power," and try to get a clearer comprehension of what it really means. Remember that it is not a power over anything or anybody; it is not a power to be used. Spiritual power is not a temporal power. Spiritual power is a state of Grace.

From

THE CONTEMPLATIVE LIFE

Erasing Our Concepts of God,
Prayer, and Grace

———•———

Religion is an individual experience, and not only is it impossible to go into heaven two by two or four by four, but even any attempt to do so must result in failure.

If a person is interested in a spiritual way of life, in seeking the realm of God or finding a solution to human problems, it is necessary that that person embark on his mission alone. This does not mean that if one's husband or wife also wishes to set forth on such a mission he or she should not do so, but because of the very nature of this search, each one must find his way within himself, alone. No two people can progress at the same rate because no two people are at the same level of consciousness; and therefore, the religious life is one which must be lived within the individual, regardless of how much is shared outwardly. No one can achieve this life for another: each must achieve it for himself.

In the writings and recordings of The Infinite Way is found the account of my own search for God: the mode, the means, and the achievement. This has been set forth merely to show what one individual has achieved, and these books and recordings are offered to you in the hope that you will read, study, or hear them, and put them into practice; and, insofar as they prove successful, live with them and through them.

In a few brief years, many thousands who have followed the particular way known as The Infinite Way have, in a measure, found their peace, their harmony, safety, security, and their supply. In reading and studying The Infinite Way, however, you are in no sense bound to it. You are, at all times, a free spiritual agent, free to come to us or to any of our students who are active in the work, but just as free at any time not to come—always free to find your own way. You have no obligations; you have no embarrassments; and if The Infinite Way does not prove effective in your individual case, you are at liberty always to seek further until you do find the particular teaching which is yours.

You are under no obligation to me or to the message of The Infinite Way. There is nothing you can join, so there are no memberships or ties to dissolve. Come, enjoy, eat, drink, be satisfied, but let each one of us maintain his oneness with God. In such a way lies true freedom, true liberty, and the obligation each one has is to his Maker and not to any man. What a satisfying thing that is to remember!

Day and night and night and day, I owe no man anything but to love him. My sole obligation is to love my God and my fellow man. There is no way of expressing the joy and the freedom this gives all of us; there is no way of explaining what takes place in the consciousness of an individual who knows that he is free in God.

When people come together in large groups, there is a tendency to rely on that togetherness, or that union, for their demonstration of peace, harmony, and security, and they thereby lose. The idea that in union there is strength has been drilled into people from infancy, but this is not true, except in the spiritual sense of union with God, not union with one another.

Couples have married, believing that in such union would be their strength and later have found that each had to find his or her strength individually—that strength could not be found collectively. Nations have united, but these unions have usually lasted only as long as they have not interfered with or jeopardized the selfish aims and ambitions of the parties involved.

When people unite humanly for the purpose of finding safety, security, peace, harmony, or health, they must fail because the only way to achieve these is in the degree of their oneness with God, consciously realized—their oneness with their Source. That is something that no one can do for another. Each must achieve this for himself.

No Theory or Concept of God Is God

There is a difficulty in embarking on a spiritual way of life, and one which everyone has to surmount if he is to remain on the spiritual path. That difficulty concerns itself with three words, but once you are able to rise above the limitations of those three words, you will find that the spiritual path is much easier than you had ever believed it could be, and much more joyous and fruitful. For a time, however, the struggle lies in these three words, the first of which is God—G-o-d.

The hardest part of your spiritual journey is to rise above the concepts of God that you have always accepted. Whether your concept of God has come from a church, from your parents, or from your own experiences in life—regardless of where or how you acquired your particular concept of God and regardless of what that concept may be—it is not God.

There is nothing that you know about God that is God. There is no idea of God that you can entertain that is God. There is no possible thought that you can have about God that is God. It makes no difference what your idea may be or what your concept may be, it remains an idea or a concept, and an idea or a concept is not God. And so every student must eventually realize that he has to rise above all his concepts of God before he can have an experience of God.

Regardless of the concept of God entertained, whether Hebrew, Protestant, Catholic, or Oriental, it has done very little for the world. This world is in a sad plight, and every known concept of God has failed to bring peace on earth—not only collectively, but individually.

The world is in a state of unrest because of fear of aggression on the part of Russia and China or because of the upheaval in Africa. The threat to world peace arising out of the situation in these areas would not of itself be too upsetting to anyone, except for the fact that very few persons have within themselves that which makes them independent of world conditions. In other words, they have no assurance within themselves that there is a God who can and will lift them out of these world problems and show them how to surmount them.

Just in one generation, there have been three major wars, and neither the Hebrew, the Protestant, the Catholic, nor the Oriental God has stopped these wars or their horrors. They never ended until one or the other of the combatants had nothing left with which to fight.

For the most part, men feel that they have nothing within themselves that can give them any assurance that, regardless of human conditions, the evils of war, poverty, or disease will not come nigh their dwelling place. The answer to all this is that whatever concept of God a person may entertain or however correct that concept may be, it still will not give him freedom, peace, safety, or security. Only one thing will bring these things to an individual, and ultimately to the world, and that one thing is the God-experience: not a theory about God, not a concept of God, not an idea of God, but a God-experience!

For nearly two thousand years, religion has eliminated that factor from its teaching. It has given the world everything *but* the God-experience: it has given it noble ideas; it has given it great ideas of philanthropy and charity; it has given it great beauty in music, art, and literature—everything, in fact, except God. But we could well dispense with all that religion has given us, if only it would give us God. We can live without all these other things, if only we can have God.

The attainment of God is an individual experience and cannot be given to a group of individuals, although it may be given to many individuals in a group. It is possible at a given time for a dozen persons in a group to realize God, but they will not receive that realization as a group. Each one receives it individually by his own preparedness for it, by his own devotion to the attainment of God-realization.

Healing Comes Through in a Moment of God-Realization

Those of you who, in the capacity of practitioner or teacher, have been the means of spiritual healing for others are well aware of the fact that you do not know how to heal and that you have no healing powers or capacities. You know, better than anyone else, that the Master was right when he said, "I can of mine own self do nothing," [1] that he spoke truly when he said, "If I bear witness of myself, my witness is not true," [2] because you have found that the only time you have been re-

[1] John 5:30.
[2] John 5:31.

sponsible for healings has been when, in some measure, in your meditation or treatment, you have actually felt a Presence or a release from fear, which could not have come except by the grace of God. Only when you attained a certain level of consciousness, a very specific level of consciousness, in which you either realized God's presence or realized the absolute nothingness of anything that was not ordained of God, have you ever been able to bring forth healing.

To those of you who have experienced healings through a practitioner or teacher of the metaphysical or spiritual world, let me say that the healing did not take place because God was favoring that practitioner or teacher and conferring upon him special healing powers. The healing had nothing to do with anything of this sort. It had to do with the fact that the one to whom you turned was able to catch a glimpse of the God-presence or power, of the spiritual nature of creation, or a realization of the nonpower of anything and everything that does not emanate from God. It is in such moments of realization that healing comes through.

So it is that those who expect only to be healed should, of course, in some degree try to realize the nature of God, but those of you who engage in an active healing ministry must understand that all your knowledge of truth is of no value when the chips are down. In other words, when you are faced with a person threatened with death or with an incurable disease, do not rely on the wisdom or on the statements of truth you have read or learned in books or lessons. Rather understand that unless you realize and feel God's presence, or unless you actually feel the nothingness of that which is presenting itself as the appearance, the healing will not take place.

Statements of truth and learning the correct letter of truth are necessary steps in our progress, of course, because it is in this way that the healing consciousness is attained, but too much attention is usually given to statements of truth and not enough to the actual experience of truth.

Prayers That Seek Favors of God Are Futile

The concept of God that most persons entertain is that God is a great power and that God can overcome all negative and erroneous powers, that God can heal disease, that God could, if He would, stop a war or prevent accidents. None of this is true; none of this is true!

And that brings us to the second word, the second stumbling block in our progress, the word *prayer*. As long as men and women pray to God to heal the sick, to give them supply, or to bring peace on earth, they are just playing around with marbles. They are not even seriously approaching the subject of spiritual living. Rather are they back in paganistic days, praying those ancient prayers of "O God! Destroy my enemy"; "O God! Give me success in battle"; "O God! Save our side— be with us." All of this dates back two, three, four, or five thousand years to those days when people thought of God as some kind of superman who sat high up on a throne and could be prevailed upon to destroy their enemies and, at the same time, give them success. Why success to them and not to their enemies?

Similarly, prayers were uttered: "Give us rain"; or, "Stop this too much rain"; "Give us crops"; "Let us have more abundant fish in our nets"; "Make the game more plentiful." Prayer of this sort belongs to those pagan days in which the concept of God was that of some kind of super-being who was sitting around waiting to be persuaded to grant favors.

Such prayers were not effective then, and they have not been effective during the past two thousand years in which they have been perpetuated by the churches. But the world continues to use these outmoded forms of prayer and to live with outmoded concepts of God for much the same reason that contemporaries of Christopher Columbus, once they had gone on record publicly as having accepted a square world, found it difficult to acknowledge that after all perhaps Columbus was right, and the world was round. In spite of knowledge to the contrary, they insisted on clinging to their square world. And so it is that once people have come out publicly and declared that it is right and proper to pray to God to destroy their enemies or to pray to God for bread, meat, wine, and water, it is a very difficult thing for them to admit that they were wrong.

One day it will be recognized that in this twentieth century an era has begun in which concepts of God and prayer will have to be re-examined universally as well as individually. There are many places around the globe in which it is evident that a beginning in this direction has been made.

But we are dealing now only with you and with me as individuals, and if we expect to enter this spiritual path, it must be done by recognizing that God is not Santa Claus, and Santa Claus is not God. God is not withholding anything that you could pray for. God has nothing to give you that God is not, at this moment, giving. The God whose kingdom is within you already knows your need, and it is His good pleasure to give you that Kingdom.

Therefore, the first step on the spiritual path is to acknowledge that you need not pray to God in the sense of telling or asking God for what you need because God is an all-knowing God, an infinite Wisdom that already knows all that is to be known, and that God is divine love, whose nature it is to give you the Kingdom.

The Is-ness of God

You cannot know what God is because no one in the history of the world has ever been able to embrace God by means of his human mentality. King Solomon said that his entire Temple was not big enough to hold God, and you may be assured that the mind of man is not capable of embracing God. So, it is useless to try to ask what God is. Rather acknowledge that God *is*.

Acknowledge that as you have looked out upon this universe and witnessed the orderly movement of the sun, the moon, the stars, and the tides, and the unfailing rotation of the seasons, as you have witnessed the divine order in apple trees producing apples and rosebushes producing roses, you must admit that there is a Cause that operates through law and through love.

When you have acknowledged that this universe has a creative Principle, a Cause, a Something that sent it into expression and form and that maintains that expression, this relieves you, individually, of all responsibility. It enables you to relax and realize that that which sent you into expression must likewise be that which maintains and sustains you and all mankind.

Once you have acknowledged that God is, and that God is that which functions as Law, as Love, and as the creative, maintaining, and sustaining Principle, you have set yourself free of all concepts of God and you can rest in that acknowledgment. You can rest assured that that which is maintaining the integrity of all nature can maintain the integrity of your and my individual life.

The Prayer of Acknowledgment

By this time, you will have begun to wonder, "What has happened to the kind of prayers I used to pray?" and you will realize that they have dropped away from you. Now you will know that your acknowledgment of God as the creative and maintaining Principle is about as high a form of prayer as man can conceive of in the realm of words or thoughts. In other words, to acknowledge that there is an infinite Something, even though invisible, to acknowledge Its qualities of intelligence, law, and love, and to acknowledge Its power as the sustaining influence, this is prayer: this is the prayer of acknowledgment.

"In all thy ways acknowledge him, and he shall direct thy paths." [3] Acknowledge this, and eventually you will be elevated to a state of consciousness in which you will pray without words and without thoughts, because after you have received this conviction of a Divinity, of a divine Presence, Power, Law, and Love, there are no more words. You have no words to address to It, but rather you have come to realize that God, whatever Its nature or being, can speak to you, reveal Itself to you, and bring you an assurance of Its presence, Its power, Its jurisdiction and government in all things.

When you become receptive to that God whose Kingdom is within, you will arrive at a point of recognition:

> The kingdom of God is within me. I do not have to go to holy mountains; I do not have to go to holy temples or holy cities because the place whereon I stand is holy ground.

With that assurance, you can then turn quietly within and realize:

> "Speak, Lord; for thy servant heareth." [4] I know now that it would be folly for human wisdom to try to instruct the Divine. I know now that it would be folly to ask God for anything, as if God were withholding from me.
>
> I know now that I need only be receptive and responsive to God's grace, that I need only turn within and wait and be patient, and the presence of God will announce Itself, and when

[3] Proverbs 3:6.
[4] I Samuel 3:9.

He utters His voice, the earth melts. When I hear the still small voice, the discords of human sense dissolve.

I know now that "I can of mine own self do nothing." [5] *It is only as I can bring forth the presence and the power of God through my consciousness and release it into this world that it is possible to say to the storm, as did the Master, "Peace, be still.*[6] . . . *It is I; be not afraid."* [7]

Regardless of the pictures that present themselves to you— the sins, the lack, limitations, injustices, and inequalities— you do not fight them. You do not pray to a god to do something about them, but you turn within in the realization that the presence of God is within you, and in that quietness and still- ness, you hear: " *'I* will never leave thee, nor forsake thee.' [8] As *I* [9] was with Moses, with Abraham, Isaac, Jacob, and Jesus, so *I* am with you. *I* will be with you unto the end of the world."

In one way or another, you will reach an inner confidence that you are not alone in this world, that you are not battling your problems alone, but that it is literally true that He that is within you is greater than He that is in the world and that He performs whatever is given you to do.

These statements as mere statements will do nothing for you except to· serve as reminders of the truth that really is. There is a *He* within you that is greater than all the problems that are in the world. There is a *He* that actually performs all that is given you to do. Scriptural or inspirational passages merely give you the confidence to become still and let that *He* come into expression, let that *He* bring you the assurance:

"It is I; be not afraid.[10] . . . *I will never leave thee."* [11] *I will be with thee. I will go before thee to make the crooked places*

[5] John 5:30.
[6] Mark 4:39.
[7] Mark 6:50.
[8] Hebrews 13:5.
[9] Wherever the word "I" appears in italics, the reference is to God.
[10] Mark 6:50.
[11] Hebrews 13:5.

straight. I go before thee to reveal mansions—mansions, man-
sions. I am the way—rest. I am the truth—rest.

Do not struggle for what you shall eat, or what you shall drink,
or wherewithal you shall be clothed, for I am your meat, your
wine, and your water.

Eventually, you will understand that your prayers have not
been answered because you have been expecting God to send
you health, and this cannot be. God is the only health there is,
and the only way to have health is to have God. God
is the health of your countenance; therefore, have God, and
you will have health. God is your meat, your bread, your wine,
your water; therefore, God cannot give you these and God
cannot send you these. *God is these,* and the only way that you
can permanently and abundantly have bread, meat, wine, and
water is to have God.

It is useless to pray to God for longer life, for God cannot
give it to you. God is life, and only in having God do you have
life. Without God, there is no life, for God is life. And to know
this truth is life eternal.

Do not even pray to God for safety or for security, for God
has none to give you: God is the fortress, and God is the high
tower, and if you want safety and security, have God. When
you are in God, and God is in you, you will have no need of
concrete shelters; you will have no need of swords, nor will
you have fear of anyone else's swords. No individual who has
ever had the assurance of God's presence ever fears death,
ever fears bombs or bullets because with the realization of
God's presence comes the conviction:

Neither life nor death can separate me from God. Neither life
nor death can separate me from the love and the care of God.
Neither life nor death can separate me from God's life, God's
supply, God's Soul, God's law, God's love; and therefore, I need
not concern myself with whether my status is life or death, be-
cause either way I am in God. God can never leave me, nor

forsake me; God is with me to the end of the world because God and I are one, inseparable and indivisible.

Preparing the Soil for Spiritual Fruitage

This assurance cannot be given to us from a book, even though we may read comforting passages there; and this assurance cannot even be given to us by a man, even though we may hear him speak words of faith and trust. This assurance must come welling up in us from within ourselves. That is what I mean by preparation. Those of us who are devoting some part of our day and night to God-realization are preparing ourselves for this very revelation or assurance that inevitably comes from within. Paul told us that as creatures, that is, as human beings, we are not under the law of God, neither indeed can be. It is only as we prepare ourselves that this inner confidence and conviction eventually dawn.

The Master gave it to us this way: there are three types of soil: the barren soil, the rocky, and the fertile. As human beings, we are the barren soil, entirely separate and apart from God, and God has no way at all of announcing Himself within us; there is no way for the revelation of God to come to us.

After we have started out on our spiritual path, it is not long before we find that we have become stony soil. In other words, we do have realizations of truth occasionally; we have revelations and demonstrations; we have a glimpse of something, and then it is gone from us. It does not remain with us too long. We have a demonstration of harmony, and then all of a sudden that seems to be far in the past. But as we continue to abide in the Word and let the Word abide in us, as we continue to seek for deeper and deeper revelations and realizations of God and prayer, eventually we find that we are becoming more fertile soil, and the seed of truth can now take root in us.

Every word of truth that we read, every word of truth that we hear, every word of truth that we declare is a seed of truth, and the further we go in our study and meditations, the more fertile our consciousness becomes and the more of these seeds will take root and bear fruit.

We all go through much the same experience—everyone in the past has gone through these same experiences—but eventually we all come to the realization that to know Him aright is life eternal. This, I would call the greatest revelation ever given to man: *To know Him aright is life eternal:* life harmonious, life perfect.

But let us understand what it means to know Him aright. To know Him aright means to drop every concept we have ever had. The Master said that we cannot fill vessels already full; we have to empty out the vessel, come with a perfectly clear and clean consciousness, and begin all over again.

When our prayer is, "Father, reveal Thyself," we should remember that we are speaking to a Father that is already within us, not a Father that we have to go out and seek, not a God that is afar off. We are beginning with the realization that what we are seeking is already within us. Therefore, we can do our praying, whether we are at business, or doing housework; we can do our praying or our knowing of the truth, whether we are walking, driving a car, or riding in a bus. We can literally pray without ceasing, because regardless of the activity in which we may be engaged, there is always room in our consciousness for a remembrance, for a realization, of God within us.

The Universality of God's Grace

There is a third word about which there are many misconceptions, and that is the word *grace.* God's grace is not given to some and withheld from others. God's grace is free to everyone.

God's grace is within us, and it is operating within us, needing only to be recognized.

What stops us from receiving God's grace is that while once a week we may say with our lips, "Thy grace is my sufficiency in all things," ninety-nine other times during the week we plead, "Give me food; give me clothing; give me housing; give me employment; give me companionship." Ninety-nine times out of a hundred, we deny the truth that we utter the one time; whereas the whole one hundred times we should refrain from desiring anything from God, putting our entire hope in this truth:

Thy grace is my sufficiency in all things, and Thy grace is operative and operating now.

It will help to remember that when it rains it does not rain exclusively for the Jones family, the Browns, or the Smiths. When it rains, it just rains. When it snows, it snows; when it is warm, it is warm; and when God is passing out food, clothing, housing, raiment, companionship, and money, it is not for Jones, Brown, or Smith: it is universal. God's grace is universally available. As long as we do not personalize it and expect God to give or send it to us, we will have His grace infinitely and eternally. It is only when we begin to localize it and ask God to let it rain in our garden that we are likely to find that it misses our garden.

God's grace is universal, and God's grace is our sufficiency. God's grace governs the universe, but God's grace is not addressed to anyone except to the Son of God, which you are and which I am. Let us have no addresses to which God's grace is to be sent because God is not interested in one person more than in another.

Let us revise our concepts of prayer and, above all things, let us realize that we cannot pray for something for ourselves, for our child, or for our parents. Our prayer has to be a realization of the omnipresence of God, omnipresent in Russia and Africa and the United States. The omnipresence of God—the omnipotence of God—the omniscience of God—universal, impersonal, impartial! Once we begin to pray this kind of prayer, we shall begin to experience answered prayer.

God's grace cannot be directed into specific channels; God's grace cannot be directed to certain persons: God's grace already is operating universally, and what brings it into our experience is our acknowledgment and realization of its universality. As we begin to understand the universal nature of God's grace, God's love, and God's wisdom, and stop attempting to channel it, we shall begin to perceive that we, ourselves, are inside God's grace, and the beneficiary of it.

ACROSS THE DESK

Grace is God's gift of Himself; Grace is omnipresence: it is the impartation of God to an individual in realization, but the realization of God constitutes the receptivity to Grace. God's gift of grace is never a thing or a condition, but always the fullness of God, although our limited state of receptivity may make it appear as a specific healing—as supply or release from some form of bondage. If God's grace appears in limited form, it is usually because we are seeking some specific good. When we rightly understand The Infinite Way, we seek the realization of the fullness of God—the fulfillment of God.

In turning within daily for the acknowledgment and awareness of God's presence, the effect of God's grace soon becomes apparent as the appearing of the activity and forms of good in our experience. The desire for specific gifts of God must be surrendered in the greater love for God, which is satisfied with nothing less than Himself. Our lives cannot be complete until we have received the Grace of His presence. Then we live constantly tabernacled with Him, in continuous communion with His life and His love.

Men seek many freedoms: freedom from false appetites, from disease, from lack, and from unhappy human relationships, but instead of seeking freedom from these limiting conditions, they should rather seek freedom in His Spirit because freedom is attained by His grace—by the attainment of His presence. If the desire for His grace is strong enough, the struggle for these freedoms can be given up and thereby real freedom attained.

In our morning meditation, we can consciously remember: "I will never leave thee, nor forsake thee";[12] and in our evening meditation, "Lo, I am with you alway, even unto the end of the world." [13] And throughout the day, as the pressure of living pushes down upon us, we can inwardly sing: "I am come that they might have life, and that they might have it more abundantly." [14] We can pause at each meal to remember inwardly: Thy grace is my sufficiency in all things. Whenever any sense of bondage tries to tempt us, we can rejoice that "Where the Spirit of the Lord is, there is liberty." [15]

The main concern of the world today is with reports of repeated threats to every kind of freedom—political, religious, and economic—yet none of these evils shall "come nigh [our] dwelling," [16] if we dwell consciously in the realization of His presence.

To bring to fruition the dawning in consciousness of His grace, we must remember the major principle of life: There is but one Power, and this Power is within us. There is no external

[12] Hebrews 13:5.
[13] Matthew 28:20.
[14] John 10:10.
[15] II Corinthians 3:17.
[16] Psalm 91:10.

power to act upon us or our affairs for *all* power is spiritual, and its kingdom, its realm, is within us. Thou, Pilate—of any name or nature—can have no power except that which is of God.

Fear not—*I* am with you.

Contemplative Meditation

———————•———————

The entire harmony of your life and the success of the activities of your life depend upon your remembrance and practice of meditation.

A meditation should be directed toward the realization of oneness with God. You should not be thinking of any desired demonstration or of any desired good in your life, of any particular person, circumstance, or condition. Your entire attention should be given to the realization of God, always bearing in mind that the kingdom of God is within you, neither lo here nor lo there, but within you. You will never find it by looking for it in any place other than within your own being.

Once you realize that what you are seeking is within, you will give your entire attention, thought, and activity to that point within you: not within your body, but within your consciousness.

Do not think of any part of your body, of any organ or function of the body: think only of some point within your consciousness and remember that somewhere within you there is a point of contact, a point wherein you and your Father become consciously one. You and your Father are already one, but that relationship of oneness is of no benefit to you until there is a conscious realization of it.

There are far too many students who, because they have been taught that "I and my Father are one" [1] and that they are children of God, believe that this is all that is necessary to bring harmony into their experience. This is not true. There must be an actual contact; there must be an actual experience of oneness. Something must take place within them that brings the assurance that they have realized the Presence.

Let Each Meditation Be an Individual Experience

This awareness of having made a contact may take any number of forms. At times when this contact is made, it is followed by a deep breath, or there may be an awareness of receiving an impression as if some message were being given to you, or there may even be the still small voice that sometimes is audible.

We can never know in what way the realization of God's presence will be made evident to us, and therefore we must never outline how it is to appear or what form it should take. We must never expect to see visions or believe that it is necessary to hear a voice. We must never outline what the experience will be because it can take place in one form today and in another tomorrow; it can appear one day one way and another day another way; but if we are outlining in our mind what should happen, we are trying to mold the experience according

[1] John 10:30.

to some preconceived idea instead of letting the experience unfold itself to our awareness.

As you meditate, remember that you must have no object, no purpose, no goal, and no desire other than the experience of God-contact or God-realization. You must not have in mind any object that you wish, or any desired demonstration. You must never have in mind the healing of mind, body, lack, or fear. Never, never, must you have any goal or any object other than the attainment of God-realization and the recognition of the Presence within you.

A Contemplative Form of Meditation on God

If you cannot quickly feel at peace with a kind of listening attitude, then you might begin with a meditation in which you contemplate God and the things of God. You might begin with the word God, letting anything come into your thought on the subject of God that wishes to unfold:

> *God is closer to me than breathing. God is already where I am, for "I and my Father are one,"* [2] *and not even life or death can separate me from God.*
>
> *God is the very substance of my form. Even my body is the temple of God because God formed it.*
>
> *God formed this entire temple of the universe: "The earth is the Lord's, and the fulness thereof."* [3] *God made it in the image and likeness of His own substance.*
>
> *God is really my identity, constituting my individuality. If I am a painter or a musician, God has given me the inspiration and the ability and the skill; if I am a novelist, God has given me the ideas with which I work and the skill to express them; if I am in a business or a profession, God is the intelligence that governs my activity.*

[2] John 10:30.
[3] Psalm 24:1.

As a matter of fact, if I am healthy, it is because God is the health of my countenance. God is my fortress. I live and move and have my being in God, and that is why we are inseparable and indivisible.

God in me is the kingdom of God within me, and in this oneness is that divine relationship of Father and son.

"Son, thou art ever with me, and all that I have is thine." [4] *My sonship with God entitles me to all that God is and all that God has, not by virtue of my being good, not by virtue of my deserving or earning it—because in my human capacity I can hardly be worthy of God—but because I am the son of God, because the relationship between God and me is a relationship of oneness, because God has decreed, "Son, thou art ever with me, and all that I have is thine." Because of this, God's grace is mine.*

God's grace is not something to be earned or won or deserved; God's grace is not something that takes place in the future: God's grace is functioning within me now. God's grace functions to support, maintain, and sustain me. God's grace functions as my inspiration, my skill, my ability, and my integrity.

I have no integrity of my own of which to boast, no honesty of my own, no morality of my own—nothing of which I can boast—because God constitutes the integrity of my being. God constitutes my capacity for work, and God constitutes my capacity for thought and for inspiration. "Son . . . all that I have is thine"; therefore, God is my all-capacity, my infinite capacity.

God constitutes the infinite nature of my supply. My supply is not limited to my activity, to my knowledge or wisdom, to what I can earn, or to what anyone can give me. My supply is limited only to the infinite nature of God's gift: " 'Son, thou art ever with me, and all that I have is thine': thou art heir, joint-heir, to all that I have." My supply is as infinite as God's capacity is to bestow.

"The earth is the Lord's, and the fulness thereof." All this earth, the skies and the sun and the moon and the stars, and all the fish of the sea, and all the birds of the air, all the perfume of the flowers—all of this is mine because "Son, thou art ever with me, and all that I have is thine."

4 Luke 15:31.

God is closer to me than breathing. God is with me if I mount up to heaven; God is with me if I make my bed in hell; God is with me if "I walk through the valley of the shadow of death." [5] *I need fear no evil for God's presence is with me, and God's presence goes before me to make the crooked places straight. God's presence goes before me to prepare mansions for me; God's presence is the very meat, wine, and water of my daily life; God's presence is the assurance of my infinite supply.*

Because God is my hiding place, God's presence is my protection, my safety, and my security. I find my safety and security within me; I carry it with me in life and in death, because I carry with me the presence of God.

In this meditation, all that you have done is to contemplate God: the presence of God, the allness of God, and your relationship to God. You have dwelt in a continuous contemplation of God's allness, God's mightiness, God's grace, God's love; and having come to the end of your thoughts for the moment, you now become quiet and wait for God to speak to you. You keep silent while your ears are open as if the still small voice were about to speak to you. This voice may speak in actual words; it may come forth merely as an impression or a feeling of God's presence; or it may leave you with nothing more than a deep breath.

In one way or another, however, within the next twenty, thirty, or forty seconds, you will feel It and have a conviction that you are not alone, but that there is a Presence within you. The moment you have gained that awareness, you have made your conscious contact with God and have attained the conscious realization of your oneness with God. Your oneness has always existed, but now you have taken the further and all-important step of attaining conscious oneness or a conscious realization of your oneness.

[5] Psalm 23:4.

Fulfillment Is Attained by Conscious Oneness

This is when the miracle really begins because in the moment that you attain conscious realization of your oneness with God, you also attain your oneness with all forms of good necessary to your experience. These, then, begin to come to you without taking thought for them. In other words, when you attain conscious oneness with God, you attain oneness with the evidence of your supply; you attain oneness with companionship; you attain oneness with home; you attain oneness with employment, with inspiration, art, literature, or music. You attain oneness with everything necessary to the fulfillment of your life.

The scriptural promise, "In thy presence is fulness of joy; at thy right hand there are pleasures for evermore," [6] becomes literally true in the experience of every person who attains conscious oneness with God because he then attains his oneness with his rightful companionship, his rightful home, his rightful sense of supply, his rightful business, his rightful artistic, literary, or musical skill. Whatever it is that represents fulfillment in his life is attained by virtue of conscious oneness with God.

It has been demonstrated for thirty years in the experience of our students that as they have attained this conscious realization of their oneness with God, events in the outer world began to change, and either new sources of supply, new sources of activity, or new professions were opened to them. Call it what you will, by whatever name or form, these students have found that fulfillment began to be expressed and eventually there came a sense of true completeness.

In the consciously realized presence of God is the fulfillment of life. You may never have painted a picture in your life, but if you have dreamed of doing so, you may do so now;

[6] Psalm 16:11.

you may never have had music in your life, but if you have dreamed of it, you will have it as a part of your experience now. In other words, something within changes the outer experience.

As human beings, we live completely cut off from God, exemplifying the Master's statement: "If a man abide not in me, he is cast forth as a branch, and is withered; and men gather them, and cast them into the fire, and they are burned." [7] As human beings we have only our own wisdom and experience, our own physical strength, health, and dollars, and all of these are limited. But the moment that we adopt the teaching of the fifteenth chapter of John of abiding in *Me* and letting *My* words abide in you, then we are as a branch of a tree that is one with the vine, and all that God is, is flowing through that vine into expression through us, and we now have conscious contact with the infinite Storehouse which is the creative, sustaining, and maintaining Power behind this universe.

In spring it is particularly easy to observe the fullness of the beds of grass, the leaves on the trees, the buds and the blossoms, and the abundance of all these. A few months previously there was no green grass, there were no leaves, no buds or blossoms: all was barrenness. Then suddenly there is fullness. How could this happen except through the activity of an invisible Presence and Power which, at the right season of the year, bursts forth into visibility as new grass, new buds, new blossoms, new fruit, and fills all nature with an infinite, beautiful, practical, and useful abundance? And all of this from an invisible Withinness unseen to the human eye.

This same unseen, infinite manufacturing Plant operates in your consciousness. It is invisible, and while you can never become aware of it through your physical senses, you can become aware of the fruitage of it as you begin to see more abundant supply and happier relationships in every area of your life.

[7] John 15:6.

When this occurs, you will begin to realize that this is the outer evidence of that invisible Essence, Spirit, or Storehouse which is likewise providing all nature with fulfillment. It is this that fills rivers, lakes, and oceans with fish and the air with birds, but the reason all these forms of life receive their abundance and experience their fulfillment in due season without ever taking thought is because there has been no break in their relationship with the invisible Source.

With man this is different. With man there has been a break, and as a human being, he has no contact with God. He is not under "the law of God, neither indeed can be," [8] until he restores to himself his original relationship with his Father. Then his life will change just as did that of the Prodigal Son when he returned to his father's house and was given the robe and the ring of divine sonship.

Beginning the Journey Back to the Father's House

When we realize our barrenness, the futility of human life, and how difficult and what a struggle life is physically and mentally, and how little help we seem to be getting from any divine Source, we begin to wonder if there is a God or if there is any way to approach God. Then begins our return journey to our Father's house, a journey that is accomplished within our consciousness, not by going to holy mountains or holy temples or holy teachers. All these may play a part in our lives, but they are not essential.

The first essential is the realization that within us is the kingdom of God and that this Presence and Power must be contacted or found within us. From that point on, we will be led along the way: we may be led to certain books; we may be led to certain teachings or teachers, all of whom can play

8 Romans 8:7.

an important part in our unfoldment. We may eventually find that within us something almost indescribable takes place, and we may become aware that angels are ministering unto us —not the feathered kind, but nonetheless angels, divine inspirations—and that which we recognize as spiritual help of one sort or another. We may find that we are being guided and being led in ways that are entirely foreign to us—ways we never knew existed.

That is because now the son of God is within us, the son of God which is our real identity, our real Selfhood. The outer expression which is called William or Mary or Martha is but the outer seeming sense of the reality which is our invisible Withinness. In other words, in this human sense of life, we are two persons, not one. The Master said: "I and my Father are one.[9] . . . [but] my Father is greater than I";[10] and Paul said: "I live; yet not I, but Christ liveth in me." [11] They both meant the same thing. They both meant that there is this outer person whom we call Jesus or Paul, or Mary or Martha, but there is also the greater Self which is the real Self, the spiritual identity, the son of God. The moment we make contact with that, we no longer live our own lives, but we find that there is a spiritual Presence, a spiritual Power, a spiritual Guide, always coming through to us provided we give It the opportunity.

Admittedly, it is undoubtedly more difficult to live the spiritual life today than it was many years ago, because never before have there been so many outward distractions to keep us from our periods of inner communion with God. There is a price tag on the life of the Spirit, and the price is the setting aside of sufficient periods in the day and the night for inner communion. This inner communion begins with contemplative meditation, leading eventually to a deeper meditation in

9 John 10:30.
10 John 14:28.
11 Galatians 2:20.

which there are no longer statements of a contemplative nature, but there is a communion in which we receive impartations from the depths within us. This is God speaking to us instead of our assuring and re-assuring ourselves.

The contemplative form of meditation is a necessary step for most persons and one that must be used for a long time, until the inner communion is so well established that one can instantly settle into an inner peace and immediately become receptive to the impartations that unfold from within one's own being. This in time leads to a further step in which we go from a communion with God to an actual, realized oneness with God, and in this there are no longer words or thoughts, but only a divine state of Being in which one realizes oneself as the life of all that exists.

Many students of metaphysics have been accustomed to thinking of prayer and treatment as a means of attaining something through God, but in this work of The Infinite Way that is never done. On this path, at no time is truth ever used to gain any end or for the purpose of making any demonstrations; at no time is God considered an instrument whereby to get something. In The Infinite Way, there is no purpose or goal beyond God-realization, and once God-realization has been attained, that realization takes care of everything that happens in life.

In the preceding chapter, the word *Omnipotence* brought forth the idea that if there is Omnipotence or All-power, then there cannot be any other power. With this realization, we instantly lose our fear of material conditions, forces, or powers, and even our fear of mental forces or powers. We rest in the assurance that since there is but one power we have nothing to fear. The so-called evils of the world have no power or presence, and they should not be fought, nor should any attempt be made to be rid of them. They should be recognized as illusory appearances.

Just as the concept of Omnipotence dissolves our fear of other powers and permits us to rest in the assurance of one power, so does the word *Omnipresence* allay our fear of any other presence because, as a matter of fact, there cannot be All-presence *and* another presence. When you grasp the real significance of Omnipotence and Omnipresence, you have set yourself apart from any of the evils of this world, which are instantly recognized as appearance, illusion, or maya—call it what you will.

Omniscience Changes Your Concept of Prayer

What really changes your life, however, is an understanding of Omniscience because this changes your whole concept of prayer. There are fifty centuries of erroneous prayers in our background, fifty centuries of praying amiss. There have been only a few brief years of praying aright in the whole of the last fifty centuries, and therefore, we really have some overcoming to do in order to correct the erroneous sense of prayer into which we were born and under which we have been brought up.

Think of the meaning of Omniscience; look it up in the dictionary and try to get a full and complete understanding of All-wisdom and All-knowledge. Then think of what you have really been doing when you have prayed to God and told God what you need, and sometimes even on what day you needed it. Think of what you have been doing when you have been asking God to heal your child or some dear soul who needs it, as if God were not omniscience. Think of what you have been doing when you pray God to send you supply.

Did not Jesus know what he was talking about when he said: "Your heavenly Father knoweth that ye have need of all these things.[12] . . . for it is your Father's good pleasure to give you

[12] Matthew 6:32.

the kingdom" [13] ? Did not Jesus know about prayer when he said, "Take no thought for your life, what ye shall eat, or what ye shall drink; nor yet for your body, what ye shall put on" [14] ? Are we not violating that teaching when we pray to God for supply, for home, for companionship, for a vacation, or for an automobile? Are we not really paying only lip service to an omniscient God?

The word *Omniscience* reminds us of what we have been doing in our prayers. Have we not been guilty of telling God something? Have we not been reminding God of something? Have we not been asking something of God that we think God does not know anything about? Have we not been telling God of someone who needs Him?

Think what you do when you go to God with anything that you wish to convey to this Omniscience, to this All-wisdom, All-knowledge, All-power, All-presence; and then you will quickly learn how to transform your prayer into a righteous prayer, a prayer that is a resting back in God in an inner assurance that "before they call, I will answer; and while they are yet speaking, I will hear," [15] that before you know your need He knows it, and it is His "good pleasure to give you the kingdom." [16] Think of how this will change your prayer as you learn to look upon God as the great All-wisdom, All-presence, and All-power.

Suppose that we had to remind God to put apples on apple trees, peaches on peach trees, or berries on berry bushes; or suppose that we had to remind God that we need or do not need so much rain, or remind Him every evening that it should become dark and the stars should come out and the moon. God is doing all these things without our advice or peti-

[13] Luke 12:32.
[14] Matthew 6:25.
[15] Isaiah 65:24.
[16] Luke 12:32.

tions, and can we not trust Him enough to know our needs without reminding Him of them?

If God knows enough to continue to put the fish in the sea and the birds in the air, if God knows enough to keep the tides in their places, ebbing and flowing on schedule, if God knows enough to keep this earth and all the other planets in their orbits, surely God knows our need, and if God has the love to supply all the needs of this world, God has enough love to supply us with ours. Only our egotism would interfere with our receiving it, only the egotism that believes we know our need better than God does, only the egotism that believes we have more love for our children than God has for His: only such rank egotism can prevent the free flow of God's grace to us.

Once we have overcome this egotistic sense, we can relax in the realization that God is omniscience, omnipresence, and omnipotence; and we can stop taking thought for our life, for what we shall eat, or what we shall drink. We can stop taking thought and begin to acknowledge God, and as we acknowledge Him in all our ways, keeping our thoughts stayed on Him, we find that God is operating in our experience and that as a need arises it is met usually before we know that the need is there.

So it is that prayer is our point of contact with God; it is through prayer that we establish our conscious oneness with God; it is through prayer that we establish our conscious awareness of God's presence; it is through prayer that we acknowledge that even "though I walk through the valley of the shadow of death, I will fear no evil: for thou art with me";[17] it is through prayer that we rest in the assurance of God's presence, God's grace, and God's law. Then we relax and find that this invisible Presence does for us exactly what it does for the trees and the grass in their seasons, and for all the rest of this vast universe.

[17] Psalm 23:4.

Practicing the Presence

When we are acknowledging God as Omnipotence, Omnipresence, Omniscience, we are practicing the presence of God, keeping our mind stayed on God, and we are setting up within ourselves an inner stillness that later becomes a receptivity to the presence of God, Itself, to that which has been called the birth of the Christ.

The birth of the Christ is that moment in our individual experience when *nothing* becomes tangibly something, when, where there was a lack of something, all of a sudden there now becomes evident a Presence, tangible and real, a power, a companion, a saviour, a guide. From that moment on, we consciously abide in the Presence.

Because of the realized presence of God within us, it would be impossible for there to be any strife with anyone. In the human picture we may disagree, but there could be no conflict of a really harmful or destructive nature between us if even one of us had realized the Presence. As this Presence lives in us, it becomes impossible for us to take up a sword, to hate or envy, be jealous, malicious, or destructive.

The entire secret of peace on earth is the establishing in our consciousness of this realized Presence, which acts as a leveler in our consciousness, making us all equally children of God. This makes it possible to realize what the Master meant when he said, "Call no man your father upon the earth: for one is your Father, which is in heaven" [18]—one creative Principle.

So we learn not to call our country, *our* country, or our flag, *our* flag. We give it its due, but we recognize that we are all of one spiritual household. This does not mean only those on our particular path. It means that every individual on the face of this globe actually has but one Father, one creative Principle,

[18] Matthew 23:9.

and in our recognition of that we are brothers. The fact that there may be cultural, educational, or economic levels that separate us at the moment has nothing to do with the basic truth that we are equally one insofar as our spiritual relationship is concerned. We all have but one creative Principle, one Father; and some day we shall all begin to act as though we really believed that.

If we are to do that, it will be necessary for us to change our concepts of prayer and begin to treat God as if that omnipotent, omnipresent, and omniscient God really were closer to us than breathing. Our function is to rest in God. But we must never try to bend God to our will or try to get God to do something for us that we want, because we will not succeed. Whenever we are tempted to try to get God to do something, remember that we are trying to bend Him to our will and then we will be released from any such paganistic concept of prayer, and we will pray:

> *Mold me to Thy will; bend me to Thy will; make me yield myself unto Thy will so that Thy will, and not mine, be done in me. Let me not have a will of my own; let me not have a desire; let me not have a wish: Let me completely yield myself to Omniscience, Omnipotence, and Omnipresence, and be a beholder of what takes place in my life as I permit an All-knowing, All-power, All-presence govern my life.*

ACROSS THE DESK

Resurrection, in its mystical sense, means resurrecting the Son of God out of the tomb of the physical senses. It is also resurrection in the sense of rising out of the physical sense of body into the realization of spiritual consciousness as governing all form.

The revelation of life lived by Grace instead of under the law consists of the revelation of the consciousness of the individual as a law of resurrection, healing, and protection to the body, business, home, and well-being in every form, and we begin to see how consciousness—the consciousness of the individual—even without taking thought and without being directed, becomes the law of harmony unto our experience.

From

CONSCIOUS UNION WITH GOD

The Basis of Spiritual Healing

———•———

Spiritual healing is brought about through the realization of the Christ in individual consciousness. God, the individual Consciousness of this universe, is the one and only consciousness. However, since God is the consciousness of me and God is the consciousness of you, and because there is only this one consciousness, truth becomes effective in the consciousness of anyone who tunes in to it. Therefore, any truth that reveals itself within our consciousness instantaneously reveals itself to the person appearing as our patient.

Sometimes, people who are not associated with us in any way, either as friends, relatives, students, or patients—someone in a hospital or a prison, someone on a desert island, someone who is reaching out for help to his highest concept of God—may be healed even though they do not know us and we do not know them; or even if they do know us, they may not know that we are on this path, and, therefore, would not know why they were healed.

There is only one Life, one Consciousness, one Soul; but that One is the consciousness of you and the consciousness of me. That is why we do not have to try to reach anyone. When we are in this conscious oneness, we become so much a part of one another that what one is thinking about Truth, or God, the other is hearing, but no transference of thought is involved and should not be so construed. We are not one in our humanhood: We are one in the Christ, and all that is being imparted is the divine idea flowing in consciousness.

For that reason, those who are aware of the principle of one power need never be concerned about suffering from other people's thoughts. All the suffering on earth, regardless of its form or nature, is a product of the universal belief in two powers; and therefore, universal harmony will only be restored when God is revealed as Omnipotence. There is only one mind and that mind is the instrument of the one Spirit, or God. Human thinking, which is the product of a mind unaware of its proper function as an instrument of God, never rises higher than the person in whose mind it is taking place.

For example, if someone were sitting here repeating, "Two times two is five," our own mathematical sense would be a protection to us, and we would not accept that incorrect statement. He might say, "You are dead!" but our own sense of life would be a protection, and we would not be troubled by such erroneous thinking.

In some forms of mental practice, experiments have been conducted which prove that an individual cannot be induced to do anything which violates his own integrity unless it is by his own conscious choice. No amount of human thinking consciously directed at a person can ever make anyone violate his own integrity; and therefore, when anyone does wrong, it is because he himself is consciously violating his own sense of right. It all lies within one's own being.

Spiritual Freedom

The disciples understood little of Jesus' mission. In the three years that they were with Jesus, although they had almost daily contact with him and with his thought and work, there were few who gave evidence of being deeply touched by his message. He was not able to bring about much spirituality in Judas, and he did not have too great success with Peter, and even less with most of the other disciples. John, of course, caught the full and complete message.

The coming of the Messiah has been prophesied for centuries, but the Hebrews had no concept of the Messiah as a teaching or as a divine idea. They thought that the Messiah, when he came, would be a man who would lead them into freedom. Freedom from what? Freedom from bondage to Caesar, from being slaves of Caesar; freedom, probably, from some of the practices imposed by their religion, because the people of Jesus' day were looking for a physical freedom, a temporal freedom, and probably they thought that the Messiah might come as a king to give them that freedom. In this they were disappointed. They did not understand that Jesus' mission was not of this world.

Jesus came with the divine idea of spiritual freedom. He hoped that by setting the people of his day free in their consciousness— free from slavery to person and thing—they would be free in fact. But the Hebrews were looking for a human emancipator who would free them from intolerable conditions, and they failed to understand the mission of the Christ. For that reason only a few of them caught the vision and benefited by it.

Today, let no one make the same mistake about the mission of The Infinite Way. Its purpose is the unfoldment and revelation of spiritual being, the harmonious and eternal manifestation of God, Good. It does not attempt to change, correct, or reform any person. Therefore, our work lies within our own being and consists of reaching that spiritual consciousness in which there is no temptation to accept the universe and individual being as other than God appearing as the universe and as individual being.

In the commonly accepted sense of metaphysical healing practice, health is usually sought as the opposite or absence of disease, goodness and morality as the opposite of badness and immorality; but in this unfoldment, we do not attempt to heal the body, remove disease, or reform sinners. We do not seek health in what Jesus called "this world" because *"My kingdom* is not of this world,"[1] that is, the Christ-work is not in the realm of human concepts. We understand health to be the quality and activity of Soul, always expressed as perfect and immortal body. Even a harmonious human body does not necessarily express health because health is more than the absence of disease: It is an eternal state of spiritual being. Furthermore human goodness is but the opposite of human badness and is not the spiritual state of being which we must realize and achieve in our approach to life.

Although this message does not concern itself with human health or disease, material wealth or poverty, personal goodness or badness, nevertheless, the attainment of the consciousness of God appearing as individual being results in what appears to human sense as health, wealth, and goodness. These, however, represent the finite concepts of that spiritual harmony which actually is always present.

When we are no longer in bondage to the belief that we are slaves to some person or circumstance and when we are no longer slaves to dollar bills, we shall be truly free forever. Then it will make no difference to us what kind of a political or economic system exists in our world. We shall be abundantly provided with whatever form of supply is necessary under the particular form of government under which we are living. And if we were in prison, we would still be free. We would be like those people of old who said, "Imprison me, you cannot! My body, you can put in jail—but not me!"

---

[1]John 18:36.

Mind, or consciousness, cannot be confined to a room or to a chair. The mind can wander around at will and can be trained so to rise above corporeal sense as actually to be out in this world with the sense of being free of the body, although we do not leave the body. It is not possible to leave our body because our body and we are one, but we can leave the corporeal sense of it and be so free spiritually that we are confined neither to time nor space. That is what happens when we gain our spiritual freedom.

In that spiritual freedom, we surmount all sense of limitation.. For example, we do not stop using dollars, but we do not worry about them. The dollars will come, and even though we continue to use them, we shall no longer be limited or confined by the concept that dollars constitute supply.

As long as we think of money as supply, we will not demonstrate spiritual freedom as related to supply. Even if our income should be doubled, we should not congratulate ourselves on having made a demonstration, if we still believe that money is supply! Money is not supply. *I am supply: Consciousness is supply.* This indefinable Essence, called Spirit, which we are, is supply, and that is omnipresent, omnipotent, and omniscient.

Understanding the Nature of God

Our entire spiritual life depends upon our ability to know God, and unless we understand the omnipresence and omnipotence of God, we shall make no progress in this work.

Throughout the ages, many names have been given to God: Abraham knew God as Friend. In the ancient Hindu Scriptures, dating back thousands of years and comprising some of the earliest literature given to the world on the subject of God, God is referred to as "Mother" and sometimes as "Father." The great modern Hindu mystic, Ramakrishna, knew God as Mother Kali; but often terms, such as "Mind," "Principle," "Soul," "Light,"

"Spirit," "Love," and other of the well-known synonyms for God, will also be found in the Hindu Scriptures. Yet because it was the nature of the primitive Hindus, as of the primitive Hebrews, to personalize, they brought God closer to themselves in the way which they understood best—as a loving Mother and occasionally as Father.

In the nineteenth century, Sanskrit scholars translated many of the great Hindu classics into the German and English languages so that, for the first time, the West had the opportunity of becoming familiar with Hindu terminology. The result was that many of its concepts for God seeped into the literature of the nineteenth century. The term "Father-Mother" as a synonym for God gained widespread acceptance through its incorporation into the teaching of Christian Science by Mary Baker Eddy. Through her use of this term in Christian Science literature, it later was incorporated in many other metaphysical teachings. And so God has been known as Mother, sometimes as Father, and also as Father-Mother. None of these terms was meant to indicate gender or to mean that God was either male or female. Rather, such endearing terms connote the tender, loving, and protective qualities of a mother, and the stern, law-giving, protective, sustaining, and maintaining qualities of a father.

So, when God comes to your individual consciousness, He comes in such a tender way that you may still use the term, Father or Mother. More and more people, however, are beginning to think of God as Light and Life; and, when God is realized in individual consciousness as Life or as Light, there is no sense of male or female, just a sense of God as the universal life which permeates all form. God is the life which permeates your form—the life permeating the form of the tree, of the animal, and of the flower, impersonal, but nonetheless life.

God is Spirit, and Spirit is the substance and the essence of which all things are formed—all that is in the earth and sky, air and water. Spiritual creation is formed of this indestructible and indivisible Substance, or Spirit, called God.

Spiritual Consciousness Reveals Reality

You may wonder then, why there are such things as rotting trees or erupting volcanoes. Are they, also, of the essence of God? No, they represent our concept of that which actually is there. In the kingdom of God, there is never a rotting tree, nor are there any destructive or disruptive forces operative. The German mystic, Jacob Boehme, saw through the trees and through the grass to reality. To all mystics, it is as though the world opens up and they see the world as God made it.

God is the underlying substance and reality of all form, but what we see, hear, taste, touch, or smell is the product of the human mind, or mortal, material, finite sense. The sum total of human beings in the world, under what is termed material law— medical, theological, or economic—has set up this finite sense of the universe which they see, hear, taste, touch, or smell.

Nothing is what it appears to be. All of us could look at the same object, and every one of us might see it differently. Why? Because each one of us interprets it in the light of the education, environment, and background of his individual experience. To understand that what we see represents only our concept of that which is actually there is important, because on this point we make or lose our healing consciousness. God created all that was created, and all that He created is good. Therefore, this whole world, whether seen as human beings, animals, or plants, is God manifest. But when we see it, we do not see it as it is: We see only our finite concept of it.

This is vitally important because it is on this premise that all spiritual healing is based, and a lack of recognition of this point accounts for ninety-five percent of the failure in spiritual healing. Many metaphysicians are trying to heal the physical body, and it cannot be healed, because there is nothing a metaphysician can do to a physical body, but when he changes his concept of the body, the body responds to that higher concept. Then the patient says,

"I have been healed!" He has not been healed: He was perfect in the beginning. What was wrong was not in the body, but in his false concept of himself and of his body.[1]

If you can grasp this idea, it may save you from making the fatal mistake of trying to heal somebody or somebody's body. When I see your body through spiritual sense, I behold you as God made you, and you will declare that you have been healed. God's creation is intact; it is perfect and harmonious, and that perfect and harmonious creation is right here and now. But this cannot be seen with the physical eyes. It can be discerned only through spiritual vision, spiritual sense—through spiritual consciousness, or what is called Christ-consciousness.

Do not try to reform the outer picture. When you meet with thievery, drunkenness, or any form of degradation, do not look at it, but through it. Do not look with the eyes. Close the eyes or at least turn away. Look through the individual, beholding through your spiritual sense the reality of his being, and you will bring about what the world calls healing. With your inner, God-given, spiritual sense, look into the heart of every man and see the Christ, and there you will find the most wonderful healing force there is in the world. Then let your feeling guide you. Get a sense, or a feeling, of the Christ sitting right there in the center of individual being, and when you reach that Christ you will have an instantaneous healing.

To bring about a healing of sin or disease, do not be concerned about a human being or body. Become silent within your being: Feel the presence of God, the presence of Good, the divine or inner Sense, and then you will not be tempted to think of any one person. It is not necessary to think of the name of the person turning to you for help, of his form, or of his disease. The all-knowing Intelligence knows, and therefore when you feel a sense of Soul which takes him in, you will have witnessed a healing.

[1]For a more complete explanation of this point, see the chapter on "The True Sense of the Universe" in the author's *Spiritual Interpretation of Scripture* (San Gabriel, Calif.: Willing Publishing Company, 1947). Pp. 203-214.

Conducting a Healing Practice

In conducting your healing practice, be careful that you do not smugly repeat statements of truth to your patients, that you do not give them beautiful quotations from Scripture or metaphysical writings, unless you yourself have had some measure of consciousness of that truth. Remember, it is far better to say nothing to your patients other than a "Leave this with me," or an "I will help you," or "I will be with you," or "Call me again in the morning"—far better to give them no statement of truth, but merely your assurance that you, with your realization of the presence of God, are consciously with them in prayer and realization.

When your consciousness is imbued with the spirit of truth—not merely the letter of truth, but the spirit of truth—healing will take place. Then you can explain to your patients what the truth is, giving them statements of truth which you have proved or demonstrated, and which have become a part of your consciousness. They will then not only be glad to hear these statements, but will feel their truth. Giving your patients or students quotations and statements of truth of which you yourself do not have the consciousness is like giving them a stone when they ask for bread. Rather give them a simple statement, one which you have demonstrated over and over again, and which, therefore, you know to be true. Unless you can do that, give them the healing silence. Say nothing, but feel within your being this healing Christ.

Remember this: You are not called upon to heal a person; you are not called upon to remove some terrible disease; you are not called upon to change the activity of a human body. All that you are ever called upon to do is to realize the spiritual nature of the omnipresent God and God's perfect creation. You are called upon to feel a living Presence, to feel this living Presence at the center of your being.

In every case to which you are called, the real call is for your realization of God as the life of man, God as the mind and the Soul and the law and the substance and the cause. Stating these things, however, does not constitute spiritual healing. It is feeling them; it is an actual spiritual awareness within your own being.

Do not try to reach your patient. Do not try to get your thought across to a patient. Only be sure that within your own being you feel the truth, you feel the rightness, you feel the spiritual sense of being. Then your patient will respond. Do not take your patient into your thought—do not take his name or the nature of his disease or what he looks like—and above all, never think that you must convey or transfer some thought to your patient.

It makes no difference what the claim or problem is. When the Christ of you touches the Christ of your patient, there is healing. Do not try to heal anybody humanly, either mentally or physically. Try to be silent in the center of your being and feel the Christ, knowing that all this is taking place in the one Heart, the heart of God, which is the heart of you. You must feel a conscious oneness with God. God is all-inclusive and since God is all-inclusive, you and I must be included in that God-being, so that when I am at-one with God, I am at-one with you; and when you are at-one with God, I am at-one with you; and when you are at-one with God, you are at-one with me. *My conscious oneness with God constitutes my oneness with you and with every spiritual being and with every activity of God that is included in my life.* All of these are divine ideas, the form of which we translate in terms of our human needs.

Just as your body is a spiritual body in God, neither male nor female, so when you are touching the Christ at the center of your being, which is the Christ of every individual, there is only pure love, pure Spirit. Because of human sense, however, the qualities of God are interpreted as both male and female.

In the same way, the idea of transportation can be translated into a donkey, an airplane, a streetcar, or an automobile. These represent only the human concepts of the divine idea of transportation. The truth about transportation is found in one word, instantaneity: *I*[1] am everywhere—here, there, and everywhere! That is the truth about spiritual transportation. That is why it is just as easy for a practitioner in San Francisco to heal someone in China as to heal someone who is physically present with him.

Awareness of God Is Necessary

In *The Infinite Way*, there is a chapter on "Meditation,"[2] which outlines a course in what may be called spiritual preparation. The first part of this preparation is the practice of awakening in the morning in the conscious realization of your oneness with God. "Except the Lord build the house, they labour in vain that build it."[3] If you do not consciously bring God into your experience with your first waking moment, you may have lost the opportunity of having God with you on every occasion throughout the day.

Perhaps as you read this, you may think, "Oh, God is omnipresent; God is always with me!" Do not believe that, because it is not true at all! That is one of those clichés—one of those quotations!

It is true that God is omnipresent. It is true that God is right where you are. But if it is true that God is omnipresent, then God must have been present when all our boys were killed at the front or when of old the Christians were thrown to the lions, or when in the last few decades thousands of innocent people were slaughtered in concentration camps. What was God doing while all these horrors were going on? Was He there? Then, why was He not helping? Certainly, God was there, but God is not a person and God cannot look down on you and tell you He is sorry for the suffering you are enduring. God is omnipresent in the

---

[1]Wherever "I" appears in italics, the reference is to God.
[2]By the author (San Gabriel, Calif.: Willing Publishing Company, 1947). Pp. 94-103.
[3]Psalm 127:1.

hospitals, in the prisons, at the battle front. God is omnipresent! But of what good is that to anybody? Of what good is it to you? Only this: In proportion to your conscious awareness of the presence of God is God available in every instance.

God is present! Certainly. Electricity was present throughout the ages even when people were using whale oil and kerosene oil. But of what benefit was electricity to them? None, because there was no conscious realization of the presence of electricity.

Jesus could have been traveling around the Holy Land in an airplane, too. And what about the Hebrews on their long trek across the sands? It takes forty minutes today! Think! That which took forty years then takes only forty minutes today. The laws of aero-dynamics were present and available to them, but there was no conscious awareness of them, although these laws could have been implemented had there been any knowledge of them.

Electricity is present today as it always has been, but now, because of a conscious awareness of its laws, it gives us light, heat, and power. God is present here and now, but there must be a conscious awareness and realization—really more than that, a conscious feeling of the presence of God if you are to avail yourself of that Presence and Power. Glib talk, quotations, hearsay, and metaphysical clichés are not to be confused with that conscious awwareness and realization through which God becomes a living reality to you. An indulgence in metaphysical clichés is as useless as it would be for someone living in ancient times to say, "You know, electricity is available." Yes, of course it was—if they had known how to make use of it.

This talking about God has been going on for thousands of years, and there are many godly people in churches who are talking abut God and still going through all the discords of human experience. It is not talk, however, but the conscious realization of the presence of God which is the secret of spiritual living.

Anyone who has had the actual feeling, or realization, of the presence of God, is no longer alone in the world, no longer working out his own problems alone, and no longer dependent on human aid of any kind. Always the Divine is there. The Presence that goes before him is always beside him and comes up behind him as a rearguard, but even though there is such a Presence, there must be a conscious realization of that Presence.

Toward the development of that state of consciousness there are certain practices which are steps along the way. The most important of these is training yourself to make a conscious effort to realize God's presence upon awakening in the morning. If you cannot feel God's presence immediately, you can at least learn to acknowledge the omnipresence, omnipotence, and omniscience of God; you can at least attempt to realize:

> *As the wave is one with the ocean, so I am one with God. As the sunbeam is one with the sun, so I am one with God.*

If you will take one or two or three minutes to do this, you will find that you are in a different frame of mind when you step out of bed onto the floor. When you learn not to get out of bed until you have established your conscious oneness with God, your day will begin aright.

When I awaken in the morning, I am in the habit of establishing this conscious realization of the presence of God. I consider that the most important part of my daily work because when I have done that, I have not much to do the rest of the day except look over my shoulder and watch God at work.

Every day, you should religiously follow the instructions in the chapters on "Meditation" and "Prayer" in *The Infinite Way.*[1] For example, when you leave your home in the morning, do not go out the door without consciously realizing that the Presence has gone before you and the Presence remains behind to bless those who pass that way. Do not go out without consciously doing this because your conscious effort determines your demonstration.

In the same way when you sit down to your table, do not eat until you have at least blinked your eyes and silently said, "Thank

[1] *op. cit.*, pp. 94-113.

You, Father!" This is not said in any orthodox sense of grace, but in a very modern metaphysical sense of grace. It is an acknowledgement of God as the source of your supply, an acknowledgement that it was not your own human effort that brought the food to you, and that of yourself you can do nothing; the Father within you has placed this food before you.

There is no way to jump from being a human being to being a spiritual being, but little by little, we must begin to spiritualize our thought until we find ourselves in the kingdom of heaven. We must learn that regardless of what we are doing throughout the day, it is only because of the presence of God that we are doing it. Jesus said, "I can of mine own self do nothing[1]...the Father that dwelleth in me, he doeth the works."[2] and Paul said, "I live; yet not I, but Christ liveth in me."[3]

You must see that every bit of good you ever do or experience is the Christ acting in and through you; it is the Spirit of God activating you. The healing activity is the activity of divine Consciousness, the activity of the Christ of your own being, which takes place within you.

[1]John 5:30.
[2]John 14:10.
[3]Galatians 2:20.

States and Stages of Consciousness

Even though for many years the metaphysical world has believed that mental and spiritual healing are synonymous, actually they are as far apart as are material and spiritual healing. Mental and material healing are much the same except that they operate on different levels of consciousness. The mental is a little higher and finer than the material, but essentially they are two strata of the same belief.

On the other hand, to use the terms, "mentally spiritual" or "spiritually mental," is exactly the same as saying, "a godly devil." The spiritual and the mental are just that far apart, not that one is right and the other is wrong, but they function on such different levels of consciousness that they are as far apart as the poles.

The present day mixture of the spiritual and the mental stems from the beginning of modern mental practice, which originated in the last quarter of the eighteenth century in Germany with

Franz Anton Mesmer, a reputable and learned physician, who named his discovery animal magnetism. He it was who discovered that there is a vital fluid—invisible and mental—which passes from the practitioner to the patient and which acts hypnotically through suggestion.

One of Mesmer's students, the French mesmerist, Charles Poyen, migrated to Portland, Maine, and there found an apt student named Phineas P. Quimby to whom he taught mesmerism, then known as hypnotism, or animal magnetism, and for sometime these two engaged in this activity primarily for entertainment purposes.

Mr. Quimby, later known as Dr. Quimby, however, had a young patient, or student, who worked as his assistant and who developed the faculty, under hypnotism, of discerning the mental causes of the physical diseases of people coming to him on the platform. Dr. Quimby, then, by recognizing the power of the mental thought, erased the disease. As a result of some remarkable healings which took place, he gave up the entertainment phase of his work and became a very well-known healer. People flocked to him from all over the country, and there are reports of amazing healings.

Dr. Quimby was a very good man—a religious man in a church sense—and very soon he began to introduce the words God and the Christ into the terminology of his work. Gradually, these religious terms became a part of what was in the beginning a purely mental practice. As a matter of fact, I believe it was Dr. Quimby who first made the distinction between Jesus and the Christ—Jesus, the man, and Christ, the Spirit that animated him. Up to that time in the theological world, Jesus and the Christ had been thought of as one. In metaphysical language today, however, Jesus is understood to be the man, and the Christ, the power or presence or Spirit of God which animated the man Jesus.

Of all Dr. Quimby's students, the one who became best known was Mary Baker Eddy, who travelled for three years giving lectures for him on the science of Quimbyism, which he later called the Science of Christ, or Christian Science. Because of her religious background, Mrs. Eddy was well-steeped in the Bible and in the religious thought of her day, and she therefore utilized all the religious terms which Dr. Quimby had introduced into his mental practice.

But let us not deceive ourselves: It was a mental practice, so mental that when engaged in the healing work Mrs. Eddy often had to ask Dr. Quimby to help her because she had taken on the disease of the patient she was treating. Early letters which passed between Mrs. Eddy and Dr. Quimby show that the practice in which they were engaged was mental even though they used terms such as the Christ. It was one mind over another mind or mind over matter or one mind understanding that disease is not a power. It was primarily suggestion—the transference of the thoughts of one mind to another.

As time went on, more and more people began to be interested in metaphysical healing, coming into the work through many other avenues. Julius A. Dresser began the New Thought movement in 1892, two years before the original Mother Church in Boston was built. While it is true that most of the students and practitioners adhered closely to the mental approach, others who were of a more spiritual temperament made progress in the spiritual field.

Thus in the metaphysical field, there are two distinct branches—the mental and the spiritual—although very few people are willing to acknowledge that this is true. Nowhere in the New Testament, however, can authority be found for most of what is now known as mental practice, although that mental practice still makes use of the name of the Christ.

"Holding Thoughts" Is Not Spiritual Healing

Jesus taught: "Take no thought for your life, what ye shall eat, or what ye shall drink; nor yet for your body, what ye shall put on,"[1]

[1]Matthew 6:25.

and yet how many of our mental practitioners today are ready and willing to attempt to make a demonstration of supply or of a house or an automobile? How many patients ask their practitioners to "demonstrate" an apartment or a house in which to live, or a husband or getting rid of one. There is not a practitioner of any experience who has not at times had the very sad experience of having people come to him asking for help to secure a home, an automobile, a husband, or a wife—every kind of "demonstration" conceivable.

Even the highest level of that type of practice is against the teaching of the Christ . The Christ-teaching is to take no thought for your life, for your supply, or for your clothing. Jesus gives a long list of what *not* to ask for, tells why, and ends with this promise: "Your Father knoweth that ye have need of these things...[and] it is your Father's good pleasure to give you the kingdom."[2] Therefore, to go to God with some finite problem would be going against the teachings of the Master.

In Luke, Jesus also said, "Which of you with taking thought can add to his stature one cubit?"[3] When you sit down to "take thought" in order to add something to your supply or your health, you will fail. Furthermore, the Bible states: "For my thoughts are not your thoughts, neither are your ways my ways."[1] Yet think of all the metaphysicians in the world who believe that if they just do some right thinking—hold or send out the right thought—it will do something for them or for their patients, although in practicing this doctrine of "right thinking" they are violating the very teaching which they claim to be following.

The transfer of thought from one individual to another is the activity of the human mind. Although it often results in what we call healing or improvement, it is sometimes at best merely temporary, because if the mental practitioner is successful today, he must work twice as hard next week. What can be the end of all this mental practice but a headache! People who become adept in

[2]Luke 12:30,32.
[3]Luke 12:25.
[1]Isaiah 55:8.

mental work begin tightening up because they are working under pressure—mental pressure. Some of you may have observed the reaction on those who give or receive mental treatments; you may have watched practitioners who have carried on their work under terrific mental pressure and witnessed the confusion it has brought.

During my sixteen years in the Christian Science practice, I observed that mental practice was just as rife there as it is in other metaphysical movements. As a matter of fact, there is just as much authority in Mrs. Eddy's writings for mental practice as for spiritual practice. both are taught and can easily be found in her writings, and anyone may take his choice, depending on which-ever teaching has the greater appeal for him. Although I person-ally have never been able to indulge in mental practice, I have seen the results of those who have used it and also the results on those who have permitted themselves to come under the mental treatment of another person "holding thoughts" for them, domi-nating them and at times almost controlling them.

Those who work without this active thought-taking process remain relaxed. Instead of trying to be a force or power, they merely become the vehicle through which the Spirit works; and therefore, there is seldom any nervousness or irritability because the Spirit is ever renewing and rebuilding. The Spirit is doing the work, not their "thought-taking."

Under the dominion of the Spirit, of that mind that was in Christ Jesus, it would be impossible for anyone to violate his spiritual integrity. No one could cheat, defraud, or be unfaithful in his duty to a patient, because the Spirit would not let him—It would not give him such a thought or impulse. Moreover, when a practitioner comes under the dominion of that mind which was also in Christ Jesus, he heals without mental or personal effort, whether the patient is awake or asleep—and even when the practitioner is asleep.

When a person is working mentally he has the choice of being good or bad, with no controlling power to prevent his doing what he wants to do, except for his own highest sense of right. That does not mean that those working along mental lines are evil people; but if they are good, it is because they are good people, not because they have come under the influence of that mind which was in Christ Jesus, which would permit them to be nothing less than God in action.

No Mental Cause for Disease

How many times have you known someone who was convinced that he had arthritis or cancer or consumption and then was healed so quickly that later he was equally convinced that he could not have had anything seriously wrong with him? Quite possibly the condition was not there, but the point is: Suppose a practitioner accepts the diagnosis as presented to him and begins to work on it. Nine times out of ten he would be working to heal the wrong disease. Even if his patient brought him a doctor's diagnosis, it could still be fifty-five percent wrong. In its own survey, the Massachusetts General Hospital in one year learned that the diagnoses made in its own hospital were but forty-five percent correct, and this even with x-rays, blood tests, urinalyses, and all the other tests devised by modern medicine.

You can see that even if a practitioner were given a medical diagnosis of a case, it might be right or it might be wrong, and if he had no medical diagnosis and just took his patient's word for it, he might be seventy-five to ninety percent wrong. So what good is a treatment given for a specific claim? If the patient gets well, he might have done so in spite of the treatment.

Moreover, since disease is an unreality and since it is a belief that really cannot be localized, all this mental manipualtion—this probing to find a mental cause for a condition or a disease—is nonsense. In my entire life I have never met any person with enough hate in his sytem to cause anything as virulent as cancer or enough lust to cause consumption or tuberculosis. A person who had that much hate or lust would be locked up in an institution. People are just not that bad—there must be a different reason for it.

Some time ago I read an article about a woman with flat feet. She had had her thought analyzed by a practitioner who discovered that the woman had grieved so over her son who had been killed in the war that she lost her understanding. Result: flat feet. Another woman had athlete's foot and could not be healed, so her practitioner examined her thought and found that she had a desire for human affection. My comment at that time was that if that is true, practitioners are going to be very busy with cases of athlete's foot when there is so much need for affection in the world.

If there ever was a time when healing was brought about through handling mental causes, take my word for it they were "belief" healings, a belief of disease healed by entertaining a belief of a cause and a cure, one belief acting upon another belief. I have read the New Testament until I have worn out the book and in no place can I find Jesus saying anything about hatred, lust, or a desire for affection causing a disease. Instead, he said, that even sin had not caused a man to be born blind.

It shocked me to learn that error is not the result of a person's thinking because I had always been taught that disease is caused by wrong thinking, but I discovered in the first year of my practice that this is not true. How could a baby suffer because his parents were indulging in wrong thinking? No, he suffers from universal beliefs which his parents do not know how to handle. People do not contract colds, "flu," and polio in their "seasons" because of their wrong thinking: These are universal beliefs which they do not know how to meet, and if they cling only to this God-is-love business without learning how to handle these beliefs, they will be as badly off as if they had never discovered that God is love.

The weakness in metaphysical practice is that most metaphysicians like to talk about how wonderful God is, but dislike intensely telling anyone what to do about the appearance of sin and disease. Would there be a single person experiencing lust, animality, fear, or false appetite, if he knew how to deal with it?

There is a law of God that annuls these, but you must know what that law is. Just saying, "God is love," does not do it because we already have too much of that in the world—even among people who are sure that God is love.

Never forget that every evil circumstance in your life can be prevented. Nobody is a victim of anything but his ignorance of the laws of life. God never intended anyone to suffer from old age; God never intended that there be cripples, alcoholics, or drug addicts, and there is no reason in the world why there are, except that the world has never learned how to meet these problems and destroy them in human belief.

Evil does not exist as a God-created thing. God does not punish people even though the old Hebraic law taught that the sins of the fathers shall be visited upon the children. When the Hebrews saw how unjust such a law was, however, they rescinded it two hundred years later: ...they shall say no more, "The fathers have eaten a sour grape, and the children's teeth are set on edge."[1] Yes, they learned three or four thousand years ago not to accept such a cruel idea as that the sins of the fathers are visited upon the children, and certainly we should be at least that far advanced. And yet we have accepted laws of heredity which bind us to the belief that the ills of the father are visited on the chilren, the grandchildren, and the great-grandchildren. We must rise higher than that, and we can make a beginning by understanding that there is a law of God in operation in individual and collective being, in individuals and in groups, races, and nations.

Thought Is Not Power

There is a law of God, but we have to begin to bring that law into operation, first, by giving up our egotistical beliefs that any kind of thinking we can do is a power, or that taking a statement and

[1]Jeremiah 31:29.

drilling it into our mind will finally make it come true. Maybe it will come true. But that is hard work; it is neither permanent nor spiritual; and furthermore, it permits others to dominate our thoughts and also takes away from us our realization of the only Power there is, which is God, whose kingdom is within us.

Repeating that two times two is four will not make it so, though it might help us to remember that it is so. The repetition of an affirmation will help to impress us with its truth, but it would be far better to hear or read a truth, and better still to have Truth revealed from within our own being and let that Truth do the work, since Truth is really a synonym for God. Why depend upon the manipulation of Truth? Why not let Truth do it alone?

How many people are there who really and truly believe that there is a God? Oh, yes, they accept God and talk about Him. But how many of those who claim to believe in God at the same moment cling to a medicine or to a thought? Neither the medicine nor the thought can ever be God. God is not thought. Thought is not God-power: *Thought is an avenue of awareness.* That is one statement you might memorize, not in order to make it come true, but if ever you should be tempted to manipulate thoughts, remembering that statement will bring you sharply to the realization that no amount of thinking is power.

When the truth came to me that thought is not a power, but only an avenue of awareness, I was startled for a moment. Then I saw that through my thought—through the avenue of thought—I could become aware of people around me and know whether they were dressed in brown or green or black, but no amount of thinking I could do could change the brown to green or the green to black. Not my thought, nor all the thought in the world, could change that. Thereafter, for me, thought became an avenue of awareness.

Through thought, you can become aware of the great truth that you are the Christ of God. That is what you are and have been since time began. It has always been true. "Before Abraham was, I am"[1]—and nobody's thinking that can make it true. It is true

[1]John 8:58.

because it is a law of God. "Lo, I am with you always"[2]—even unto the end of this human belief of things. That *I* will be with you and that *I* is the Christ, the mind that was in Christ Jesus, the Soul, or Spirit, of God.

One grain of the Christ does miracles when left to operate without mental manipulation, without the mental desire to reach out to the consciousness or the mind or thought of the individual seeking help. How many times have you had the experience of being in an office with a practitioner of highly developed spiritual consciousness and feeling some beneficial effect, some uplift, or some sense of peace? But do you believe it is necessary to be in the same room or in the actual presence of the practitioner to have that experience? Does the body or the brain have anything to do with it? No, you could sit in your home in China and receive the same divine impulse from any individual in whom the mind of Christ is even in a tiny measure in the ascendancy.

Availability of the Mind
That Was in Christ Jesus

We must go further than mind science and mental healing, and come to that place where we work in accordance with the revelation or teaching of Christ Jesus. Jesus lived, "not by might, nor by power, but by my spirit."[3] Is there any better way to heal than that, or any way that will leave your patient freer to function normally without undue influence from other human beings? "Not by might, nor by power, but by my spirit," by *My Spirit*, the Spirit of God, by that mind which was also in Christ Jesus, which is not only the mind of the Christ, but the mind of you and the mind of me.

The mind that was in Christ Jesus is as available to you today as if Jesus were sitting in this room. If you do not believe that this is

[2]Matthew 28:20.
[3]Zechariah 4:6.

true, try this experiment: Sometime when you are feeling tired or ill and have the opportunity to be by yourself, close your eyes and ask yourself whether the mind that was in Christ Jesus was inside his brain or inside his body, or was he stating a profound truth when he said" "Before Abraham was, I am.[1]...Lo, I am with you always, even unto the end of the world.[2]...If I go not away, the Comforter will not come unto you."[3]

If you believe those words to be the truth, you will relax in this realization: "All right! Mind of Christ Jesus, Father within, the Christ! As long as You are with me, I can sit back and rest in peace!" Then rest in that peace and see if you do not have an instantaneous healing without "taking thought."

At first you may not be healed of your more serious claims and problems because most of us are still in that place where we might not be able to accept such healings without thinking we had seen a "miracle." But begin in small ways with the lesser problems. Rest in the mind that was in Christ Jesus and see if it is not as available to you here and now as if Jesus were in the room.

Regardless of where the practitioner is, you are not going to reach out to him as a person, but to the mind that was in Christ Jesus, which is the mind of the practitioner. You must never limit yourself to the human mind of any person. The mind of Christ Jesus realized is the mind of you and of me, available to all, whether close or far. That is the secret of living in Christ-consciousness, the secret of The Infinite Way. Paul's statement, "I live; yet not I, but Christ liveth in me,"[1] is true, and every time anyone reaches out to a person of realized Christ-consciousness, he is reaching out to the Christ, which is living through and as that person.

Be grateful that every truth is a universal truth, not only about Jesus Christ, but about everyone in the world who will open his consciousness and accept it—accept it, not about a human being,

[1]John 8:58.
[2]Matthew 28:20.
[3]John 16:7.
[1]Galatians 2:20.

because a human being is limited to his human, educated mind or to his experience, personality, and birth, but accept it about any individual who will open his consciousness and recognize, "Yes, anything that was true of Moses, Elijah, Elisha, Jesus, John, or Paul is true of me. Otherwise it would not be truth, but only personal sense."

Therefore, if you want to have that mind that was in Christ Jesus continuously, open your consciousness. You need not exercise mental power; you do not have to direct your thought to a certain part of the body or to a certain cause for the disease or to any person, because error is not in any person's body or thinking.

The minute you begin to know that the mind that was in Christ Jesus is your mind, from that moment on, it is doing something to your body, your business, your income, and your human relationships. It may seem slow in the beginning, unless you experience a tremendous light such as Saul had when he became Paul. In that case, it might be quick; but even with Saul, it was nine years after he had had his great experience before he became Paul and went out on his first mission. It took that long for the truth to digest, unfold, and come forth.

So with us. Sometimes we catch a tremendous light but may not understand its full significance until some time later. I noticed this in the early days of my healing practice when I was sending out a weekly letter. Even though I knew the truth of what I wrote, it was only on re-reading those letters two years later that I understood certain statements and felt an inner conviction, or realization, of them.

You will find this to be your experience also because many truths with which you intellectually agree today may only register with you one or two years from now. Often it takes time to rise from the level of egotistical sense to a higher consciousness. If you were at a high enough point of spiritual consciousness, what you have read so far in this book would lift you into heaven. But the fact is that one statement registers with one person here and some other statement with another one there. These words are coming through from the Spirit, but it takes a degree of spiritual awareness to be able to digest and grasp them .Often I find that many statements I have made on different occasions startle me when I hear them again, and I wonder where I ever got that.

Living in "My Kingdom"

One statement from Jesus, "My kingdom is not of this world,"[1] has been my life and my blood and my bones for many years. After having been told that "My kingdom is not of this world," what would you think of me if I began to do some mental work for next month's rent? What would you think of a person who, after having been told that the Christly kingdom has nothing to do with this world, went around worrying about whether he was married or single? If those things are not a part of this world, I do not know what is! It is true that in one sense, we are always in the world, but not in it and of it in the sense that we have any concern for it: We let it unfold—its people and things—and become a part of our being, normally and naturally.

To illustrate: You are reading this book, and yet perhaps in the very room in which you are sitting is a radio or a television, only waiting the turn of a knob to bring you every manner of entertainment—low comedy or inspiring drama, rock and roll or symphony. But you are reading a book on spiritual living! Ask a few thousand or a few dozen people if anything in the world could be more boring, duller, or more uninteresting than such reading.

Then why do you like it? Why do you spend your time doing this? Because you are already living in a different world from that of most people, and it has not been necessary for you to die to get there. One spiritual quotation, one spiritual thought gives you more joy than the most spectacular moving picture. Why? Because you are no longer in a world where that is the measure of

[1]John 18:36.

your joy. You have left that world—not through the act of dying or of doing anything ridiculous like stopping eating or giving up the wearing of clothes, not through anyting of an eccentric nature. And yet you have left that world.

Take another illustration: How many thirty-cent thrillers and crime novels do you imagine were sold in our country today? Yet here you are, instead of paying thirty-five cents for one of those, you pay three dollars and ninety-five cents for this book! What is wrong with you? Nothing! You are simply living in a different world. You have left that other world.

Another thing, how many people are there who actually believe they cannot make a good honest living without doing a little chiselling or cheating or without using some political influence? You, however, have learned that there is a principle at work within you which enables you to live completely in accord with the law of Christ Jesus, with the law laid down in the Golden Rule, and you can adopt a principle such as that for yourself and be abundantly cared for—and I mean abundantly—if you want to make the effort to claim it.

That is what I mean by living in a different world. There are those who could never agree that human ingenuity, physical force, mental pressure, and unlimited capital are not necessary. But you know that by the application of spiritual principles you can live a normal and harmonious life, attracting to you all that is a part of your fulfillment. You can experience this fulfillment not through affirmations, but by realizing:

> *My oneness with God constitutes my oneness with every spiritual idea, and that spiritual idea will express itself as home, friend, student, patient, book, or teacher—anything of which I have need.*

You do not have to go about demonstrating things. You need only demonstrate your oneness with God by opening your consciousness to that truth, accepting it, and letting it become part of your consciousness. Then that truth does the work.

The moment that you begin taking thought for anything in the world that can be known through the physical senses, you are taking thought for this world, and "My kingdom is not of this world," in dealing with the problems of your personal life, you may be doing mental work for right activity, business, supply, companionship, or marriage—all the time having in your mind some particular location where all this must take place. Yet right at this very moment your demonstration may be in Africa, but in outlining the manner and method in which you want your life to unfold, you have closed your whole mind to the direction in which fulfillment lies because Africa may not have entered your thought at all.

If, however, instead of taking thought for anything that had to do with person, place, or thing, your entire work had been for the conscious realization of the mind that was also in Christ Jesus, you then might possibly have heard it voiced within, or might have received a letter telling you what was waiting for you in Africa, China, or somewhere else.

In other words, it is sinful to limit. It is sinful to put any kind of mental limitation on your demonstration. How do you know where it is going to be, when, or with whom? If there is a God governing His own universe, how can you and I have the presumption to limit or outline that demonstration? The truth is that we have no right to outline. We have the right only to abide in the principle of spiritual living which is to take no thought for our life.

The Body Is Life Formed

The telephone bell rings, and a voice cries, "Work for life; I am dying"; but the Bible says: "Take no thought for your life."[1] So my response to that call is "Yes, I will work to realize God." Life

[1]Luke 12:22.

is a synonym for God. Can you not see that if you do any mental work for life, you are probably thinking in terms of life as the opposite of death, but since God is the only life, life has no opposite?

A practitioner once said to a patient, "There is no life in your body"; but the patient naturally wanted to manifest life more abundantly, if not in, then certainly as a body. Too many of us are trying to get rid of our body, denying the body. Can you picture what we would look like without a body? Do not deny the body or throw it away; it is very good to have. You have a body and God gave it to you—not your parents. Not one of you who is a parent knows enough to make a body. God forms the body, not parents, or as I once said to a mother, "At best, you were the oven in which your child was baked."

God is Spirit and expresses Itself infinitely and individually and has Its own way of producing Its image and likeness. This which we see is only our concept of an already divine activity. Human parentage, or so-called human creation, is not spiritual; it is not of God. If it were, everyone would be harmonious and normal, and there would be no diseased or deformed children. It is only because we have left God out of it that we have such conditions.

Most people look upon this experience of human birth as if it were just an animalistic thing. That is a false interpretation. It in not animalistic: It in itself is divine and wonderful. It is we who turn it into something of an animal nature. We must learn to reinterpret it. And when we learn to do that, there will be more happy marriages and fewer divorces.

The only reason for divorce is that a man and a woman see one another merely as man and woman. It is a hard thing for a man and woman to live together for many years unless there is a common meeting ground, and even more important, a spiritual bond. If only, long before marriage, they could come to the realization that they are not seeking marriage or home or companionship, but are really seeking the presence of God in visible form, there would be more happy marriages, and every child born of such a union would then be God made manifest.

Immortality, Not Longevity

So we come to this point: What is the motive for your study? On that depends your future in this work. I do not mean that those of you who cannot grasp what I am saying may not go back to the mental level again. If necessary, that is what you will have to do until you are able to rise to the spiritual level. But to those of you who have caught a glimpse of the meaning of spiritual living, the whole of your future is going to depend on whether or not you can determine to seek only the consciousness of the presence of God and be satisfied to let the *things* be added. The extent to which you are able to do this will be the measure of your demonstration.

Is your motive in this study merely to change sickness into health, loneliness into companionship, or homelessness into a home? Or, are you ready, at this moment, to stop taking thought for the things of this world which do not belong to the spiritual kingdom and honestly pray:

> *All I want is the kingdom of God on earth. All I desire is the reign of God in my individual experience, the government of God in my individual affairs.*

When we reach that point, we are seeking the kingdom of God and His rightness, not our sense of rightness—more dollars, more companionship, more health—but *His* rightness, the spiritual sense of good. If we understood the spiritual sense of supply, we would find it to be far different from our present sense of it, just as the spiritual sense of health is far different from the human standard which allots sixty or seventy years as the normal span of life. But His Rightness—His standard of supply, His standard of health—would enable us to live abundantly on earth as long as we desired, or as long as we did not get lonesome for those who had gone on before us.

There are people living on earth today who are said to be two hundred years of age, and one man reputedly over six hundred years of age. Such advanced years are possible if the desire is for the spiritual sense of God, health, and immortality—not merely for the physical sense of health or life or longevity.

Is immortality merely living a long time? Is it merely longevity? No, immortality is life eternal without beginning or ending. No spiritual seeker would believe that his consciousness can come to an end even though he might believe that it is inevitable that his body will drop away. But that is a thought which should be corrected at once. Your body does not drop away or age unless you permit it to do so. You are the one who must make the conscious decision that life is eternal and that your body, the temple of the living God, is under the jurisdiction of that life.

Since life is eternal and life is consciousness, how can consciousness be dead? The continuity or life can be understood when you realize that through your own consciousness of being you have existed eternally and that you will exist eternally. In your inner enlightenment, you can go on existing without that moment of passing, that transfer, which the world calls death but which is only *transition*. When you can make the transition out of the world of mortal beliefs, you have made the transition from "this world" into the world of spiritual reality in which you live without taking thought.

Living by "My Spirit"

Let no one believe that living without taking thought has anything to do with becoming a mental blank. On the contrary, the moment you learn to live without taking thought, you will be the most mentally active person in the community because then you are not governed by your own limited sense of mind. The mind that was in Christ Jesus begins to function as you: If you want to write, you will be a writer; if you want to paint, you will be a painter, because there will be no more limitation.

You do not become a mental blank and you do not live in a vacuum, but you are so animated by this spiritual consciousness that even when you are sleeping you are thinking. You are not taking thought which is quite a different thing, but you are receiving divine impulses through the mind, your avenue of awareness, which interpret themselves to you as thought, and you are continuously aware of an infinitely expanding experience.

Never believe that living without taking thought will lead to laziness of any kind. Rather does it bring such activity into life, the wonder is that you ever go to sleep. There is no end to the activity that comes to the person whose being is animated by the Christ-mind. When that Christ-mind takes over in your experience, inspiring and creative thoughts, the thoughts of God— God's thoughts pouring out as man—are flowing forth from you instead of your digging around in your brain for some used-up thoughts or cold truths.

And what is a cold truth? A cold truth is something you remember as a quotation, something which comes to you out of stored-up memory. When a thought comes to that consciousness which is receptive and open, it comes as a hot truth, a live truth, and it carries with it healing or brings with it inventiveness and new ideas. That is what happens when we receive a direct impartation from the divine Consciousness.

A person can dig into all the old books from ages past—and these truths really go back a long way—but the truths found in them will be of no value until they find lodgment in an open consciousness, at which time they become alive. Therefore, the most important aspect of this teaching is not imparting knowledge or giving out statements of truth because every statement I am giving you now has been known throughout the ages.

The real value of this teaching is to develop in you a state of spiritual receptivity, so that you can be receptive to the Christ-mind; to open your consciousness, so that you can receive these truths; to open your consciousness to the inflow of the Christ, so that your open consciousness becomes the living Christ, and thereby becomes the light of the world.

Many people believe that soon there will be another coming of the Christ, but I am convinced that you and I are coming in proportion as the Christ is awakened in us. Every one of us is now coming into that state of consciousness where we can accept Jesus' statement that the Comforter will come to us when we stop relying on people and human modes and means. When we can open up our consciousness to the whole infinite Christ, then Christ, the Christ of the second coming, will come to you and to me. I can not believe, though, for a minute, that any second coming of the Christ will be experienced by the person who has taken no time to learn to know the Christ.

We must *experience* the Christ, not by hearsay but by actual demonstration, by actual contact. Some students know that such an experience is possible, and in working with those of receptive thought, I have observed that I can lift them to where they can see the same vision that I see—not through the transference of thought, but through their own individual unfoldment. They have heard "the still small voice" and received impartations through developing their capacity to meditate.

Watch the presence of God open your consciousnes to the inflow of good. Do not outline in what form it will appear, through or with who, or where or when. Open your consciousness to God and let It become evident or manifest—not with mental work, not by repetition or affirmation, "not by might, nor by power, but by my spirit."

From

THE MASTER SPEAKS

Reality of Spirit

———•———

The most important part of our work is finding the answer to the question, What is God? So long as we think of God as some kind of a super-man sitting on a cloud or a man on a cross or some unknown and mysterious being, we do not bring even a small amount of spiritual power into our experience.

Gratitude, appreciation, and recognition are a natural part of spiritual revelation and realization. Nevertheless, we might repeat over and over, "Thank you, Father" from now until doomsday; but unless we actually understand *what* God is, *who It* is, and *what It* is we are thanking, and *why* we are thanking *It*, such outward expression is of little value. What is It that we are acknowledging; what is It we are thinking about; what is It we are seeking as the source and foundation of our unfoldment? God— but what *is* God? For thousands of years God has been considered as something separate and apart from us. Today, however, we are no longer willing to accept a far-off God, because we have come to understand that God is the Soul of our being; God is the Mind, the Spirit, the very Substance of which we are formed. God is the center of our being. God is the infinite consciousness of our being. Our "Thank you, Father" is, therefore, not only an expression of gratitude, but it is a recognition and realization that the Father, or God, is the divine consciousness of our very own being.

The value of that recognition is that whatever we find to be true of God is universally true. It is true of us and it is true about every individual, everywhere, and at all times. "His mercy endureth forever."[1] This truth is universal and eternal throughout all generations. Whether we are thinking of people who. to our human sense of things, have passed on or whether we are thinking of people who are now on earth or those who are yet to come, remember this: God is their very own consciousness and they are always under divine protection, divine guidance, and divine illumination. We have no personal responsibility, therefore, toward them. To understand *what* God is, is to see God as the very life of individual being. If we realized God as the life of individual being, we would never again be concerned about whether anyone is, to appearance, alive or dead; because we would know and understand life as the only reality.

Conscious Awareness of the Presence of God Is Necessary

This leads us to another very important element in this work. The only benefit we derive from any truth teaching is through the activity of our own consciousness. Therefore, unless we understand every word of truth we declare, we are deriving no benefit from it. We must be consciously aware of the truth of every statement we use. We must not be satisfied to be human beings walking up and down the street, believing that afar off

[1]Jeremiah 33:11.

somewhere there is a God with whom we can leave our problems. To say glibly, "Oh, well I am going to leave it to God," as if there were a God out there to whom we could shift our problems is of little value. But we *can* leave our every problem to God, when, through a correct understanding of the revelation of truth, we rise to an understanding of the true nature and character of God. When we have a conscious awareness of the truth of being, God becomes the very activity of our being and we can then leave everything to God. In themselves, the statements, "Thank you, Father, " or "I and my Father are one," are of no value; but the conscious awareness—our conscious knowledge of the meaning of those statements—make them God-power in our experience.

Consciousness is God—your consciousness and my consciousness. One infinite, indivisible Consciousness, which appears individually as your consciousness and mine—this is God. It is the activity of your consciousness and mine which results in the fruitage of our harmonious daily experience. We cannot sit with a dull, sleepy, or thoughtless mind and believe that there is a God-power acting somewhere for us. God-power is the activity of our consciousness. This God-power appears as the activity of our consciousness. God-power is our consciousness at work, and it is our consciousness when it is imbued with truth, an awareness of truth, and not merely the declaration of truth.

It is on this very point that truth students have made some of their greatest blunders. They have believed that the recitation of these truths is a virtue or has power. This is an incorrect assumption. It is not the activity of the human mind that is power; it is the consciousness imbued with a knowledge of truth that is power. Jesus said, "And ye shall know the truth, and the truth shall make you free."[1] He did not simply say, "The truth will make you free." He could have said just that. A study of the words of the Master shows how sparing he was in his use of words and how very careful he was in his choice of words. He could have saved several words by saying, "The truth will make you

[1]John 8:32.

free." But he did not do that. He went to the trouble of saying,"...know the truth, and the truth shall make you free." If we are to follow his teaching, we must become aware of the meaning of the truths that we read and declare and make these truths an active part of our consciousness, of our conscious awareness. Then they bring a *feel* with them, and that *feel* is the power made manifest.

Since Spirit is God, Spirit is real; Spirit is vital, alive; Spirit is allness. Spirit is totality. But although this is true, there must be a conscious awareness of the reality of Spirit. In that conscious awareness, we have the power that produces the harmonies of our daily experience.

Even before 1492, the oceans existed, and beyond the seas, rich and fertile lands. But to those who believed the world was flat, to those who accepted appearances for reality, the total extent of the ocean was only about eight miles. They looked out and saw where the sky and the ocean met and, of course, seeing that, they believed that they could not go beyond that point. This limited sense, based wholly on appearances, actually bound them to the limitation of their own little country and the waters nearby.

All this time, in reality, there was no such limitation. Never once did the sky touch the water. The oceans, the seven seas, were always open and free for travel, and yet, for centuries, every person sat in his little corner, a prisoner to the idea of the sky's meeting with the ocean in the distant horizon. All this was changed by one man who was not blinded by appearances, but who, in turning away from appearances, reached the conclusion that the world was not flat, but round. Of course, if the world is round, the sky does not come down and touch the water, nor does the water rise up to the sky. The sky is always in its own place, and the water is in its own place. Neither one is a barrier to the other. That one man, through the activity of consciousness, through his unlimited vision, refused to be hypnotized by everybody else's belief. He, able to think independently, unhypnotized and free, caught the vision which enabled him to sail forth opening up new worlds.

So it is with us. If we sit back and give credence to the beliefs of the world just because people have believed them since time began, then we, too, are limited. Today most of us are limited by our sense of body; we believe that wherever we are at this moment is the extent of our being. Actually, that limitation has as little foundation as the limitation imposed on those who believed the earth was flat. A few have had the actual realization that they are not confined to a body. In that realization they can instantaneously be anywhere in the world: as a matter of fact, they are already there, only not consciously aware of it. We, as infinite individual consciousness, can be anywhere and everywhere in this world; but we have not as yet gained the conscious awareness of that fact.

It should not take very long to prove that we are not *in* the body. Let us look at our own feet, and then ask ourselves two questions, "Is that foot I?" or "Is that foot *mine?*" Let us wait until we have a distinct answer within ourselves. Let us not go any further away than our feet, and see if we can really find ourselves in our feet. If we are not there, then at least we shall have discovered that we are not confined somewhere down in our shoes or in the bones or flesh of our feet. Through this kind of an exercise, we shall come to the realization that that foot is not I, but *mine.* I *possess* my foot, but I am not *in* my foot.

Let us continue the journey and go to the legs. Are we in the legs or are they our legs? Are they not our vehicle, our possession, our instrument, the instrument we use at this moment for the purpose of walking? Let us be sure that we understand that we are not doing this just as a pastime. We are doing it because this little idea contains within itself the entire secret of life as it has been revealed for thousands of years. The fact is that we are not body and we are not *in* a body.

We go from the legs all the way through every member of the body, until we reach the topmost hairs of our head. As we proceed, let us not hesitate to stop, at any or every point, and ask ourselves if this is I or if this is mine: Am I there? Am I in the muscles, the nerves, the stomach, or the solar plexus? Am I in the heart, liver, or lungs? Am I even in the brain, or is all of this *mine?* Is all this merely an instrument for my use? As we continue the search to find in what part of the body we are localized, searching tirelessly, the revelation finally comes to us, "I cannot find myself in this body. There is not a particle or part of this body in which I can find myself entombed. I am not there at all! All the time that I thought this was I, it was *mine.* I thought that when I looked in the mirror I saw myself. I never did. I saw only my body; I was not there."

We must understand this basic premise thoroughly because merely rehearsing it or agreeing with the author that we are not in the body will not be of much benefit to us. We, ourselves, must have the conscious awareness that we do not exist *in* the body; that we are not to be found inside the body, search though we may, from our toenails to our topmost hair. Having reached this conclusion, the next thing we must ask ourselves is, "Since I am not in the body, where am I?" Yes, that is the great mystery: Where am I? Who am I? What am I? One thing we shall immediately be sure of and that is that we are not confined even to a room, and we are not confined to a body.

The next thing that must come to us is, "Since I am conscious of my body, and I am conscious of this room, and I am conscious of this building, and I am conscious of my home, and I am conscious of my family, and I am conscious of my friends, and I am conscious of my business; then it seems to me that all I find is that I am conscious of this; I am conscious of that; I am conscious of the other. *What is there to me but consciousness?*"

Proceeding along these lines we find that our business is our consciousness of business; our home is our consciousness of home; our body is our consciousness of body. None of these things exists separate or apart from our consciousness. None of these things exists outside our consciousness. None of these things exists outside the government and the power of our consciousness. We learn, moreover, that the body exists only at the standpoint of our consciousness. If we were not conscious of the body, we would not have a body, or it would not be of any value to us, because we would not be conscious of it and, therefore, would be unable to use it.

Only that of which we are conscious is important in our experience. When we have no consciousness of body, it is as if we did not have a body, and we lose all interest in it. If we have no consciousness of our bank account, it ceases to be of any use to us. All the money we might have in the bank would be of no avail, if we did not have the conscious awareness of that bank account, where it is, and what its purpose is. Without this awareness, even a bank account would be of no value to us.

If we do not have a conscious awareness of the presence and the power of Spirit, It does no healing work for us. That is the reason one person is able to do successful healing work, while another fails. The only difference is that one has a conscious awareness of the Spirit which does the work, whereas the other has not yet attained that conscious awareness of the Spirit. It takes a *conscious awareness* of the Presence to do the work. Everything in this life is dependent upon our conscious awareness. It is logical, therefore, to say that *all there is to us is consciousness*. All we are is consciousness.

Developing Spiritual Consciousness

Our great purpose in life should be the development and unfoldment of our spiritual consciousness or spiritual awareness. For that purpose it becomes necessary for us to begin with the knowledge that we are not feet, legs, or torsos, but that *we are a state of consciousness*, appearing to the world as body .We are infinite consciousness; we are divine consciousness. Apart from consciousness we are nothing, but as consciousness, we are *infinite*. This we must understand. It is absolutely necessary first, to understand that we exist as consciousness; and secondly, to become conscious of this reality of existence.

As we look out through our human eyes and see only so much bone or so many pounds of flesh, then, of course, we cannot be satisfied with ourselves or with life. As we learn, however, through our developed spiritual consciousness, our awakened consciousness, to behold Him as He is, then we shall begin to see that we are not flesh and bone; we are consciousness. We can be satisfied with that likeness. That is the reason The Infinite Way teaches us never to look at a person, but to look through him, especially through the eyes, where we can catch glints and glimpses of that light, which is the reality of being. We are consciousness: you are consciousness; I am consciousness. In proportion as we become conscious of one another—as we really are—then we enjoy one another, and each one of us takes his rightful place in the scheme of things.

Physical or mental healing is based on the belief that we exist somewhere between our feet and our head, and it attempts to do something about a physical existence. Spiritual healing has an entirely different basis. Spiritual healing is dependent on the individual's becoming consciously aware of the truth that we do not exist *in* the body or *as* the body, but that we exist as infinite, divine consciousness.

Jesus did not say that he was the body. He said, "I am...the life."[1] He did not say that he knew the truth. He said, "I am...the truth."[2] When we begin to understand what this means—I am life eternal; I am truth—then, we can also see that the body or anything else—music, paintings, sculpture, literature—can be the subject and the object of our consciousness;[3] and we can come into an awareness of it as it is, not as it appears to be to the unillumined or ignorant sense, but as it really is.

Here is the great wonder of this world and of this work: *There is a Christ.* Whether we call It the Christ of the Christians, Immanuel of the Hebrews, or Tao of the Chinese; there is a Christ. That Christ is infinite, invisible presence and power. It is actually the seat of our being, the center of our being. It is the one

[1]John 14:6.
[2]John 14:6.
[3]This subject is dealt with more fully in the author's *The Art of Meditation*, Harper and Brothers, New York, 1956, pp. 123-29.

divine, individual reality of each one of us. But to experience the presence and power of the Christ, it is necessary to be consciously aware of the Christ as the reality of our being, as the seat and source of our intelligence, our eternality, and our immortality.

From this time on, it will be less than useless for us to talk about the Christ, or about God, or about Spirit; or even to read inspiring writings about God, or about the Christ. We have been through thousands of years of hearing about God and praying to God and expecting to meet God in the next world. From this point on, the time has come for the actual realization and demonstration of God. We are making an about-face and we are recognizing the I-Amness of the Christ. We are recognizing the presence of eternal Life here and now—not in some future event, and certainly not in some past event which has gone beyond the possibility of recapturing. Our work lies in attaining the I-Amness of the infinite Christ. Christ has always been the infinite, invisible divinity, but we now come to the conscious awareness of the Christ as the foundation of our health, as the foundation of our wealth, as the foundation of the happiness of our home.

Realization of the Christ Appears as Form

In my work the treatment is always this: *realization of the Christ.* When I sit quietly and peacefully in a receptive state of consciousness, sooner or later, I feel something within that I know to be the divine Presence, the Christ; and I find that It, that Presence, that Christ, meets these claims, whether they are mental, moral, physical, or financial. It, Itself, enters into human relationships, bringing peace where there was strife—that is, when that peace is desired. Many times people do not want the peace of the Christ. They want their own human will satisfied. They may want to see a fight settled amicably, but they want it settled on their own terms. A person may want his health, but he wants it, not the way by which the Christ may bring it to him. In anyone the Christ touches, It always dissolves the elements of sensuality, envy, jealousy, or malice. The Christ very often operates in our consciousness to dispel even inherited or environmental traits which are not conducive to spiritual living; but many people do not want that to happen to them. They want to hold on to their lust for power, their lust for place, their lust for money, or their lust for something else—and yet expect to get their healing, too. They want the healing, but they do not want to surrender the personal sense of self.

This does not mean that in our practice of The Infinite Way an attempt is made to discover what is erroneous in an individual's thought and then try to correct it. No, no, no! Never would we be guilty of trying to find out what error lurks in another person's thought. But, by abiding in this spiritual sense of truth, harmony, and peace, whatever of material or mortal sense exists as a state of thought is dissolved. The treatment, therefore, for anything and everything, is "Peace, be still." That is all. Just those words, "Peace, be still!" are enough if they come from a state of consciousness which is at peace and which has found the center of its being.

If I were to try to correct something in your mind or body, the treatment would fail. If, however, I forget the world and what is called form, and find my center of being—find my peace, the realization of the Christ—then quickly the answer comes, "I have been helped," or "I am healed." It was not anything which I knew, or any power which I, of myself, possessed; it was this Christ.

If we do not have this consciousness of the presence of the Christ, we lack the one element which does the healing work. The Christ is always present with us; the Christ is the reality of our being; but the need is for the *conscious awareness* of the presence of the Christ. We develop that through studying and hearing the Word, coming together with other students on the path, and the revelation within our own being brought about through meditation. Reading, association with others on the path, and meditation bring us to that state of consciousness where all of a sudden the inner realization comes, and the Christ unfolds and discloses Its glory to us.

Our consciousness of truth appears outwardly as form. This Christ, which is Spirit, appears tangibly as form. It may appear as a new heart or liver or lung for somebody; It may appear as a new bone in his body; It may appear as husband, wife, or companion; It may appears as an opportunity; It may appear as a parking place on the street. It appears in the tiniest forms—a little pin, if that is what is needed at that moment. We do not sit back and try to form it. We do not sit back and sigh that we are going to need the pin, parking place, or a new piece of flesh. Our only responsibility is to attain the consciousness of the presence of the Christ, the awareness of our oneness with the Christ. We sink back into our inner being; we feel ourselves at the center; and out of It flows the infinity of God. We do not direct It any place. We are just a center of peace, a center of Christ activity, a center of love, and a center of life. The more continuously we maintain that attitude, the more does that love appear outwardly as money, patients, students, customers, or whatever the need may be.

Our consciousness of truth appears outwardly as form; but we do not have to outline what that form shall be. We are required only to live and move and have our being in Spirit—to live as Spirit, as Soul, as Consciousness. We are responsible only for maintaining our spiritual integrity, and this is attained and maintained in the degree that we see Soul, Spirit, and purity, as the life and harmony of every individual. This means every individual, not every mortal.

We are not dealing with the mortal picture. We are not looking at it or trying to improve it. We are looking through it to the reality of being, with our spiritual wisdom, with our intuitive sense. Who, by searching, can find out God? Nobody. We never can find God with the intellect, our human sense, or our reasoning power; we find God only in our inner, intuitive, spiritual consciousness. In a moment of awareness, something within suddenly says, "No, it is not I, but He. I am He."

Something within gives us the feeling of a divine Presence, of oneness. As we realize this, we spiritually discern the reality of our neighbor's being—even our enemy's being, since we are told that it really does not do us any good to know all this truth about our friends only; the scribes and the Pharisees did that. We, who have taken the name of Christ, must see that this is true, even of what appears to human sense as our enemy. Many of us think of an enemy as a person, but we have no greater enemies than death and disease. Ultimately, we must come to see through the illusory picture of death and disease to life eternal, and then we shall not experience death.

The world will go on experiencing the death of the body until, in consciousness, it overcomes the belief of death. In other words, as long as we entertain an awareness of death, that awareness will appear in the form of death. Our inner awareness appears outwardly as form. When we have the inner awareness of life eternal, it will appear outwardly as immortality, spirituality, harmony, peace, joy, power, and dominion.

Evil a State·of Hypnotism

Does wrong thinking, then, appear outwardly as sin, disease, and death? No, it does not. It comes to us merely as an appearance or a belief, and we accept that appearance or belief as if it actually were an external form. Can a person who is hypnotized into believing that there is a white poodle on the hypnotist's platform, even produce a white poodle there? No! All the hypnotized thinking in the world will not produce a white poodle. It will only produce an appearance or a belief which the victim claims is a white poodle. Wrong thinking will never produce sin, disease, or death. We are not creators; God is the creative principle, and It creates only Its own image and likeness. Our wrong thinking and the world's wrong thinking, therefore, will never produce sin, disease, or death. Such wrong thinking will only objectify the belief as an illusory picture like our "white poodle" and then look at it and say, "How am I going to get rid of it?" It is not even here, so how can we get rid of it? There is no such thing as sin, disease, or death; and all the wrong thinking in the world that we can do will not produce such things. But the universal belief in a selfhood apart from God does produce these erroneous pictures which we see as claiming to have substance, law, and reality; but which they do not have. All such pictures are as unreal as the white poodle which the hypnotized man believes he is seeing. Let us remember, he is not seeing it; he *believes* he is seeing it.

There is no way to remove that white poodle except to awaken the subject out of his state of hypnosis. How do we do that? One with God is a majority. If there were one person of spiritual vision in the audience who could laugh out loud and say or even think that there is not a white poodle to get rid of, the hypnotized man would awaken out of the dream. It is only because everyone is in agreement with him—the blind leading the blind—that is happens. If someone would consciously realize that he is merely witnessing a form of hypnosis, such a realization would quickly awaken him to the fact that hypnosis is not a power. It is a *belief* in a power apart from the one Life.

Whenever we are confronted with any form of disease, sin, death, lack, or limitation, let us be quick to realize, "This is a hypnotic picture, and I do not have to do anything about it." In this way, we can very well have an instantaneous healing. Even if the healing is not instantaneous, our holding to that truth will ultimately reveal the harmony which already is.

We must realize that there is no disease: there is only hypnotism; there is only a hypnotic picture appearing as disease. Spiritual healing is not using truth with which to overcome error. It is not using the power of good to overcome the power of evil. Jesus answered the impotent man: "Rise...and walk."[1] This was not using a power to heal disease; it was saying, in effect, "There is nothing to be overcome." He did not use the power of God to

[1]John 5:8.

do something to Pilate or to ward off the Crucifixion. He said, "Thou couldest have no power at all against me, except it were given thee from above."[2] Then he let the Crucifixion proceed and he proved life eternal.

A spiritual healer is not a person who develops a technique of using truth to overcome error or of using treatment to overcome disease. A spiritual healer is that state of consciousness, which knows that God alone is the reality of all being, and that anything else is a state of hypnosis. The recognition that he is dealing with a state of hypnosis, rather than with a person or with a condition, is the healing consciousness.

[2]John 19:11.

The Healing Ministry

———————•———————

My oneness with God is my oneness with spiritual wholeness. The only place where disease has no reality and where it disappears, is in one's spiritual sense of life—in this intuitive spiritual sense of life that you feel when you are in the silence, when you are touching Reality. In this life, there is no sin, no disease, no lack, no limitation, no war. There is nothing going on in this spiritual sense of life but spiritual good. That is the reason I say that most of our work should be done silently and not audibly. Giving a person who has asked for help a barrage of metaphysical truths, to me, is nothing but nonsense. To me, the only way to respond to a call for help is to say, "I will help you right away." Just as fast as is possible, get back into that silence, where you can *feel* the very presence of God, where you can discern Reality. Then the patient will be free. When I have a headache, if a practitioner were to say to me, "Now, you know it is not real; of course you have not got a headache"; I would be inclined to reply, "Oh, go jump in the lake! I want freedom! I do not want a lot of conversation!" If the practitioner really and truly believed that the headache was not real, I would be healed long before he could assure me of its unreality. It is not how glib we are at blurting out these metaphysical truths that is going to help anybody. It is the recognition within of spiritual Reality. This you touch somewhere within your own being, and when you do, the whole human picture fades out and you begin to see divine Reality.

We should get out of the habit of telling and repeating testimonies. Testimonies are legitimate when they are used to exemplify some point of spiritual practice. You may want to illustrate a certain principle and use a testimony of healing as an example, but aside from that, give up the habit of testifying, either to your own healings or to those for which you may have been responsible, or to others of which you may have heard.

There is another important point to be considered in the healing work: this ministry is probably the most sacred of all human relations. The full explanation of that statement will unfold as you continue the work. It is a sacred relationship, and for that reason, confidences should never be breached. In the first place, we should neither mention the names of our patients or students, nor disclose who they are except as such information becomes known of its own accord. Never discuss one patient's problems with another, even when they are those of husband and wife, or when the problem concerns mother and child. Never be tempted to discuss one person with another. It is not good, and it might prove harmful.

The Healing Ministry Requires a Dedicated Life

In this work where patients rely so greatly on the help of practitioners, especially in cases involving pain or fear, it is necessary that the practitioner accept the full responsibility and be at the service of his patients. For that reason, two things are important in the conduct of a practitioner's office. One is never to let the telephone be occupied for more than two or three minutes, and if possible not more than one minute. A practitioner's telephone line should be kept open. A patient should not telephone a practitioner and find a busy signal once, twice, three times. Such delay sets up a human sense of irritation or fear that is not conducive to healing. Certainly, it is impossible for a busy practitioner to keep his telephone line open all the time .But if there are too many calls for one telephone, he should have two. A practitioner's home is his office—just a branch office, that is all. A practitioner no longer has a home in the old sense of the word. In many ways, in entering this work, one gives up one's personal life.

The second point to be emphasized is the importance of a practitioner's being within reach of his telephone. A practitioner should not be away from his home for social engagements; and if he finds it necessary to be away, there should be some provision .made for leaving a message as to where he is and where he can be reached. In other words, this is a ministry; and when one enters it, one must be willing to give up one's personal life.

As far as possible, this dedication must become the practitioner's rule of life in order to maintain his own consciousness on a high level. The only thing that heals is the ability to maintain that consciousness, and that is not done if one is indulging overly much in social activities—making social calls and entertaining friends and acquaintances. The teaching of the Master on this point is very clear. In entering the healing ministry, one gives up all for Christ—even father, mother, sister, brother, husband, wife. This does not mean that they are given up in the sense of putting them out of one's life, but they are relegated to a secondary place, which is their rightful one. The *practice* must come first, and then, if there is any time left over for husband or wife, he or she can have it; but you may be sure that it will not be much.

That sounds hard, does it not? It sounds difficult. But actually, that is the way a healing ministry is carried on. It is the way a person must live if he looks upon this as a ministry and not just as a pastime.

In working with patients, especially during periods of pain and fear, I encourage patients to call me frequently: Call me in an hour; call me back in twenty minutes; call me back in two hours. When I first work with a person, particularly a person who comes to me with any claim of a painful or fearful nature, I encourage frequent calls, especially during the night. I have done some work where I have had the telephone ring every twenty minutes all night long. I have seen the crisis passed in many cases—actually healings brought about—through that persistent reaching out for help.

Another aspect of this work is the handling of the mail. From the very day that air-mail was inaugurated, I have used air-mail for all letters that have had to go over two hundred miles. When a patient or any person writes to a practitioner, he is really waiting for an answer. It is an incomplete job until he receives that answer. He may get his healing long before he gets the answer. It is not a question of healing; it is a question of courtesy and consideration. For that reason, our part is to get our answers off as quickly as possible, and to take whatever steps are necessary to have them delivered as quickly as possible. If it seems wise not to wait for an air-mail letter to be delivered, send a telegram, or make a telephone call. Let your patient know as quickly as possible that he is being taken care of, that the work is underway. That is all a part of the healing ministry—part of its service. It is the kind of service which is demanded of every person who expects to work in this field. I say this, primarily, for the benefit of those who will come to you for help, but I say it also, for your own sake. If you hope to be successful in this work, follow these suggestions. No one is ever going to be successful in this work if his heart and soul are not in it; and if one's heart and soul are in it, then he will want to seek the highest form of service there is.

Spiritual Maturity a Necessity

Will you be surprised if I tell you that one of the great sources of our trouble as individuals—even as students on this path—is the fact that we refuse to grow up spiritually and become spiritual adults? For that matter, men and women even refuse to grow up humanly and act like adults. An adult is a person who has arrived at the state of consciousness where he is an individual in his own right, where he is no longer dependent on mother and father, sister and brother, and where he does not transfer that dependence even to his children. An adult is one who, even humanly, should be able to stand on his own feet, and not be a mental parasite, fastening on to his elders or on to his children. How many people there are, even in this work, who are still leaners or parasites, leaning on mama or papa, on sons or daughters, or on sisters or brothers, and then wondering why they do not attain their freedom.

Spiritually, this is even more important. All demonstration in this work is based on the degree of realization of the truth that I and my Father are one. Now, ask yourself this question: "just how seriously do I believe—to what extent do I believe—that I and the Father are one? To what extent am I completely leaning, depending, or relying on this truth or to what extent am I expecting something, some understanding, some support, some companionship from mother, father, husband, wife, child? I am not talking about *enjoying* our relationships with our relatives and families; I am talking about the degree in which we are bound by them and to them We either make them subservient to us and do not give them their freedom from us, or on the other hand, we do not accept our freedom from them.

Many of our individual troubles in the world come from our failure to maintain our spiritual integrity. Out in the world of men and women, people do not even maintain their human integrity. Parents will not free themselves from their children, or children will not free themselves from their parents. There is much too much of a clinging to relationships which have long since served their purpose, instead of breaking loose from them. The birds are better off than we are; they push their young out of the nest and set them free to fly. We do not give our children their freedom if we can avoid it; we rarely ever set them free. And it is seldom that a husband or wife is given the freedom and independence to which he or she is entitled. There is too much of a clinging to human attachments, a holding on, perhaps because of jealousy or fear—for the most part, I think it is fear.

On the spiritual path, there is nothing more satisfying in the world than the relationships between friends, companions, students, or patients; nor is there anything more comforting than the understanding that can come between a man and wife in this work. But this understanding must be based primarily on our recognition of our oneness with God as the chief relationship. When we have established in consciousness our oneness with God, we become one with everybody and we can have the most satisfying relationships—and yet there will not be a dependence on any person as such.

We can take the work of a practitioner as an example. A practitioner who becomes dependent upon a patient for support, or supply, would soon lose his whole healing gift. If a practitioner became dependent on his practice for his living, he would lose his healing gift. It does not mean that practitioners may not derive their living from that source; they very well may; but their *dependence* on it would destroy their effectiveness as practitioners. Unless a practitioner can establish in his consciousness daily that "I and my Father are one¹ and all that I have is thine"¹ and, in this realization, set the patient free, there is again that clinging relationship, which is detrimental to both practitioner and patient.

The same principle applies to the relationship between teacher and student. The moment that a teacher becomes dependent on a

¹John 10:30.
¹Luke 15:31.

student for anything in the world, they are both lost, since the only true relationship is their oneness in Christ—their oneness because of the divine relationship of oneness with God. My oneness with God constitutes my oneness with everybody who has ever been through class with me. But it is such a beautiful oneness that there is no dependence, and there is no interdependence—just a cordial, "Hello," and a friendly, "Goodbye."

Each of us must establish, within his own consciousness, his freedom. Freedom is not a human characteristic: It is a spiritual quality; it is an activity of God, a quality and a quantity of God; it is of the nature of God. Therefore, only in Soul, in Spirit, can we find our freedom.

We find that our health is also a spiritual quality. Health is not in the body, and that is why we are not healing conditions of the body, since health is not a quality or activity of body. Health is an activity of the Soul, which the body reflects. The moment we find our freedom of Soul, we find freedom of the body.

In the same way, economic freedom is not found in dollars, and it is not found in marriage; and we have discovered that it is not found in investments. Economic freedom is found in Soul. Economic freedom is a quality and an activity of Soul. If you make a conscious contact with your Soul, within the depths of your inner being, you will have found your economic freedom. True, it may seem to come through a husband or wife or an investment. It may seem to come through the practice, through the healing ministry, but that will only be the seeming—the appearance. In reality it will be coming from the Soul.

Therefore, if our income should be cut off in one direction, there is nothing to fear because, since Soul is infinite, not only in its capacity, but also in its expression, new sources of income will immediately unfold from another direction. No person will ever find his economic freedom, any more than he will find his physical freedom, until he finds his freedom in Soul, in Spirit, God—in his conscious oneness with God.

Very few people are willing to grow up—to grow into emotional, mental, and spiritual maturity. Within themselves, actually they do not want to be free. For many years I have watched this parade of human life, and I know how many people cling to the very circumstances from which they could be set free, if they really desired freedom and were willing to pay the price of freedom.

First of all, we cling to a bodily sense of life. In other words, we are afraid of what is going to happen to the body .As a matter of fact, the Bible tells us that unless we lose our life, we shall not find it. In other words, unless we lose that physical sense of life—that sense of life in body—we shall not find our spiritual sense of life. We have to lose our material sense of existence, in order to find the incorporeal or spiritual. That does not separate us from our body but it separates us from the false concept of body.

You will never lose your body, since your body and you are one. Your body is merely your consciousness formed, and you cannot separate consciousness from its form. You will never lose your body. Even should you decide to die some day, you will find that you have not lost your body. It will still be right there with you—right where you are. You will not leave it behind. When we agree—even in a measure within ourselves—to be free from the corporeal sense of body, no longer to be afraid of what happens to the body, we begin to find some measure of freedom.

We have to agree, moreover, that we do not care what happens to our dollars, since dollars do not constitute supply. Dollars are merely the form as which supply appears. If there were not dollars, there would be carrots or green peas or chickens. But it really does not make any difference in what form supply appears. If you have the consciousness of supply, you will have abundance, no matter what form it may take. If you touch that place within your consciousness where you realize that your own consciousness itself is the essence and substance of all form, then you will not have to be concerned about a physical body or a material dollar; and in that consciousness will come freedom from human dependencies and interdependencies. We have fashioned ourselves from our beliefs. We have fastened ourselves to someone's life, feeling that life is empty unless we are near some human being. We expect to have mother close at hand, or father, son, daughter, husband, or wife; and we clutch them to us. But when you have found your oneness with God, what a wonderful sense of freedom comes! In finding that oneness with God, you find yourself at one with everybody in the world in a beautiful and satisfying relationship. Each one shares the best side of himself with you and keeps the worst side away from you. Your associates come to you with all that is best in themselves and share that best with you. Watch it, as you learn to find that sense of freedom.

Setting Your Patient Free

At this point we are going a step further in spiritual living than has been taken perhaps by any other teaching that we know. The reason that this is possible, is because we have no organization or anything to which we can belong; we have no rules, and therefore, each one of us can set the other completely free in Christ. If there is an organization, or if we belong to an organization, there is a limiting sense of obligation which says: "I must support this, or this is dependent on me. This church needs my support or I need the church's support." But do you not see that only when you have come to some spiritual unfoldment in which there is no attachment to a person or thing, no dependence on person or thing, are you set free to find your own complete spiritual freedom?

Every person who goes into the practice must understand the meaning of spiritual freedom. Never for a minute believe that any patient who has come to you for help is under any obligation to come back to you tomorrow or the next time he needs help. When a patient asks you for help today, set him free. If you never hear from him again, or if he never comes back to you again, he has violated nothing, because you have no ties on him. You have no right to have ties on a patient or a student. They are free; they are free in Christ: they are free to come; and they are free to go.

Every patient should be set free the minute you have completed your treatment. He is free. No patient should have to report back to you if he does not want to; he does not have to telephone you if he is not coming back; he does not have to pay you; he does not have to do anything for you.

In this work it is very wise, in so far as possible, not to think of people as owing you for last week's work, or last month's work. Let nobody owe you anything. What anybody pays you today,is paid up to date. If to his sense there is an obligation, and he wants to pay something more next week or next month, that is his business. But in your thought, set him free. Do not keep a set of books showing that somebody owes you money from last week. Such accounting is very bad business in the healing ministry. Nobody should owe you anything except for today; and if he does not pay it, he does not owe it to you. You hold him in no mental bondage and no economic bondage. That means that whatever cash comes in today is your day's supply, and what did not come in has nothing to do with you. You are not going to depend on yesterday's manna. In your own consciousness, you are living on the manna that flows today.

Naturally, there will be many days when more will flow than you can use that day. That does not prevent your putting it in the bank and using it tomorrow or next week or next year. The important point is: do not have a tie on your patient. Do not hold him in bondage as "my patient" or "my student," and do not hold him in economic bondage, saying: "He still owes me eight dollars." He does not owe you eight dollars or eight hundred dollars. Each day's work is complete in itself: if it is paid, it is; and if it is not paid, it is not. Remember your supply is coming from the infinity of your own being.

If you can let go of that mental clamp which would try to fasten your patient to you, you will have more freedom. What a freeing experience it is just to know that everything good is of God, and that you do not have to worry about whether your patient is going to change practitioners, or whether your student is going to find a new teacher, or be concerned about any other kind of change.

My oneness with God constitutes my oneness with all spiritual being and ideas, and the more that I can realize my constant oneness with God, the more beautiful friendships will I have. Many people are not *free* to live their own lives. Somebody has a mental clamp on them. Now, break that bondage and do not yourself hold anybody in bondage. Set everybody in your world free. If you cannot accept your freedom in Christ—if you cannot accept your freedom in your divine sonship with God, the relationship that exists between you and the infinite Being within—you are not going to go far on this spiritual path.

Find the Kingdom Within

We now come to a most important point in all spiritual teaching: Do not try to find spiritual good in the human scene, but as quickly as possible go into meditation; get into that silence, into that place where you can commune with God, and there behold Reality. In the belief of human living, you will not find God, or spirituality. True, human living is a belief and a dream, but merely to say that it is not real is not going to get rid of it. Something further has to be done, and that is the point that is overlooked by most metaphysicians. That something is *to find your spiritual base within yourself.* Find that center of your own being where you commune with God, with the divine Reality, and feel that warmth; feel that gentle Presence; and then any and every form of error will be dispelled. It does not make any difference whether the discord has been in the form of sin, disease, lack, limitation, unemployment, unhappiness, or anything else. It all disappears if, and when, you touch that center within you.

Why do you think I spend so much time on this idea of meditation? Certainly, it is not because I want to close my eyes and get away from the world. I am not afraid of facing the world, but I know that in the human world I have no power to do anything about a human situation. It does not make any difference how much I know. I know that some of you have heard me say, "There is not a word of Truth in all my books, or in all the other metaphysical writings that have ever been printed." The reason is that when it is sent out into the world it is not Truth. It is the truth about Truth. Truth is that which I *am*. Truth is something that I sense and feel and touch within my own being. It is where God and I become one. It is that point in consciousness where I disappear and God alone becomes real. That is where healing takes place, and that is the only place.

The reason we are spending time learning truth, and reading truth, is only because it is one way of leading us out of the human sense of things into the spiritual sense. But the real object of reading truth and hearing truth is to lead us back to the kingdom of God within ourselves, to where we *feel* the contact, to where we feel this gentle Whatever-It-Is—we call It God, or the Christ. "I live; yet not I, but Christ liveth in me."[1] But I could *say* that from now until doomsday; I could put it on a record and play it; but that would not make it effective. There has to come a *feeling;* there has to be something within that actually feels *Christ* living. Then, when you have that, the error dissolves; it disappears. Otherwise, there is nothing but psychological healing.

Now there is nothing wrong in being healed psychologically. That is perfectly all right. Neither is there anything wrong in being healed medically. But in *our* work, the aim is the attainment of spiritual being, of spiritual reality; and that is the reason we are not concerned with either medical or psychological healing. We are dealing with that healing which is brought about as we attain a conscious awareness, a realization, of actual spiritual being. This thing that we call "Spirit, or God" does not exist just as words or thoughts. There really *is* God. Let no one doubt it. There really is God, a God that you can meet and *feel* and commune with and be with. It is pouring forth into expression. And *that* heals.

[1]Galatians 2:20.

Therefore, when I say to a person, "I will help you; I will be with you. Do not worry; I am on the job," I do not mean anything human, because there is not anything in a human way that I can do. I learned years ago that Jesus was right when he said, "I can of mine own self do nothing."[1] He knew it, and I know it. But there is this *thing* within; there is this point of contact, at which the human experience fades out; all human power fades out; and there is just a wonderful sense of nearness, closeness, and oneness. It is something which makes you smile. You may not even have a good reason for smiling, but it brings a smile to your face as if you were saying, "All right, Father, I know you are there." That is all there is to it. But *that* dissolves the error.

Now, knowing this, why do we *ever* have a failure? It is only because we do not have a sufficient realization of our oneness, and do not stay in that awareness. That is the only reason. If we could only get more into it, and stay in it, we would have many more healings.

As we touch this center of our being, we get a response—the Life, the Fire—which goes forth and does the healing work; and that is the kind of healing work we are trying to do. It is not that which looks at a human being and says, "Well, you are sick, but I am going to get you well"; or "I am going to turn to God and see what God can do about it." It is a looking away from the human picture, a turning away entirely from the human picture, and touching the center of your being. Then the work is done.

---

[1]John 5:30.

The Ever Present Christ

———•———

There is a power called Spirit, or the Christ, and it does the work. Talking about the Christ will not bring God or the Christ to bear upon your problem. The Christ must be realized, must be felt. Then we really can say, "I can leave it with God. I can leave it with Truth." As we become convinced within our consciousness of the truth, that conviction, which is realization, makes the demonstration.

Our object is to develop this awareness, this consciousness of truth, this sense of omnipresence. As this is developed, we no longer work specifically on problems; as a matter of fact, we do not have specific problems on which to work. Life begins to unfold in a normal and harmonious manner. We have only to maintain ourselves in that atmosphere of the Spirit for that flow to come through, the flow of divine Life. When we are confronted with problems, then, it is necessary to get back within ourselves, until we get that feeling of the Presence.

As you think of God, the one Life, omnipresent as your own life; God, the one Mind, omnipresent as your own mind; you will not have the sense of twoness, or even the customary sense of God as omnipresent—God and you over here somewhere, separate and apart from It. In thinking of Omnipresence, think of It as your own being—the allness of God, the infinity of God, omnipresent as your individual being. Then there is no sense of separation or division.

The Christ is something which is controlling your being and your destiny. All you have to do is to realize this Christ, or gain the conscious awareness of It, since everyone has It. You do not have It within you, and you do not have It without you; you have It as being. When you talk about the activity of the Christ, you are not talking about a within or a without. If it acted just within our consciousness, there would be no reaching from one to another. It is a within, and it is a without.

What Is Sin?

In spiritual teaching, of course, there is no such thing as sin, in and of itself, because there is only God, expressing Its infinite being. Sin, therefore, is a human term and defines, more or less, a violation of a code of conduct. Rightly speaking, sin is the violation of any law. That law might be a moral law, or it might be a legal law, inasmuch as we consider stealing a sin. If we understood our spiritual identity, everything would flow through; and if it did, there would be no need of having personal possessions or personal ownership; in which case, you would be welcome to whatever I had, and I would be welcome to whatever you had; and that is all there would be to it. It would be a recognition that "the earth is the Lord's and the fullness thereof,"[1] and "Son...all that I have is thine."[2]

[1] Psalms 24:1.
[2] Luke 15:31.

The Master recognized this when he walked through the field, plucking the corn. When he was rebuked for it, he referred to David in the temple, eating the shewbread, which was also against the rules: I suppose that he meant that the corn in the field was for the use of the disciples or anybody else who had need for it.

Another human code of conduct relates to marriage. Marriage has been established as a human institution, because it is a protection to society against the unpredictable nature of men and women. Such laws are designed to protect men, women, and especially children. Under spiritual dominion, there would be no need for these laws, for the simple reason that under the government of Spirit, no one would ever do anything contrary to spiritual right.

That leaves us with the question, "Then what is sin?" If we forget human law and consider only spiritual government, we would have to say that sin is anything that takes us outside the government of God, government by spiritual instinct, intuition, or spiritual law. In other words, sin violates the truth of spiritual oneness. If we should desire money, that would be sin, since that would be a violation of the spiritual truth of the omnipresence, the oneness of God, appearing as the fullness of individual being. To believe that we are separate and apart from the infinity of our supply would be a sin; it would be a sin against the Holy Ghost; it really would be a sin even to desire supply. In fact, desire, in any form, would be sin, because it would be an acknowledgment of less than Self-completeness—and, of course, "Self" spelled with a capital "S" really means God of all-completeness, here and now, individually expressed. Any sense, then, of lack or limitation is sin.

Any sense of separation from good would be sin. You might say that any unhappiness would be sin, since it would be based on a sense of our own incompleteness; and spiritual truth reveals that we are already complete. We are the fullness of God's glory. If we say, "I am the fullness of God's glory made evident," and then are unhappy, or desire some thing or some one, we have nullified the sense of completeness, and in that we have sinned. We are taught that the word "sin" comes from the Greek word meaning "missing the mark"—missing the mark of spiritual perfection. That is exactly what this would indicate, that sin is any sense that we entertain of a separation from good.

God Appears As

Let us consider the word "God" in relation to cause and effect. To illustrate, let us think of a mahogany piano. We would not say that there is mahogany in the piano: mahogany is formed, or appears *as* a piano. Or we might take as another illustration a solid gold fountain pen. Again, we would not say that there is gold in the fountain pen. No, gold is formed as a fountain pen. You might say there is ink in the fountain pen. Yes, but the ink and the fountain pen are not one and the same. If you say, God *in* effect, it is like saying that there is ink in the fountain pen, or gas in the gas pipe. You have two substances. Therefore, in that sense, there is no God in any effect. That is the objection to the term, "God is man." Certainly, there is no God *in* man.

When Jesus spoke of "the Father within me," he was not making of himself some kind of a hollow tube in which God was located. He did not mean that statement in a literal sense. It was his way of referring to God *as* his consciousness, God *as* his being, God *as* his life; but not God *in* his life, not God *in* his body, not even God *in* his mind. How can you get infinity *into* anything? It is literally impossible to incase infinity *in* anything. You could not get infinity *in* this whole world; but infinity can *embrace* the world, or infinity can appear *as* a world.

To state that God appears *as* individual being is to have God and individual being as one. It is like saying that whatever the quality of gold is, that is the quality of the fountain pen, since the gold and the fountain pen are inseparable and indivisible. They are one, as essence or substance, the fountain pen appearing as the form into which gold is molded; or in the illustration of the piano, all that mahogany is, the mahogany piano must be, since mahogany and piano are one. But you certainly would not say, "There is mahogany in the piano." The only way you could say that is if you had a piano and then put a little piece of mahogany into it. But then you would not necessarily have a mahogany piano. Nor can you say, "I and my Father are one," if you merely mean that there is a little bit of God somewhere in us.

God, infinite Life, individually appears as the life of your being and of mine. God, Life, is not *in* your life; nor is God, Life, *in* your body. But God is the *substance of* your being. God is not visible; God is not definable; God is not a limited being, person, essence, or substance. God is the totality or infinity of spiritual being. Let no one try to reason out what God is, because it cannot be done. On the same basis, let no one try to reason out what man is. It cannot be done. It is playing with words, and it is cheating yourself of any hope of ever finding heaven or harmony. The only way you will ever know God is through spiritual sense; the only way you will ever know man is through spiritual sense. Trying to reason out the truth, fathom it with the mind, or think it out, is pure nonsense, and only defeats your purpose.

Spiritual Consciousness, the Seventh Sense

It is not that we are to accept anything blindly, but we are certainly not to seek God through intellectual reasoning. The things of God are foolishness to man; that is, to mortal man. "Cease ye from man, whose breath is in his nostrils: for wherein is he to be accounted of?"[1] Do not look at a mortal man and hope to find God. If you do, you will not find healing, because the spiritual world does not heal human beings. The spiritual

---

[1] Isaiah 2:22.

teaching reveals the Son of God, the Christ being, and it does not do that through human reasoning or thinking. The Son of God is revealed through spiritual intuition. Do not permit yourself to be cheated out of the wonderful glories of heaven on earth by a reliance on the intellect. You cannot achieve heaven on earth with the thinking process. Beyond the five physical senses, beyond the sixth sense which we call intuition, there is a seventh sense which operates even above the intuition—that seventh sense is spiritual discernment or spiritual consciousness.

That is why, in our treatment, instead of voicing statements, we listen for that still small voice, and it reveals to us spiritual being—God appearing as an individual. What does He look like? I have never seen Him with my eyes, but I have felt Him in my innermost being. I have felt the God-being of many people, many times. If this healing work could be done humanly or with human thinking, there would not be so little of it in the world, and instead of a few dozen practitioners, we would have millions of them. Jesus, himself, could not train more than a few to go out and do healing work. Why? Because it took a specially developed power. And that power is the power of the Spirit, not of the human mind.

John beheld a wonderful vision of heaven. He saw the heaven while he was here on earth, right while he was here with us. He saw an incorporeal universe; that is, a world without physical structure. He saw this through spiritual sense. He was able to see through what appears to us as a structural universe to that which is, and he saw it as it is in all its perfection. He saw it with that seventh sense, spiritual consciousness. His vision revealed that this is a spiritual universe, that we are spiritual beings, and that this body is spiritual. This body is the temple of God, the temple of the Holy Ghost, just as it is described in the New Testament. This body is the temple of God, and it is indestructible. It is not our body that ages or changes. Our body is just as indestructible and spiritual as it was before Abraham was, and as it will be until the end of time. The change takes place, not in our body, but in the human concept of body.

Removing False Concepts

Everyone, to some extent, is under the claim or belief of human consciousness. Remember, however, that you do not have a human mind of your own, nor a human consciousness. The human mind or human state of consciousness is a universal sense of separation from God. Actually, there is only one mind, the instrument of God. But there is a false or limited sense of that mind, which we call the human mind or human consciousness. It is not really mind or consciousness, but a *limited sense* of the one infinite Consciousness. Through that limited sense, you look at the body and see the changes that that limited sense depicts.

Let us suppose, for example, that you see a diamond, and, looking at it, you mistake it for a rhinestone. Yet, all the while it is a diamond. Where does the rhinestone exist? Nowhere; there is no rhinestone. What you are calling a rhinestone represents a finite or false concept of a perfect diamond. you accept your concept of the stone as truth until a diamond broker appraises the stone and tells you that it is a diamond. What happens to your rhinestone? There never was a rhinestone; the stone is now and always has been a diamond. your rhinestone has disappeared. But from where has it disappeared, since it never had any existence? There was really nothing to disappear, since there never was a rhinestone; the rhinestone's only existence was a belief or false sense.

In the same way, we are told that all of mortal experience—everything we see, hear, taste, touch, and smell—is illusion or a false concept. Does that mean that there is a real world and an unreal world? No. It means that this world is the world which was envisaged by John, except that John had risen above the finite concept, so that he no longer saw it through the misperception that would mistake a rhinestone for a diamond.

That is the basis of spiritual healing. The person who calls himself a patient is actually the Christ, the presence of God, spiritual man, standing in all the fullness, all the glory, or spiritual being and identity, actually God made manifest. Just as you were falsely seeing the diamond as a rhinestone, so you see the universal picture of mortal man, that "man whose breath is in his nostrils," and who, according to Isaiah, "is not to be accounted for."[1] Your first reaction is to attempt to heal that man. The moment you seek to do that, it is as if you were to say, "I should like to change that rhinestone into a diamond." But you cannot do that, because there is no rhinestone there. The diamond is *already* a diamond. The healing take place when you, yourself, recognize that the patient is not out there as an individual to be healed. The patient is a false concept in universal belief. The minute you know that truth, your patient should be healed. Ultimately, your patient is healed through knowing that truth. Sometimes when you know that truth the first time, he is healed; but sometimes, for one reason or another you have to know it a hundred times.

Among many metaphysicians, the belief persists that you must heal something or somebody, or change him, or reform him, or correct him. The only healing, reforming, or correcting, which has to be done, is that which is done in the thought of the beholder. That means in your thought and my thought. If we could catch this point, then, regardless of the name or nature of any form of error—and error actually has no more existence than the snake in the rope, or the diamond appearing as a rhinestone—healing would be instantaneous. Some day, we who remain with this long enough will develop this spiritual sense sufficiently to bring about quick healings, and, ultimately, instantaneous healings, since all that it requires is this awareness.

There is only one thing that will compel us to refrain from giving somebody a treatment: that is to realize instantly that, no matter what the picture is, it is not true, since Christ, the spiritual man, the Son of God, is *all* that is there. When that is your reaction, you have instantaneous or quick healing. Nothing less than that is spiritual healing. Spiritual healing is not using

[1] Isaiah 2:22.

the power of God to get rid of sin or disease. Spiritual power is the realization of God, omnipresent as individual being. When once you can recognize that God is omnipresent as individual being, you will never give a treatment to the appearance, but will instantly be alert to recognize, "I am not deceived by appearances."

Christ interprets Itself. The vision of The Infinite Way is that we do not go out into the world trying to correct it or improve it. Let us not have any fear of or for the world, or any sense of the world's needing saving or reforming, since all that has to do with the universal concept of a world. We are not asked to leave the world; we are asked to be in the world, but not of it. We are to be in the world, but we are to be no part of its fears, its hates, its enmities, or its jealousies. "Ye are the light of the world."[1] No one can be a "light of the world" who has any fear, doubt, criticism, judgment, hate, envy, jealousy, or malice. The "light of the world" is that individual who, through spiritual discernment, has seen that the universe is spiritual, perfect, and harmonious. This, he can only see or feel through an inner spiritual light or spiritual discernment.

The attempt to reform or to govern and control other people's lives will not work. You were not ready for spiritual teaching, and I was not ready for it until the time came; and no one could hasten that readiness by preaching at us, or by shoving books in front of us and asking us to read them, or leaving them on the table for us, hoping we would pick them up and read them. What we are called to do is, not to preach the gospel in the sense of *living* it, showing forth what it is doing in our experience. Then, strangely enough, we do not have to tell anyone about it. They can see it in our whole being; and, certainly they can see any health or supply that we show forth. So we never really need to speak. When we find our God in secret, that secret will be shouted from the housetops.

Let us, then, begin with that knowledge. Let our relationship with God be a sacred and secret one. Let it be made manifest

[1] Matthew 5:14.

outwardly only through the appearance of the new harmony of our being and of our body. Not only do we bless the world that way, but we bless the entire spiritual movement. The world is hungry for truth. It is merely looking for someone to show it forth so that it, too, can find it.

Spiritual Power

Spiritual power is a power that is generated or made manifest through our awareness of God as one power. One Power, good— that is the only power. In other words, spiritual power comes with your recognition, not that you are going to give a treatment to remove the snake from the rope, but that the rope is a rope, and there is no snake there. You need not say a prayer or give a treatment to remove a snake when all the time it is a rope. That is spiritual power. In individual experience, then, that means that as we walk up and down the world, realizing God as the infinite nature of our being, we do not look out at the world and strive to save it, or change it, or reform it. Our spiritual power consists in looking through the human being to the divinity at the center of his being, and, thereby, greeting the Christ as individual being. You never have to say that aloud. You do not have to mention it to anyone. In a store, on a streetcar, in an automobile, or whatever you may be; if you do not pay attention to the outer appearance, but always realize Christ, God, as the center of all being, the reality of all being, and realize that behind that mask is the real man, the man of God's creating—that is spiritual power.

Let us add to the great sum total of spiritual power that is abroad in the world. It is almost incredible when you think back on the experience of some of the early workers and realize how many people they healed as they walked up and down the streets. They did not wait to be asked to give a treatment. As soon as they met with deformity, dishonesty, or alcoholism, they looked right through it to the center of being, and there beheld the Christ; they knew what was appearing as this human being was a false concept, an illusion, but not an illusion out there. The appearance out there did not fool them; and in that way they brought about healing.

That is exactly the same way in which a lecturer or a teacher on a platform brings about healing in his audience. He does not take pity on someone he sees in the audience who is sinning or is ill; he does not recognize the error by saying, "Well, now, we will just bring God down here to do something about that." That is not a healing state of consciousness. That is not the Christ state of consciousness. The Christ state of consciousness looks right through the sinner and right through the disease and says, "What does hinder you? Pick up your bed and walk." It beholds spiritual being out there where the false concept seems to be, and it knows that the false concept is not out there. Do you remember the illustration of the mirage on the desert? The person who sees a mirage on the desert as if it were an actuality to be surmounted is afraid to go forward through that which appears to be water. The one who recognizes that the mirage is but a belief in thought, an optical illusion, drives right along in his car and pays no attention to the water on the road.

When you begin to realize that, since God is the only creative principle of the universe, you are not dealing with sinful, diseased, or dying humanity, you, then, have the vision of Paul. Spiritual being is the house not made with hands, eternal in the heavens. You deal only with that false concept which we recognize to be a complete illusion in mortal thought, and not an entity or identity out there. Then are you the "light of the world"[1] Then are you the healing Christ. Then do you bring spiritual power to bear in this world.

When one practitioner can bring about the healing of many hundreds of people through individual awareness, can you not realize what would happen if there were a million of them? Think what a million practitioners could do—a million practitioners, all

[1] Matthew 5:14.

motivated by spiritual power, that is, by the power to recognize that God is the center of all being, the actuality and reality of all being. We read in newspapers and magazines about spiritual power, and about utilizing spiritual power in this age. We shall never utilize any of it, however, if we think of it as a *good* power that we are going to apply to an evil person or condition. This is just as benighted an idea as it is to pray to God to reform a bad man, or offer up a prayer to heal a sick child. It is a lot of nonsense. If God knew anything about the evil man or the sick child, He would have done something about it long before anyone did any praying.

Spiritual power lies in the awareness of God as omnipresent, as the Presence appearing as individual being. You can begin to utilize spiritual power any moment that you like. All you have to do is to adopt the first commandment of Moses and the commandment that Jesus added to it, which is also an Old Testament commandment, revised. There is but one power. Acknowledge no other power but God, and see God as omnipresent, as all individual being. Recognize that good is the only power, and evil is not a power. Evil does not exist as power, but as an illusion. The second commandment, "Love they neighbor as thyself,"[1] means that if you believe that you, yourself, are spiritual, or that your mother is, or that your child is, you should then "love your neighbor"—and that means the whole world—with the same love. Know that God is just as much the reality of this person's being as of that person's being. In other words, know that God is the reality of universal being, and that there is no being separate or apart from God's being. Then you are utilizing spiritual power. When you sit down in your home in the morning to do this work, you probably think of it in connection with yourself, your family, your business associates, your friends, or with anyone with whom you come into personal contact: and it is right that this should be so. Unless we can really begin to see this truth operating in our immediate circle, we shall not see it operate in

[1] Matthew 19:19.

the wider circle. We must be able to demonstrate it here where we are, before we can expect to see it demonstrated in the far-off places or in the deeper problems of human existence.

Some time during the day or some time during the night, sit down and give earnest thought to this great truth of loving your neighbor as yourself, recognizing God as the life of all spiritual being, recognizing the one mind as governing the spiritual creation. Stay with your vision of God as the actual reality, presence, and power of all spiritual creation, and then let the truth govern what we call the concept or outer condition.

Spiritual power begins with an individual and actually it ends there. If we utilize spiritual power for the realization of God as omnipresence, we then find that it appears here, there, and the other place, and gradually, spreads, until Its light eliminates the darkness on the face of the earth.

From

MAN WAS NOT BORN TO CRY

FOUR

Christ Raised from the Tomb

———•———

The Hebrews of old foresaw the coming of the Messiah, but because they believed that the Messiah would be some kind of great king or general, someone who could lead them to victory over Caesar or perhaps even over their own Sanhedrin, a man who would turn the evil conditions of their day into good conditions, they were unable to accept the gentle Master. Instead of understanding that *"My* kingdom" is not of this world, they accepted the God of the Forty-seventh Psalm:

> O clap your hands, all ye people; shout unto God with the voice of triumph.
> For the Lord most high is terrible; he is a great King over all the earth.

He shall subdue the people under us, and the nations under our feet.

From the time of the Hebrews under Pharaoh unto this very day, the same prayer has gone up, the same psalms have been sung, and the same hope expressed that God will subdue nations, remove tyrants, and overcome the armies of the aliens. Should not thousands of years of such praying have proved that God has done none of these things up to now, and that there is no likelihood of His doing them at any future date?

In the Forty-sixth Psalm there is an indication that the nature of God has been misunderstood, and that that is one reason peace on earth and good will to men have not been experienced.

God is our refuge and strength, a very present help in trouble.

Therefore will not we fear, though the earth be removed, and though the mountains be carried into the midst of the sea;

Though the waters thereof roar and be troubled, though the mountains shake with the swelling thereof.

There is a river, the streams whereof shall make glad the city of God, the holy place of the tabernacles of the most High.

God is in the midst of her; she shall not be moved: God shall help her, and that right early.

The heathen raged, the kingdoms were moved: he uttered his voice, the earth melted.

The Lord of hosts is with us; the God of Jacob is our refuge.

Come, behold the works of the Lord, what desolations he hath made in the earth.

He maketh wars to cease unto the end of the earth; he breaketh the bow, and cutteth the spear in sunder; he burneth the chariot in the fire.

Be still, and know that I am God: I will be exalted among the heathen, I will be exalted in the earth.

The Lord of hosts is with us; the God of Jacob is our refuge.

The greater part of this Psalm refers to God as our refuge and strength, and therefore, will we not fear. It is up to us; not to God—to us. We will not fear, because God is our refuge. If we can gain an understanding of the nature of God and of the Messiah or the Christ, we shall find that earthly conditions dissolve, and that harmony can be brought into our experience, not only as individuals, but as a united world because God is no respecter of persons, of religions, or of races. God is one, and God is equally the Father of us all. When God is known, understood, and contacted, that Presence does change the course of our human experience.

Turn Away from the Worship of Personality

The belief that the Christ was a man and the worship of the Christ as a person have blinded the eyes of mankind to the truth that God is Spirit, God is love, and God is life. God is not a man, and it is not a man that is to accomplish these great things on earth.

We must never place our faith in a man or in a book. Many persons have placed their entire faith in the idea that the Bible is a holy book, but the Bible of itself has no power. It is the truth that is revealed in the Bible that does the work, not the book, but the revealed truth of Scripture. When this truth becomes a part of our consciousness, we are knowing the truth, and as we assimilate the truths of Scripture and as they become a living part of our being, we are able to demonstrate: first, that God is; next, that God is closer than breathing; and then, that God takes over our experience.

At first, we may prove only that God takes over the experience of our personal lives. In other words, as a person seeks for

God, for Truth, or for Reality, and as he becomes somewhat aware of this Presence that is already within him, miracles begin to take place in his experience: changes in health, in human relationships, and in other areas. A greater sense of safety and security comes to him, a greater inner peace, all of which are reflected in his outer life.

As this continues, it then becomes apparent that whatever it is that is taking place in this person is also in some measure touching the members of his family. He is beginning to bring more peace into his household. It very soon becomes evident that a new influence has come into the home, that something has taken place in the outer experience which indicates what has taken place in the inner life of one or more individuals of that household.

This is then noticed by neighbors, friends, and relatives, and eventually those in far places begin to be aware of this spiritual stirring, even without knowing what it is that is happening. So we find that one individual, a Moses, for example, will lead an entire people out of slavery into some measure of freedom and law. A Jesus will not only begin to reveal the nature of spiritual freedom to his immediate people, but down through two thousand years, untold numbers of persons will be touched by that same Spirit that was awakened in this Hebrew rabbi who became the Christ, and that very Spirit will be felt in the consciousness of individuals, even as it is felt today and will be for all days to come.

Millions of people are now receiving spiritual light, inner peace, and outer harmony through the Spirit that has been revealed by great mystics like Lao-tze, Gautama the Buddha, Shankara, Guru Nanak, and others who have become illumined by the revelation of a divine Presence and Power within.

The secret of all of these mystics has been their discovery of

God and the Christ, and in the teachings of every one of them is found the admonition not to worship the individual. Jesus said, "I can of mine own self do nothing . . . If I bear witness of myself, my witness is not true.[1] . . . My doctrine is not mine, but his that sent me.[2] . . . The Father that dwelleth in me, he doeth the works." [3] What is Jesus doing but turning us away from personality to the realization and revelation of the Spirit? So it has always been with the great illumined souls of the world. Each one has turned his followers away from personality to the revealed truth of an inner Presence—an inner Presence found not only in Moses, Elijah, Elisha, Isaiah, Jesus, Paul, and John, but a Presence within every living thing.

Occasionally statements such as "Be still, and know that I am God: I will be exalted among the heathen, I will be exalted in the earth," [4] reveal to us our true identity, the nature of God, and the nature of the Messiah or the Christ. If we are wise and sufficiently discerning, such inspired passages may reveal all the secrets necessary for us to know.

As the human race, we are the heathen. It makes no difference whether we are a little more of heathen, as some are, or a little less, as some others are; as the human race, we are nevertheless the heathen until one glorious moment of revelation.

Being Reborn

Paul explained very clearly that "the natural man receiveth not the things of the Spirit of God." [5] The natural man, that is, the human man, is not under God's grace or under God's gov-

[1] John 5:30, 31.
[2] John 7:16.
[3] John 14:10.
[4] Psalm 46:10.
[5] I Corinthians 2:14.

ernment. "But ye are not in the flesh, but in the Spirit, if so be that the Spirit of God dwell in you." [6] *If, if, if* so be, *when* the Spirit of God dwells in you. Ah, there is the secret!

As we continue our study of the spiritual wisdom of the world, we shall discover, as it was revealed in the Christian message and thousands of years before, that the object of our search for God is to "die" that we may be reborn. Mortality must be put off, and immortality be put on.

The whole secret of the spiritual teaching of the world is that the heathen in us must "die" in order that the son of God may be raised up in us. As human beings, we are the tomb in which the Christ is buried. As human beings, referred to by the Master in the fifteenth chapter of John, we are the branch of a tree that is cut off and withers and dies. This is the heathen; this is the human; but when the branch is one with the Vine, then do we bear fruit richly. Why? Because we are permitting the Christ to live in us, and we are living in the Christ. Now we have moved from our heathenhood to our Christhood, from being a natural man to being that man in whom the Spirit of God dwells.

Saul of Tarsus expresses clearly the state of consciousness of the human being intellectually and religiously taught, the good man humanly, the ardent seeker of God humanly, and yet a persecutor of that which he was seeking. When Saul of Tarsus "died," or was "stricken blind," his eyes were opened, and the "death" of Saul became the "birth" of St. Paul. This symbolizes the "death" of that natural man *seeking* the kingdom of God, and the "birth" of the spiritual man who has *realized* the kingdom of God.

Since the Master spent his entire ministry revealing that the kingdom of God is not in holy mountains or holy temples but

[6] Romans 8:9.

is within us, if we are to "die" to our heathenhood and be re-born of the Spirit, we must realize that whatever change is to take place in us is not going to come about because we go to some holy place or find some holy man or holy book. The change is going to take place if we will permit that holy place, holy temple, holy man, or holy book to reveal to us that the Spirit of God is within us and must be revealed within our own being, so that we accept it as a personal responsibility to seek until we find, knock until the door is opened to us, and we are able to hear:

> I *in the midst of you am mighty. I in the midst of you am God; I in the midst of you will be exalted in the earth when you recognize Me within you, when you recognize that the Spirit of God dwelleth in you, when you realize that the son of God is hidden in that tomb that you call "you."*

The Dark Night of the Soul

Saul of Tarsus, the Prodigal Son, the woman taken in adultery, the thief on the cross—what are these but you and me? They represent the tomb in which the Christ is buried; they represent the mortality of human life. It makes no difference for the moment whether we are an earnest seeker as was Saul of Tar-sus, the sinning woman, or the pleasure-seeking prodigal. The reference is still to us, to our human nature, to the mortal side of us, and in that very mortality is buried this Christ, this son of God which must be lifted up, exalted, and recognized. When that Christ is recognized, then what happens? We become still:

> *"Speak, Lord; for thy servant heareth."* [7] *I will be still that I may hear Thy voice. I will be still that this Spirit in me may utter Its voice.*

[7] I Samuel 3:9.

This Spirit is not floating around in the air; this Spirit is not sitting upon a cloud: this Spirit that is to utter Its voice is within us. The kingdom of God, the allness, the realm of God is within us, but then also the reign of God!

As we learn through our meditations to be at peace, to be receptive and responsive to this that is within us, eventually we, too, will have an experience. I realize, of course, that the vast majority of our students do not enjoy the experience when it comes. Perhaps that is because they would all like it to come peaceably, gently, sweetly, and gradually, but this is not the way it has come to most of those who have experienced it. It usually comes as a blinding experience; it often is a very distressing and disturbing period. For Paul and for every mystic it has been a terrible experience! It is called the dark night of the Soul, and it would be comforting if there were only one such night.

Unfortunately, there are many dark nights leading up to the experience of being "blinded," being "stricken dead," or being "mortally wounded." But when we are helpless and hopeless, when there is not a trace of human strength or power left in us, or human wisdom, when we have come to that place of unknowing, when there is no possibility of our having any human ability to help ourselves, in that moment the Voice speaks within and says,

> *Know ye not, I am in the midst of thee, and I am thy God. I am thy bread, and thy meat, and thy wine, and thy water. I am the resurrection, restoring unto you even the lost years of the locust. I am your life eternal.*

The Nature and Function of the Christ

Now perhaps we can begin to perceive the nature of the Christ. The Christ is not a great king; the Christ is not a general. The Christ does not conquer nations militarily or politically. The Christ conquers nations through Its gentle Spirit, because when the loud noise is over, when the destructive period is past—the dark night of the Soul—This that is within us begins to reveal Itself in humble and gentle ways, leading us step by step from the discords and inharmonies of human existence to the higher attitude and altitude of spiritual living and into spiritual Grace.

The first evidence of the Christ in our experience is an improvement in our human affairs. Our nature, our disposition, our health, even the amount of our supply, and certainly a greater harmony in our human relationships: these are the first signs of the raised-up son of God in us. All these changes, however, are only steps, because the ultimate of spiritual revelation lies in this statement: "My kingdom is not of this world." [8]

When harmony has been restored, then begins the second and final stage in which we are lifted above physical and mental harmony, above all the harmonies of this world, and begin to perceive the nature of spiritual Grace. The function of the Christ is to reveal to us a spiritual kingdom far greater than a human world with good government, or even human beings who are kind instead of unkind to one another. Right here on earth, a new universe, a new mode of life is revealed to us.

Always the disciple is instructed not to leave this world, but to remain in it, to be in it, yes, but not of it. We walk through life eating the same kind of food, making use of the same modes of transportation, and operating the same businesses or

[8] John 18:36.

engaging in the same arts and sciences, but with this difference: we do it now not for a living, but for the joy of action, for the joy of being.

Try now to make a transition in your understanding of the nature of the Christ. Perhaps you have been delaying your own spiritual progress by thinking that this Christ has the function of removing your bodily diseases, providing you with a larger income, with a promotion, or something else of a human nature. Sometimes we even think that It ought to settle our traffic tickets, or other things of a similar nature. But God is not to be used; the Christ is not to be used. It is not something to which we can turn in the expectation that It will do something for us. No, the Christ is That into which we relax ourselves, not that It may do something in our lives, but that It may be our life.

As human beings, all we think of is what we would like our life to be, and we aim our thoughts toward the Christ with a preconceived idea of what we would like It to do for us or in us, whereas the real function of the Christ is to lead us to a point where we "die," where we become completely "dead" to that life that we have been trying to glorify, so that the *I*, the Spirit within us, may be exalted, but not so that we may take pride and boast, "Oh, look what God is doing for me." There is no God to do anything *for* me or *for* you. God is infinite Being, and God lives unto God. God lives unto Itself, manifested as individual being, but never, never departing from Its own life.

Personal Selfhood Must Be Surrendered

"The heavens declare the glory of God; and the firmament sheweth his handywork." [9] Man is here, not to be glorified, but

9 Psalm 19:1.

that God may be glorified; and God is glorified only in the degree that we surrender this personal sense of life and come to the ultimate revelation as given by Paul: "I live; yet not I, but Christ liveth in me." [10] In that state of consciousness, there is a surrender of personal selfhood, a surrender of the desire to get God to do something to us, or through us, or for us, such a surrender that it lets God live His life as us. Now there is no more room for self-glory. *I* will be exalted, not *I* will exalt *you*. *I* will be exalted—God will be exalted. God will be lifted up, and God will live His life on earth as God lives His life in heaven. In other words, the Spirit of God fills all space in heaven above, on earth, and beneath the earth. We need only to realize that it is God living God's life, not God performing something for us.

This is the big barrier. All of the prayers of wanting God to do something for us, for our nation, to do something against our enemies, or to make us more successful than our competitors: this is the barrier. God is life, and since there is no life but God, we must surrender our false sense of life until God becomes our very life, and then let God live it.

Do you see why the ancient Hebrews failed to understand the function of the Messiah? They expected this Messiah to go out and destroy somebody or something for them. God does not overcome any enemies outside of us, but He does overcome the enemies within us; and in reality the only enemies we have are those within our own nature, that part of us which constitutes our humanhood.

The idea of self-preservation at the expense of any and all has become such a dominant characteristic of human beings that it is called the first law of nature. This is the most evil part of our nature, and that is the enemy within which must be

[10] Galatians 2:20.

overcome. I cannot ask God to overcome it within you; I have to ask God to overcome it within me. If I have a trace of self-preservation or if I have a trace of desire for something other than what I also desire for you, that is the enemy, the false sense of self within me which must be overcome.

If there is such a thing as God being the Father, and all men the sons of that Father, how inconsistent it is to invoke the aid of God *for* one and *against* another! The secret of the ancient schools of wisdom was that the initiate was to be trained, instructed, and enlightened until he came to the full awareness of himself as the spiritual child of God. There was no teaching about using this power to do something to somebody else, or for somebody else: it was purely one of self-development, self-realization, in order to bring each one to that point where the son of God could be raised from the tomb. But it was not taught that the tomb is in Jerusalem: the tomb is our human selfhood, the human mind, the human consciousness, the false sense of self. That is the tomb in which the Christ is buried.

The Work of the Initiate Is Enlightenment

Until our own blindness and inadequacy have been removed, we are not the light of the world; but if we can forget the world for a moment and concentrate on our own self-enlightenment, very soon we shall discover that even the small measure of light that we have become is already having an effect upon our families. As this light grows and grows and as we become more spiritually aware, it touches the lives of friends and neighbors, and as we have seen in this work, it is beginning to affect people in every part of the globe and on every continent. The illumined consciousness of just one, two, or ten is making itself felt in a world-wide way. In other words, the smallest possible group of spiritually enlightened people can save this entire world from destruction, but how futile for anyone in his blindness to try to lead someone else!

Where the Spirit of the Lord is, there is peace, there is harmony, there is justice. It does not mean that there have to be ten thousand people: it means that there has to be the Spirit of the Lord, and that Spirit of the Lord is right here where we are. As a matter of fact, the Spirit of the Lord is wherever the Spirit of the Lord is realized. There is no way to confine the Spirit of the Lord once it has been released from consciousness. Has not the Spirit of the Lord, when released through the Master, continued to operate in consciousness down through the ages? No number of years has been able to stop the operation of the Spirit of the Lord in the consciousness of those who have opened themselves to It.

Therefore, the first step is your enlightenment and mine that we may individually raise up this son of God in us, and in some measure "die" to the struggle for self-preservation. As we perceive that God's grace is a universal Grace, we begin to understand that it is not self-preservation that matters because this is only a law of human nature, and human nature is the tomb of the Christ. The real spiritual law is that we be willing to lay down our life for a friend, to lay down our life for our neighbor, to lay down this human sense of life in order that even the least of our brothers may be raised up, that we be willing to let this false sense of life disappear from us that the Christ-life may appear, and in that Christ-life serve mankind as Jesus did by leading generations of people to an awareness of the spiritual nature of life.

This is not using God, this is not using Truth: this is surrendering our personal sense of life in order that we may be used, that we may be a transparency through which God's grace can touch the life of all mankind. The purpose of this search for God, of the initiate's undertaking the work of enlightenment, of our being on the spiritual path, is that we may lose our life, surrender this personal sense of life, be clothed upon with immortality, and be a transparency through which the grace of God may reach this earth and overcome the kingdom of men's minds. It is not the kingdom of men's governments that is to be overcome, not the kingdom of his politics; it is not even his armies that are to be overcome: it is the mind and its iniquity that must be overcome; it is the enemy within our own household, our mental household, that is to be overcome. The Christ is the law of elimination, working through love to overcome the enemy within ourselves.

The Christ Destroys the Enemy Within

Follow the Master for a moment into the wilderness where he was tempted. Do you see that it was the evil within himself that was tempting him, and that he was saying unto the evil, " 'Get thee behind me, Satan!' [11] I cannot be tempted, for I am not here to glorify myself, but that God may be glorified. If I perform a miracle to glorify myself, I will have lost the kingdom of God. Get thee behind me!"

Then when his consciousness was made free of personal sense, personal glorification, self-preservation, he could go forward and fulfill his ministry because now he could not be tempted by anything external to himself. He had overcome the

[11] Luke 4:8.

world when the enemy within his gates had been overcome, and the enemy within his gates was the mortal sense of selfhood that sought to preserve itself, instead of wanting to let itself "die" in order that the *I* might be exalted, that the Spirit of God in him might be the light of the world.

When there was no longer any personal sense left, when the Master was no longer living his own life, he had the capacity to heal the sick, to raise the dead, to forgive the sinner, and to feed the hungry because then he knew that his finite capacities were of no importance whatsoever and were not to be relied upon. He had no small capacities or great capacities: he had no capacities, period. He was the transparency for the divine Capacity, the spiritual, the infinite, the All-capacity.

The kingdom of God is within you and me, and the function of the Christ is to purify you and me. We are not to call upon the Christ to do something to someone else, but we are to realize that the Christ is functioning in human consciousness to dispel personal sense, first in us, in our friends, and then in our enemies. Let us pray for the enemy that we may be children of God, pray the prayer of realization that the kingdom of God be just as much in our enemy as in our friend, awaiting only this recognition to be brought up from the tomb, raised again, and resurrected into life eternal.

Rightly to understand the nature of the Christ, we must begin to perceive that It is not going out into the world to destroy our enemies. It is to be admitted into our consciousness to destroy the enemies within ourselves. These enemies are made up of all phases of personal sense from the greatest evil, self-preservation, to the least evil which is believing that we are good, philanthropic, religious, spiritual, or moral, which we are not, and cannot be, for only the presence of God in us is good. When we lose our sense of evil and later lose our sense of good, then we are a clear transparency through which the grace of God can shine upon this world—upon our own families and friends first, and gradually, as the circle widens, it will embrace this whole world.

F I V E

Withinness

———•———

When a person comes into some measure of understanding of the nature of God, a change takes place in his life. This coming to know God aright is often referred to as illumination, and as illumination changes consciousness from a limited sense to one of infinitely greater capacity, a new life begins to unfold.

Even a faint glimpse of the real nature of God brings an understanding of the Master's revelation that the kingdom of God is neither lo here, nor lo there, but is within. With that recognition, vital changes begin to take place in your life, and perhaps the most important of these is that you are no longer consumed by fear. What is there to fear if there is a God? What could be a power over God? What could harm God? Is there a power greater than God?

To believe that there is a power greater than God is atheism. It is to have no God, because the only God there is, is Omnipotence, Omnipresence, Omniscience. Therefore, when you have a God that is All-power, that is present wherever you are, and that is infinite Intelligence, what is there to fear? How could disease or lack or limitation be present? How could death enter into the presence of All-power, All-presence, and All-wisdom?

Those who live in the realization of God as Omnipotence, Omnipresence, and Omniscience are free of the pitfalls that come nigh the dwelling place of those who do not dwell in the secret place of the most High. This does not mean simply going to church or belonging to a church, as this does not keep a person from being an atheist. The only thing that separates anyone from atheism is an actual conviction of God. Joining an organization does not do it. In fact, it is possible to join the noblest and loftiest of movements and yet not take on the nature of its teaching. A person can be a member of a fraternal lodge founded upon the most high-minded principles and still go on cheating and defrauding, but this he could not do if he had an understanding and conviction of the real meaning underlying the teaching of that fraternal order.

It is possible to join a church and still be fundamentally an atheist. Atheists can be found inside and outside the church. On the other hand, a person is a theist if he has never belonged to a church as long as he has attained a conviction of God, and not only a conviction that God is, but that God is wherever he is, omnipresent.

No Power from Without Can Operate Upon You

When you are convinced that the place whereon you stand is holy ground, you are no longer in fear—even if bombs should burst, for not even being blown to bits can separate you from Life.

If it is true that the kingdom of God is within you, no power external to you can operate in your life. No evil power can act upon you, in you, or through you because the kingdom of God within you would immediately dissolve any such power, if there were one. Nothing from without your being can enter to defile or make a lie—no external power, no external force, whether of the nature of sin, disease, or of lack—nothing, absolutely nothing. That is your protection.

You may wonder, then, why so much evil, so much sin, disease, lack, limitation, and even death have come into your experience, but if you are on the spiritual path, you must acknowledge that these discords have not come to you from without. There is no way to make spiritual progress, to bring about purification, no way to put off mortality and put on immortality without first recognizing that no power of evil has ever entered your experience from outside your own being.

When you have acknowledged this, your next step is to find out what it is within your own being that is responsible for the sin, disease, or accidents that have come into your experience. Eventually, it is borne in upon you that what is responsible for the ills of mankind is darkness, ignorance—ignorance of truth. The Master promised, "Ye shall know the truth, and the truth shall make you free." [1] It must be plain, therefore, that if you are not free it is because of your lack of knowing the truth, and this, of course, means because of your ignorance.

Ignorance is responsible for your ills, but fortunately ignorance is something you can do something about. If there were a devil or a Satan external to you, responsible for your ills, you might be justified in saying, "There is nothing I can do

[1] John 8:32.

about it but suffer it"; or if the stars and the planets possessed power to govern your life, you might also say, "I can do nothing about that." If there were conditions external to yourself that could be held responsible for your ills, you could protest, "Well, I can do nothing about them. I must bear them." But the Master declared, "Ye shall know the truth, and the truth shall make you free."

Paul went further than that when he said, "Whatsoever a man soweth, that shall he also reap." [2] He did not hesitate to lay your problems right on your own doorstep, and he added, "He that soweth to his flesh shall of the flesh reap corruption; but he that soweth to the Spirit shall of the Spirit reap life everlasting." [3] And so again it is *you—you*.

But this does not mean that you are condemned, or that you should condemn yourself. Since Jesus did not condemn anyone, but in every case, even to those who had sinned, his response was, "Neither do I condemn thee," [4] you will realize that you are not under condemnation even for your ignorance. You have within yourself the power of redemption, for it is as *you* sow. God is not responsible for your ills; God is not responsible for your death. "For I have no pleasure in the death of him that dieth, saith the Lord God: wherefore turn yourselves, and live ye." [5]

Forgiveness Is at the Instant of Repentance

Above all things, if any one of you is living in fear that God is punishing you for some sin, lose that fear in this hour, for it

[2] Galatians 6:7.
[3] Galatians 6:8.
[4] John 8:11.
[5] Ezekiel 18:32.

is not true. God has never punished anyone for any sin. There is no provision in God for punishment of any nature. According to the teachings of the Master, forgiveness is unto seventy times seven. What about the 491st time? It never comes. It would not be possible to forgive and forgive and forgive without bringing healing to the one you are forgiving. What the Master really meant was that forgiveness should continue until a healing takes place, forgive until there is nothing left to be forgiven, but never condemn, never judge.

Although a person is punished for and by his sins, he is punished only so long as the sins continue. The very moment that he looks up and turns away from them, in that moment, though his sins be scarlet, he is white as snow, and he does not have to wait for death to give him the forgiveness he is seeking. His forgiveness is at the instant of his turning, at the instant of his repentance.

Do not accept the belief that the discord from which you are suffering is of God, or that God is the author or the cause of your suffering—not even for a good reason, for there is no good reason ever revealed by the Master. The Master's whole teaching is one of forgiveness, and when you can come into agreement within yourself that God is not the author of your discords or inharmonies, of your mental, physical, moral, or financial troubles, you have taken a great step forward and have released yourself from the belief that God is holding you in bondage.

Accept Your God-Given Dominion

The realization that there is no power outside of your own being responsible for your ills prepares you for the next step, which is to understand that the suffering, the lack, and the limitation in your life are due to something *within* you, not to something *outside* of you, and that there is nobody in heaven, on earth, or in hell responsible for this condition. The fault which must be corrected is nothing but ignorance of the truth, and that you can do something about. You never have suffered and never will suffer from anything other than ignorance of truth, and that you can correct at any time.

> *All power is within me. God gave me dominion over all that is in the earth and in the skies above the earth, including the stars and the planets and their astrological implications.*
>
> *God gave* man *dominion. Therefore, all dominion—all law and all power—is within me. It is not mine in a personal or an egotistical sense as though it were of my own self. It is mine by the grace of God. God gave me this dominion; God gave me this power over all beliefs of power. God instilled His dominion in my consciousness from the very beginning. God-given dominion is my dominion over all the forces that exist.*

When you have a feeling within you that this is the truth, you begin to perceive that you need not take up the sword against any external powers because he that lives by the sword will die by the sword. You begin to understand why the Master said, "Resist not evil," [6] why he never set up a warfare against the devil, and why he never battled evil. There is no record of his fighting the devil, no record of his warring with Satan, but merely a quiet, peaceful, "Get thee behind me." [7] And we hear no more of the devil in the Master's life.

You, too, have God-given dominion over all the devils that may torment or tempt you. Always you have dominion, but that dominion is exercised only by the recognition of the truth

[6] Matthew 5:39.
[7] Luke 4:8.

that makes you free. You do not have to battle; you do not have to struggle; you have to know the truth:

> *There is a God-given dominion within me. The kingdom of God is within me, and this kingdom of God within me is the law; It is the son of God; It is the presence of God that is within each and every individual.*
>
> *God has given me dominion over all that is, and this God-given dominion within me is now operating to free me, whether it is of sin, lack, disease, hate, envy, jealousy, or of resentment.*
>
> *This God-given dominion is operative now within me. The kingdom of God within me is jurisdiction and dominion over everything there is in this world.*

Although every individual in the world has the kingdom of God within him and every individual has the Christ indwelling, It does not function except through his acknowledgment of It. It is not the truth that makes him free: it is his knowing of it that brings it into action.

You Carry Your Good With You

To acknowledge that the kingdom of God is within you—the power, the dominion, and the presence of the indwelling Christ —is an important step in the direction of bringing about your own resurrection from the tomb of sin, of disease, poverty, unemployment, or the tomb of bad business. Another important step forward is to remind yourself daily of the truth of Withinness, that all good is already within you, never to be achieved but only expressed.

When you enter an empty room there is no love there, neither is there any hate, sin, or disease. If a person went into a room to get anything, he would leave disappointed, for there is nothing in the room to be gotten. Whatever is in the room has to be brought there by the people who go into it. If there is love, it is because the people in it have brought love, and those who carry love into a room will walk out of the room with love multiplied. If anyone goes into a room with hate, envy, and jealousy, he will probably walk out with hate, envy, and jealousy multiplied.

An illustration of this, which occurred some years ago, was the case of a man who came to me for physical healing and explained that he had been to many practitioners and teachers and yet had not received his healing, although he attended church regularly and was faithful and loyal. It was just a flash of inspiration that led me to ask, "Why do you go to church?"

It took him some little time to solve that one, but finally he came up with an answer, "Oh, to learn more about God."

"You mean that after all these years that you've been attending church you haven't yet learned about God? You're still going there to learn about God?"

"Well no, not exactly. I know something about God, but if I learn more, I'll benefit more."

"And so the reason you go to church, then, is so that you will get some personal benefit?"

He had not thought about it in that way, and therefore he floundered because he could not explain his real reason for going to church. Thereupon, I pointed out to him that he would get out of church whatever he brought to it and added: "How about reversing your attitude and, the next time you go to church, go with the idea of taking something there with you? You already have some understanding of truth, of God, and of prayer. Why not go there with the little grain of truth that we will admit you have, and try to put that grain of truth to work for the benefit of those who are there and who do not yet know what the realization of God can do? Spend that entire hour with the idea that whatever you have gained of understanding you are going to share with those in that church."

The second week he came to me and announced noticeable improvement, and the third week was able to confirm a complete healing.

There is nothing in life to be gotten—not even God, nor an understanding of God. All that is, already *is*. And all that is, is already wherever you are. The kingdom of God cannot be brought to you even by Jesus Christ. He merely announced that the kingdom of God is not lo here, or lo there, but that the kingdom of God is already within you. Holy mountains or holy temples will not reveal God, and certainly there is even less hope of finding God in a man or in a book. God must be sought where God is—within you.

It is not your becoming more loving that makes love operate for you. It is the realization that the nature of God is love and the kingdom of love is already established within you.

So it is that there is no such thing as love in an empty room, and nothing of hate, envy, or jealousy either. It is just a room, an empty room—nothing more. You go into it, and whatever takes place there depends on what you have brought with you. If you have brought love, then love is there; but if you brought hate, envy, jealousy, malice, criticism, or condemnation, that is what is there. You did not find it there: you brought it there.

Do not go anywhere for love, and do not go to anyone for love or for friendship: carry love and friendship with you. Do not go to anyone for forgiveness: carry forgiveness wherever you go. Do not go into this world expecting understanding: carry understanding to those you meet, and whatever you carry with you will be returned unto you.

The Bread You Cast Upon the Waters Returns to You

"Cast thy bread upon the waters: for thou shalt find it after many days." [8] The law is that the bread that you cast will return unto you multiplied. If love is not being returned to you, that is not the bread that you are casting upon the waters. If understanding, forgiveness, abundance, and sharing have not come to you, it is because you have not cast that bread upon the water, and if you have not, it cannot return to you. All the bread on the water is earmarked, earmarked for return to the person who placed it there. Whatever the name or nature of the bread that is cast upon the water—the sweet bread of love and life, or the sour bread of envy, jealousy, malice, resentment, and persecution—that is the nature of the bread that returns. Life is like a checkbook, and the person who tries to draw out what he has not put in, sooner or later, is in trouble.

There is no love in this world, but there is love in you and in me. There is no hate in this world, but there may be hate in you and in me. If we send that love or that hate out into the world, it is there to multiply and return. I have traveled in practically every country of the globe during the past fifty-three years, and although I have met with much love, I have never yet met with hatred, resentment, or bigotry. I have never known any of these to be aimed at me, or to reach or touch me. I have spent many years in countries where bigotry and class distinction were rife, but I have never experienced or known these.

This is not because of any virtue on my part. I was born and brought up in New York City, and in such an environment a person grows up side by side with white, with black, and with yellow, with Jew and with Gentile, with Protestant and with

[8] Ecclesiastes 11:1.

Catholic, and usually he is not aware of any distinctions until he is too old to have it make any difference to him. It is a blessing to be born and brought up in a city like that and to be educated in the public schools where the boy or girl sitting next to you may be the child of very wealthy parents, and the one on the other side of you may live across the way on the wrong side of the tracks. Because of this circumstance in the formative years of my life, I grew up without any knowledge of bias or bigotry, and therefore in all my travels I have not experienced these, but have had returned to me only that which I have carried with me.

Since those early days and because of whatever measure of enlightenment has come to me, I know that wherever I travel I will meet what I carry with me. And so whether I have to go into a business office, a church edifice, or a customs station at the border, I carry with me the recognition of the indwelling Christ, the realization that every individual in his true identity is the child of God. When the Master taught, "Call no man your father upon the earth: for one is your Father, which is in heaven," [9] he was not talking only to his particular followers in the Holy Land. He was talking to the world! There is but one Father—the heavenly Father.

Consciously carry with you, wherever you go, the realization:

I have but one Father, and He is not only my Father but the Father of every person I meet, be he white or black, yellow or brown, Jew or Gentile, friend or enemy. Regardless of his background or present status, I know that we are brothers, for there is but one Father, and we are all children of that one Father. Whether anyone else knows it or not, I know it, and that makes everyone I meet of the household of God.

[9] Matthew 23:9.

When you carry that in your consciousness, it is felt by those you meet.

The World Gives Back to You
Your Attitude Towards It

You have all had the experience of knowing someone—a minister, a leader, a practitioner, or a teacher—whose very presence made you feel comforted and clean, made you feel engulfed by a wave of love. You recognized it because in the consciousness of that person there was love: he was living his Christianity; he was living his religion; he was living his godliness; and by being in his presence, the love expressed by him enveloped you.

Conversely, some of you have probably been in the presence of a person who has made your flesh creep. You could feel the hatred, the bigotry, the lust, or the sensuality that emanated from his thought, and you wanted to run away, to withdraw from it; you may have felt nervous or fidgety; and you may even have had the experience of wanting to run home and take a bath. It is as Emerson said, "What you are . . . thunders so that I cannot hear what you say." We are always expressing our inmost self even when we are trying to hide it. Mostly we hide it only from ourselves, but those who meet us know us, sometimes better than we know ourselves.

All of this is due to ignorance. If you are carrying out into this world any resentment, any hatred, jealousy, bias, or bigotry, you are doing it because of ignorance. You do not really know what you are doing. The Master was right when he said of those who crucified him, "Father, forgive them; for they know not what they do." [10] It is not sinfulness on your part if you carry fear out into the world: it is ignorance. You do not know what you are doing. When you do know, you can change that by knowing the truth:

There is an indwelling Christ. The Spirit of God is within me, and the Spirit of God is in every individual I shall ever meet.

Carry that out into the world, and the world will change its attitude toward you.

Try to understand that nothing can enter your experience except through your consciousness, not a thing. It is through your consciousness that you take in or give out either ignorance or wisdom.

You impart yourself to others. People will be drawn to you if they feel warmth, joy, spirituality, and good because in the presence of those qualities they are finding only the love of God flowing through.

You can carry that attitude out to the salesmen or the buyers you meet, to the customers you serve and to the salespeople who serve you. By carrying the realized presence of God to them, many a time they are healed, and you may send them home from their work more blessed than they have ever been.

You are always imparting yourself to others by your state of consciousness. This fact reveals the true nature of the Christian life. The Christian life is not a way of going to God for something; it is not a life of getting: it is a life of giving.

There is no way for God to reach this world except through consciousness; there must be a consciousness through which It comes. That is the secret of healing. You cannot receive spiritual healing from just anybody on the street. It takes someone who has developed his consciousness to the point of being a

[10] Luke 23:34.

transparency through which God functions, and the greater the degree of that transparency, the greater healing work he can do.

Know the truth, the truth that all power is given unto you—God-power and God-dominion over all the sin, disease, lack, and limitations of the world. Know the truth that the indwelling Christ in you and in every individual in the world is the resurrecting and healing Christ and is ever-operative, even without being told what to do, or to whom. Carry that realization with you in your association with other people, until more and more you are told, "I feel comforted when I talk with you," or, "A burden falls away when I am with you." Then you will know that you have entered the Christian life, and that great reservoir of Withinness at the center of your being is flowing forth into expression as love, peace, and joy.

INSTRUCTIONS TO A STUDENT

You are trying to heal *persons,* and it will not work. You are meditating to realize God, then peeking to see what God does about the error. In proportion as you attain spiritual awareness, you will find that harmony is, and that you do not have to try to establish it, but only to recognize that it is so. Spiritual consciousness does not heal: it sees through appearances to what actually is.

Healings rarely take place as we, or the patient, expect. What we would like is to have the pain stop instantly, the fever dissolve, and the lump disappear. If the patient is receptive, what actually occurs is that a change of consciousness takes place. There is less reliance on, and joy in external things and conditions, and a correspondingly greater love for, and understanding of, the Invisible, and then outer harmony becomes evident.

If some patients do not respond outwardly, it is because they have not yielded inwardly. We do not change the appearance. Our realization of the Christ opens the consciousness, and that changes and purifies it. Then, and only then, does the outer appearance conform to the inner consciousness. In fact, the outer condition is the state of consciousness externalized. There can be no outer change until an inner awakening occurs.

All spiritual light comes only after darkness. Do I not indicate that over and over again? When we are happy in our health, supply, and relationships, there is no spiritual progress. As the material conditions or persons fail us, we are driven to the Spirit. Just note how often you feel pleased because of apparent harmony, and you will see why you must be jarred out of merely human good.

ACROSS THE DESK

It is a great joy to watch the unfolding of The Infinite Way, principally because the increased activity is an indication of the students' success in living and practicing the specific principles which constitute the message.

To understand the nature of God is the great secret. Once the student perceives that God is not like anything he may have believed Him to be, and in proportion as the nature of God is revealed to him, an understanding of prayer and meditation comes quickly. Only through prayer and meditation is the activity of the presence of God made practical in our daily affairs. Above all things, to understand that there is not a giving or a withholding God, not a rewarding or a punishing God, is to find peace, quiet, and release from anxiety and fear.

Do not feel that you must eternally chase God: rather, be still and let God catch up to you. Let God find you as you let

God's love flow through you to your neighbor and especially to your enemy-neighbor.

There is a Christ, and to "be still" brings the experience of divine Grace because of this ever-present Spirit of God in man. "Be still." There is no need to tell God, to instruct, or to plead with Him. "Be still." The All-knowing already knows, and the stillness brings the fruitage of God's knowing; God is love, and that stillness brings the fruitage of God's love; God's grace is ever with us, and that stillness reveals the fruitage of God's grace.

From

CONSCIOUSNESS UNFOLDING

Peace

---•---

Peace I leave you, my peace I give unto you: not as the world giveth, give I unto you. Let not your heart be troubled, neither let it be afraid.

John 14:27

My peace, the peace of Christ! More healings have been brought about through absolute silence than through all the arguments metaphysicians have thought up in the whole history of the world. When you are called upon for help, sit down and get at peace. Think no thoughts; just sit and wait. Wait. Be patient, and wait for the peace of the Christ to descend upon you. In that moment of peace, without a word, you will witness healing.

The only value a treatment has is to lift us to a point or place in consciousness where we are ready for spiritual consciousness to unfold. We are now in a different position from the one in which we found ourselves, when we were functioning with treatments.

We have come to that place in consciousness where we are ready for the next higher step. Even if mental argument, affirmation, and denial were necessary to us in the early days of our work, we can now leave such forms alone.

Learn to sit down and relax. Whether the case is sin, disease, death, or unemployment; whether or not it is serious, sit down and relax. Do not try to "handle" it. Do not try to "work" on it. Do not try to "treat" it. Sit back and, in silence, create a kind of vacuum for God, for the Christ, to rush in. Sit down and relinquish the thought that the human mind is a healer: Christ is the healer. The essence of the whole work we are doing is this: God is. God is so let God work in us and through us to Its own end, and as Its own creation. Instead of continuing to use the words, God, God, God, let the actual realization of God do the work, since God is.

"My peace I give unto you: not as the world giveth."[1] The world can give us a certain kind of peace. It can give us a lack of noise, a quiet country place, or an ocean trip. That is the peace that the world can give. People travel to far places, but they travel with themselves, and they return home with themselves. We cannot, any of us, get away from ourselves. If we have a problem, we take it with us, wherever we go.

We must stop all such futile efforts. The human mind is not the Christ. For many years, mental efforts have been tried. The words of the Bible are, "My thoughts are not your thoughts, neither are your ways my ways."[2] What good, then, is all this "thinking" that we have been doing? The truth of the matter is that the human mind plays no part in any healing. The only factor in spiritual healing work is the Christ. Spiritual healing means that healing which comes from one's realized Christ consciousness, rather than from mental argument or external means, such as medicine or surgery. "My peace I give unto you." In that peace that "passeth understanding." in that quiet, in that

[1] John 14:27.
[2] Isaiah 55:8.

stillness, the peace of God, the power of God is made manifest, and it does the work.

In our work, many people seem to come, wanting only loaves and fishes, instead of seeking for God Itself. With that we need not be concerned. We are not to be concerned with what they appear to want. We just "sing our song." Those who can receive it, will; others may not be ready. You will find that more healings take place through a smile, through the simple recognition of the presence of God, than will ever take place through any mental striving; and they will be purer, sweeter, and more lasting healings because they will be the descent of the Holy Ghost, the Christ, Itself, coming into consciousness and dispelling the errors of sense.

Peace: A State of Non-Resistance to Error

Just what is required to "walk on the waters," to dispel the storm? Is it some mental argument, denial, or affirmation? All that Jesus said to the storm was: "Peace, be still."[1] That was all—just, "Peace, be still." Everyone who has done healing work knows that the healing has taken place when the sense of peace, that realization of the Christ, has been experienced. He may not know how, or why; but let me tell you the how and the way of it. It is because the state of consciousness of the practitioner in that peace did not fight, oppose, or resist the error or claim. That is the reason for the healing.

This, I learned through an actual experience in the first year of my practice. A man, suffering from tuberculosis, was brought to my office by a friend of his. When I agreed to help him, he mentioned the difficulty he had in eating solid food because of pyorrhoea and asked for some help for this condition, also. I assured him that I would help him with that, too, but in my

[1] Mark 4:39.

youthful enthusiasm, I forgot all about the pyorrhoea. However, the following morning, he called and said, "What have you done to me? I have just spend five minutes with a stiff tooth-brush having a wonderful time and I could not move my teeth."

That gave me something to think about. It was my first experience with "forgetting" something; but my second experience was to come soon after, when a telephone call came for help for a severe headache. The patient who was in my office at the time the call came recognized the urgency of the call and at once proceeded to leave. Before she had reached the door, the telephone rang again, and the young woman who had been suffering from the headache reported that the pain had disappeared. It had been an instantaneous healing.

Such things do not happen to a person in this work without causing him to question, "How?" Either these things are accidents, isolated instances which might have happened anyway, or they reveal a principle. As I studied and observed closely any and everything which would help to reveal the secret, I learned this: Healing is not brought about by the human mind; it is done by a state of consciousness imbued with the Christ. Christ consciousness is the understanding that disease does not exist as a reality and does not have to be fought. The very act of "forgetting" shows that the practitioner does not take it too seriously.

The one who is showing forth the Christ light, the Christ healing light, is the one who is not making a reality of error, is not fighting it; but, in a peaceful recognition of the fact that God is the life of individual being, quietly realizes, "Not by might, nor by power, but my Spirit."[1] One person, sitting in a room in silence, in a state of receptivity, can have that silence and that peace which he experiences felt by a roomful of people. How then can we measure what can happen with little groups scattered around the world, all maintaining this great power of silence?

If your consciousness is imbued with silence, with peace, then it is imbued with power. Healing takes place through the

[1] Zechariah 4:6.

consciousness of the practitioner. The state of your consciousness will determine the healing of those who come to you, not that the healing power is yours as a person. The healing power is the presence of God, the Spirit of God, appearing as individual consciousness. You do not have this healing power unless you have a consciousness that is at-one with devine Love, a consciousness that is at-one with the peace "which passeth all understanding."[2]

When you go out into the business world, if you really want to be successful—if you want to sell something, buy something, or bring to consummation any kind of business transaction—do as you do with healing: Go with peace in your consciousness. Do not go out with a fearful or doubting consciousness, or with a fretful consciousness; or you will impart this state of your consciousness to the one with whom you do business, and he, too, will feel it. Go with this silence in your heart; go in a state of peace. If necessary, before making your business call, go off somewhere for a minute or two, sit down, and get that sense of peace before you start out. Then see what that sense of peace will do; see what it has already done. The state of peace in your consciousness is a state of receptivity.

Peace: *The Experience of God*

Ultimately, we are going to learn the greatest of all secrets—the secret that hitherto has been known only to a very few—the secret of what God is. If we study the scriptures, if we study the philosophies and religious teachings of the world, we are likely to come to the conclusion that God is something very far-off, something that is very seldom contacted, and something that very seldom answers prayer in accordance with our wishes, needs, or desires. Because the world has no knowledge of what God is, it keeps on, generation after generation, praying for world peace

[2] Philippians 4:7.

and not achieving it, praying for life, health, immortality, and yet not achieving them.

If we are Christians, we should at least know *where* God is, because Jesus told us that "the kingdom of God is within you."[1] That alone would have been a wonderful foundation, if only we had believed it. If our fathers, grandfathers, and others who preceded us had spent the past two thousand years seeking the "kingdom of God within," then, by this time, it would have been found and made manifest. Instead, all the generations which have preceded us, have turned to some master on a platform, or have turned their eyes up to the skies, or have looked in every direction except the one where they were told to look—within. The time has come, in this century, for us to begin looking for that kingdom within our own being, for that is where we shall find God. Although I can tell you this, you, yourself, will have to have it revealed to you from within your own being. Then, you will find that God is life eternal and God is infinite consciousness. But you will find, also, one thing more than that. you will find that this divine, universal Consciousness is manifesting Itself as your individual consciousness so that, ultimately, you will be able to say, "I and my Father are one."

We must know the nature of God and we must *experience* God. We should not go on for the next ten years as we have been doing up to now, just talking about God: The time has now come when *we must experience God.* Let us not pass lightly over this part of the teaching, because it is the most important part of it all. We must see God while we are yet in the flesh, and that means you and me, individually, here and now, without waiting to die. We must experience God through our periods of silence, our periods of peace.

Each time you sit down, think of the statement of the Master: "Peace I leave with you, my peace I give unto you"[1]—the peace that passeth understanding. Let yourself be enveloped with that

---

[1] Luke 17:21.
[1] John 14:27.

peace. You will find the presence of God in that peace, and in that presence of God you will find power, joy, dominion, healing— healing not only for yourself, but for all those who have brought themselves within the atmosphere of your thought.

In the old method of metaphysical practice, the first thing we did when a problem was brought to us was to "answer it back," to think up some wise saying, some metaphysical or scriptural statement in some form or other, and quickly to affirm or to deny it. We are always denying some error and affirming some truth. In this new approach, we are not going to affirm, and we are not going to deny. We are going to sit quietly, achieve a sense of peace, and let that sense of peace do the work. We are going to prove that it is not the action of the human mind that heals.

You see, the danger of believing that your affirmation or denial is necessary, or that you have to think some kind of a thought, is that if you were in a position where you could not think, you would be without hope. But that could never be true, because so long as God is present, that is all that is necessary. When a thought is unfolded to us from within, however, that is an entirely different thing. That is a divine revelation of God, announcing the presence and the power of God. It is for that very reason that we spend so much time developing "the listening ear," the state of receptivity.

Begin now to change your old basis of treatment. If necessary, do it drastically; do it by forcing yourself to take no thought. I am asking you to come into a higher consciousness of the presence of God, a consciousness higher than that which you can attain through the action of the human mind. Let us move a step higher into that state of consciousness in which we would be if we were students of Jesus, who said: "Take no thought for your life, what ye shall eat. . . . or what ye shall drink. . . . your Father knoweth that ye have need of these things. . . . Consider the lilies, how they grow: they toil not, they spin not; and yet I say unto you, that Solomon in all his glory was not arrayed like one of these."[1]

[1] Luke 12:22, 29, 30, 27.

So it is with us. Let us remember to adopt for ourselves that peaceful attitude of assurance and confidence, which fills us with the peace and the power of God. That consciousness is the very presence and power of God, Itself. When we are not thinking or struggling with thought, when we are not fighting error, our consciousness is the presence and power of God. This divine Consciousness is not really in effect—is not really effective—so long as the human mind is moving around in a circle. It is true that you cannot ever get away from the presence of God, but you do not benefit by It in such a state. You benefit only in the degree that peace descends upon you.

Paul experienced this peace as the descent of the Holy Ghost, as the Spirit of God in man. These are terms used to describe what appears to us when we are not thinking, when the only thoughts filling our consciousness are God's thoughts. In the silence, God fills our consciousness far more than when any thinking of ours is taking place. It is hard for us to imagine this state of being because we are so used to the idea that we must be thinking, or that we must be holding a thought. This is not true. If we could have silence for the space of half an hour, true silence, we would find ourselves in heaven. Silence is God in action. Therefore, when a problem confronts us, whether our own or another's, let us sit down and find that silence, and then let the solution appear.

Suppose that someone comes to us today with a problem. The problem may be one of unemployment, a sinful habit, or a state of ill health. Instead of refuting it, let us look through it in the realization that it exists only as an appearance. With "the listening ear" say, "All right, Father, throw the light on it, so that I may see it as it is." Then, watch what kind of treatment will do for you. In other words, when we see railroad tracks coming together, instead of asking, "Now what must I do to separate those tracks?" let us say, "Father, show me those tracks as they really are." Then we do not have to think about it any more.

Do not try to improve a person, or his health. Do not accept into your consciousness the thought that there is a person in ill health. Sit in a state of receptivity, relaxed, in a state of silence, a state of peace. Let that peace permeate your whole being, and when you have accomplished that, sit with a listening attitude, and watch the light dispel the darkness, watch intelligence dispel ignorance. Instead of your being the healer, you are a witness watching this state of peace do the healing. Be a beholder of the activity of the Christ, or God. Watch It work in you, and through you, and ultimately, *as* you.

"Though I speak with the tongues of men and of angels, and have not charity."[1]—have not love, it availeth nothing. It would not make any difference how wonderful my speech, how marvellous the statements of truth which roll off my tongue. If these statements and this speech are not imbued with a sense of God's allness, they will be of no avail in the healing ministry. It is not the speech; it is not the letter of truth which is important: It is the degree in which the consciousness of the practitioner is imbued with the understanding of God as love and life; the degree in which the practitioner has lost the ability to fear, to hate, or to love error of every kind.

We read in John: "Not that any man hath seen the Father, save he which is of God, he hath seen the Father."[2] There is the crux of the whole matter. No mortal, nor any human being, can see God or know God. Only the Son of God, the Christ consciousness of you and of me, can ever witness and behold the presence of God. In other words, it is not our human mentality that will know God. Never with the human mind shall we see or know or understand God or spiritual living. But the Son of God, the Christ consciousness, our spiritual sense, can behold God.

A Developed Spiritual Sense Is Requisite

There is the heart of the Christ teaching. And that is where the human world has failed—trying to know God through thinking, trying to know God with the intellect, trying to "explain" God. It

[1] I Corinthians 13:1.
[2] John 6:46.

cannot be done. God is discerned only through spiritual sense. Only through a developed spiritual sense can you and I, individually, discern truth, the things of truth, and the formations of truth—the spiritual universe. We develop that spiritual sense in many ways: through our reading of metaphysical and scriptural literature; through teaching and being taught spiritual living; through association with people who are on the same path. Being together in one place, of one mind, develops that spiritual sense, which is called "the mind that was in Christ Jesus." Paul called it, "the Christ that liveth in me." In most cases it is a *developed* sense, and we must *consciously* develop it.

You can help to bring about the realization of God by acknowledging God throughout the day, and once or twice during the night. Realize God as the centre, the reality, of your being. Realize God as the mind and Soul of you, functioning as your individual being.

> I am the living bread which came down from heaven: if any man eat of this bread, he shall live for ever: and the bread that I will give is my flesh, which I will give for the life of the world[1]

This bread, which is understanding, is the World made flesh. As you, through the human mind, behold your body, you are beholding only the mortal and material concept of body, and that is all that you will ever behold with the human mind. But, through the development of this I which I am, this Father consciousness or Christ consciousness, you learn to look out on the universe through spiritual sense, and you, ultimately, begin to see the "body not made with hands, eternal in the heavens." That was John's vision of the Christ, his vision of heaven, while yet on this earth, while he was right here, walking, talking, and moving about among his people. He saw what no human brain or human eye can ever see. He saw the temple not made with hands; he saw the spiritual universe, the spiritual body. That is what you will behold when, instead of using thoughts, you become a state of silence, a state of peace. When you have felt that divine Reality,

[1] John 6:51.

then you have seen the temple not made with hands, that body which is life eternal.

> Then Jesus said unto them, Verily, verily, I say unto you, Except ye eat the flesh of the Son of man, and drink his blood, ye have no life in you.[1]

That, again, is but the Christ revealing Itself. Unless you eat and drink, unless you absorb, unless you realize, unless you see the temple not made with hands, you will not have life eternal. To eat and to drink means to take in, to absorb, to realize. The more you look out on the world through human reasoning, through human thinking, the more you have of a fleshly body which dies somewhere between sixty and a hundred years of age. But the more you take in, that is, the more you carry in your consciousness this truth of being, the truth about God and God's creation, the more will you manifest intelligence and life as long as you are using this body.

> Many therefore of his disciples, when they heard *this*, said, This is an hard saying; who can hear it? When Jesus knew in himself that his disciples murmured at it, he said unto them, Doth this offend you?[1]

The human mind is always offended at truth because truth is a reversal of everything that the human mind knows. Imagine saying to the human mind that when it is still and doing nothing, great and wondrous works of healing can be accomplished! That is an insult to the human mind. Think of saying to the man who prides himself on his intellect that all of his mental gyrations will not do as much for him as one moment of silence will do!

> It is the spirit that quickeneth; the flesh profiteth nothing: the words that I speak unto you, *they* are spirit and *they* are life. But there are some of you that believe not.[2]

[1] John 6:53.
[1] John 6:60, 61
[2] John 6: 63, 64.

What was it they could not believe? It was that the Spirit quickeneth and not the flesh, that it is the silence, the peace, that really does the work, and not the mental gymnastics, not what is learned in books or through the intellect. We, like the disciples, are not going too well, either; we are not making such great progress. Today, just as in Jesus' time, the human mind is offended; it feels itself rebuked at the suggestion that there is a Spirit which works without words or thoughts, that there is a Spirit in man which can lift him up and guide him through life, and can still all the storms of life without his thinking a thought, saying a word, or giving a treatment.

> But there are some of you that believe not. For Jesus knew from the beginning who they were that believed not, and who should betray him. And he said, Therefore said I unto you, that no man can come unto me, except it were given unto him of my Father.[1]

And what happened?

> From that *time* many of his disciples went back, and walked no more with him.[2]

Is it strange that so few, even in this day, can grasp the great fact that it is the Spirit which quickeneth, that there is a Spirit in man that does the mighty works of healing and regenerating? The human mind takes offence when we try to give it up.

> The world cannot hate you; but me it hateth, because I testify of it, that the works thereof are evil.[3]

The world will never hate anyone who uses the world's weapons, or who uses accredited and accepted forms of activity. The world hates only those who say that all that is unnecessary, that there is a higher power, the power of Spirit. It is then that persecution sets

[1] John 6:64, 65.
[2] John 6:66.
[3] John 7:7.

in, not that any persecution is necessary. Today, we are learning
to let the impersonal Christ absorb all the persecution, instead of
allowing our human selves to take it on. We accept persecution by
believing that the message we are presenting is "my" particular
message, "my" particular truth. Instead, we should realize: "This
is not my truth, but the Christ truth, and if you are going to hate
anything, hate it, and not me. I am merely showing forth what
the Master gave of the Christ teaching of the presence and the
power of That which is invisible to human sense, of That which
is the state of your own being, the divine Consciousness of your
own being, the Comforter which is within you. If the world
wants to hate that truth, let it do so." That is the secret of the
Master, that my peace "passeth all understanding,"[1] and that
peace is power.

The Inner Meaning of the Temptations

> Then was Jeasus led up of the spirit in the wilderness to be
> tempted of the devil. And when he had fasted forty days and forty
> nights, he was afterward an hungred. And then the tempter came
> to him, he said, If thou be the Son of God, command that these
> stones be made bread. But he answered and said, It is written,
> Man shall not live by bread alone, but every word that proceedeth
> out of the mouth of God.[1]

Here we find the great inner meaning of the temptations. That
passage is the cue to the principle of this entire teaching. The
temptation was to demonstrate an *effect* to demonstrate bread, to
perform a miracle in the outer world, to centre the thought and
attention on the things of this world, that is, on the outer need.
But the mind of Jesus knew that such is not the way of
demonstration. The way of demonstration is this: "Since God is

[1] Philippians 4:7.
[1] Matthew 4:1-4.

divine consciousness, and since consciousness is the substance and the activity of all form, then as long as I live and move and have my being as consciousness, all form will appear without my taking thought." And that was Jesus' answer to every temptation.

That must be your answer also. Instead of "working," that is, doing mental work, when any problem confronts you, remember that you have accepted the two great statements of the Master: "Take no thought for your life, what ye shall eat; neither for the body, what ye shall put on",[2] and, "Seek ye the kingdon of God; and all these things shall be added unto you."[3] When temptation comes to you to try to utilize this truth to secure a job, to perform a healing, or to do something in the outer realm, say with the Master:

> *I do not live by bread alone, but by every word that proceedeth out of the mouth of God. I do not live by outer demonstrations. They are the "added" things. They are the things that come to me of their own accord through my realization of God, the divine Consciousness, forever disclosing Itself as my individual consciousness. As long as divine consciousness is my consciousness, then It is the source of my supply, and I do not have to perform magic. I do not have to set up the personal "I" to be a demonstrator. The one I, the great I Am, is governing, maintaining, and sustaining Its own image and likeness. If, then, I try to perform a miracle, if, then, I try to make a demonstration; I am setting up an "I" apart from God; I am setting up a selfhood apart from God. God is forever maintaining Its own.*

That is why the human mind makes trouble. That is why the human mind set up the prodigal, who went out into the world. He was not satisfied to live on the inheritance of his father, but wanted to go out and make his own way in the world. And you know where he ended up.

> Then the devil taketh him up into the holy city, and setteth him on a pinnacle of the temple, And saith unto him, If thou be the Son of God, cast thyself down: for it is written, He shall give his angels charge concerning thee.... lest at any time thou dash thy

Luke 12:22.
Luke 12:31.

foot against a stone. Jesus said unto him, It is written again, Thou shalt not tempt the lord thy God.[1]

If we have God, Itself, as our consciousness, do we need to produce angels, do we need to demonstrate "effects" of any kind to hold us up, to support us and help us? Do we need aught beside Him, or It? When we look to anything but God, are we not becoming idolaters? Are we not looking for a "lesser than God" to bear us up? And is not that the sin against the real God? Is not that the sin against our own spiritual sense of life? When we are tempted to turn to "man, whose breath is in his nostrils," when we are tempted to rely on some human form of God, even though it may appear to us an an angel, let us remember Jesus' temptation. Have I any need of angels? Have I need of any help? Have I need of any lesser forms of help, even that of human thinking?

> Again, the devil taketh him up into an exceeding high mountain, and sheweth him all the kingdoms of the world, and the glory of them; And saith unto him, All these things will I give thee, if thou wilt fall down and worship me. Then saith Jesus unto him, Get thee hence, Satan: for it is written, Thou shalt worship the Lord thy God, and him only shalt thou serve. Then the devil leaveth him, and behold, angels came and ministered unto him.[1]

The temptation comes to all of us, at some time or other, to turn away from our highest sense of Soul, so that we can improve our lot, tempting us to help the situation by coming down from our standpoint of oneness to a lesser form of treatment, tempting us to come down to a reliance on something separate and apart from God. And that is where we shall have to resist temptation, and learn to sit in silence, in that state of peace that sees no power in the appearance. Since God is the individuality of your consciousness and mine, we need no other help than the awareness of that; we need no lesser form of treatment; we need no human

---

[1] Matthew 4:5-7.
[1] Matthew 4:8-11.

help, not even in the form of mental help. We need only the constant consciousness of God as our consciousness.

I began by saying that we must all come to the place of knowing what God is. I come back to that again now. God is the principle of this universe, but God is manifest as individual consciousness. Your individual consciousness is principle or law unto your individual universe and experience. Your outer experience is determined by the degree in which you realize God—divine Law, divine Life—acting *as your individual consciousness*. It is still God, even when it is your individual consciousness, and this does not mean that each one of us is, or has, a separate God. It means that God is the infinite. indivisible consciousness of the individual, but it is still infinite, and is still all power.

As we walk or drive about, living, moving and having our being in the consciousness of this ever present God as our individual consciousness, how far are we ever away from God, or from the guidance, direction, and protection of God? When we know God to be the divine reality of our being, we know that God is very close—nearer than breathing, closer than hands and feet. That is the secret. It is not enough to know that God is life eternal. We must know it to the nth degree, as Jesus did, by realizing, "I am life eternal." He did not say, "God is the way." He said, "I am the way." In other words: "All that God is, I am; all that God has, I have because I and the Father are one."

When you want to help somebody, do you see that you cannot turn away from your own consciousness—God consciousness—to give that help? Rather, let your own consciousness be imbued with peace; let it be filled with the same confidence that Jesus demonstrated in the overcoming of the temptations. Too much do we neglect that story of the temptations. Remember that Jesus was up on the mountain top, but he was there with his consciousness, not separate or apart from it; and remember, furthermore, he knew that his own consciousness was the source of all good.

Every one of you, at some time or other, is going to be called upon to help somebody. Some of you are going to be called upon to help many, and no lesson will be of greater value to you than what I am telling you now. Beginning today, at this very moment, remember: It is your consciousness that does the work for your family, for your business, for your home, for your body. It is not some far-off God. It is your own individual consciousness when your consciousness is imbued with silence and with peace. All you have to do, and all you will ever be called upon to do, is to achieve that sense of peace.

Do not wonder what great truth you ought to know. There are probably no greater truths in the world than those you already know; but there is one thing that you must practice and achieve and that is a state of peace within your own consciousness, coupled with the realization that it is your own consciousness which is the healing Christ. When we know that *we* have the mind "that was in Christ Jesus." then, we know that we *already* have that mind which is the healing Christ: We already have that state of peace which comes from the realization that error is not power—error is not a thing. In fact, *error isn't.* You do not have to fight it, or wrestle with it, or attempt to manacle it, or sit up all night to be sure that it does not overcome you. What you must do is to learn how to find your peace.

As you walk up and down the world with a sense of peace in your consciousness—and that sense of peace comes to you only in proportion to your realization that God *is* and error is *not*—as you achieve that sense of peace, you have the Christ consciousness. All that the Christ consciousness is, is your individual consciousness when you no longer fear or hate or love error of any name or nature.

We have not done the healing work that we should have done, and in nearly every case the reason is the same. We wonder when the mind of God is going to do something, or when divine Love is going to begin to work, or how we are to attain divine Love or the healing Spirit. And so we cannot and never will do the work that we should because the mind of God is your mind; divine Spirit is your spirit; divine Love is the love with which you are imbued. The state of consciousness which does the healing work is your own mind in a state of peace. If someone comes to you for help, it is your responsibility to arrive at that state of peace that "passeth all understanding." and that state of peace becomes the "peace, be still" to error of every name and nature. When a person calls upon a practitioner for help, it is that practitioner's responsibility to "live and move and have his being" in this state of peace, and if he is not already in it, to attain it, so as to bring about the healing. When that consciousness reaches a state of peace, harmony, well-being, and confidence, it becomes the transparency for healing.

Your individual consciousness and mind, in a state of *transparency*, is God! God is the consciousness of the individual, and it is that which heals.

From

LEAVE YOUR NETS

Knowing the Unknowable

———•———

Truth is infinite. Yes, truth is infinite, but that truth is within you. Then, how great is your capacity? How big are you? Infinite! Infinite, because infinity cannot be confined in anything less than infinity. Because of that, the true nature of your being is infinite, and from the depths of your being, infinity must flow. Nothing can be added to you: not even truth. Therefore, the only truth of which you can ever become aware is the truth that is already within your own being.

There are many ways of bringing truth to awareness and to conscious realization, bringing it into expression and activity. It is possible to retire to a mountain or a valley somewhere, take a little cabin for a month, six months, or a year or two, and just meditate day and night, and day and night, and day and night, remain alone, away from the world, carrying perhaps only a book of scripture, meditating, abiding in quietness and in peace, and praying and praying and praying. Eventually the truth that is within your own consciousness will begin to flow, to unfold, to come forth, and to reveal itself. In the end, if you are faithful and persevere, you will know all the truth that has ever been revealed since the dawn of civilization. That is one way.

Another way is through following some system of spiritual teaching in which there is a teacher with a measure of spiritual consciousness who, through his written or spoken word, is able to open the consciousness of those who come to him. One state of enlightened divine Consciousness can be to thousands desiring illumination what the sunlight is to the bud, opening it into the flower.

"I, if I be lifted up from the earth, will draw all men unto me." [1] "I, if I be lifted up" can draw all those who are searching and seeking to my level of consciousness. To no one does this apply more aptly than to the teacher of spiritual wisdom. The spiritual teacher can be a teacher only in proportion as he has received some measure of spiritual light—not because he has read books or because he knows and can recite statements of truth. Knowledge, as such, does not constitute a spiritual teacher. True, it may be one of the essential qualities of a teacher of mathematics, music, or engineering, but a spiritual teacher can impart only from the measure of his spiritual consciousness. And why? He is not going to teach truth at all. He is merely going to open consciousness so that the truth already within can flow forth.

When truth is recognized to be an integral part of your being, not even the search for truth will be left to you. How can you

[1] John 12:32.

seek and search for that which is already embodied within your own consciousness? You might as well say that you are a seeker for integrity or honesty, loyalty, fidelity, or morality. Are you seeking those things? Why not? Because you know that they are already embodied within you. Even if at this moment you are not manifesting the fullness of integrity, loyalty, fidelity, justice, and benevolence, even if you are not giving expression to these in their fullness, you know that they are within you and that you cannot go outside to get them.

And so it is with truth. So it is with family, companionship, home. There is no use to seek or to search for them because you will never find them. As a matter of fact, it should very quickly become evident to you that all seeking for things—all desire—is sin. You will soon recognize that every desire, even every good desire, is just an error that is separating you from your good. Why? Because the desire is for something you believe you do not have, but if or when you get it all will be well. If, however, the nature of your being is infinite, that cannot be true: you must already have it. It is already embodied within you, and as you learn to commune with the Father, it will begin to flow forth from you.

As a human being, you are limited: you can go no further in this life than your environment, education, or personal experience can carry you. You are subject to what the world calls laws: natural laws, laws of limitation, laws of matter, hereditary laws, medical laws, theological laws. Like a cork, floating on the ocean, you are a victim of every wave and every force that comes from every direction: from the water, from the wind above, and probably from beneath the water.

As a human being, man is always a victim and a target. He is forever being played upon by one kind of force or another: economic, political, the weather, climate, or food. If you permit

yourself to live as a human being, you could live a life of continuous fear and doubt, a life of wondering what is going to
happen next and from what direction it will come. As a matter
of fact, that is the kind of life the world is living.

But it is not necessary for man to be a victim of the times, the
tides, or conditions. By bringing himself into harmony with divine law, he becomes, not the victim of circumstances but, in the
measure of his understanding, the master of them.

Throughout all time, the world has had the example of those
great men—saints, seers, prophets, sages, or saviors—who made
a direct and personal contact with the Source of all good. Furthermore, there is an extensive literature filled with accounts of
those we might term average men and women who have also
made that contact with their Source, and who then began to
show it forth in their daily living, enabling them to be a blessing
to all who came within range of their consciousness.

Unfortunately, at first the only medium these individuals had
for imparting their experiences was through the spoken word,
and for that reason only those who could personally come into
the presence of the great masters of the past could receive the
benediction or blessing of that contact. As the printing press
brought about the wider dissemination of scriptural and other
inspirational and spiritual literature, it became possible for more
persons to have at least some contact with the letter of truth, and
in a lesser degree even with the consciousness of the writers of
truth. For that reason, during the last five hundred years many
more persons have learned how to become at-one with the Infinite Invisible.

Today it is possible for anyone to bring divine Grace or the
power of the Infinite into his individual experience and thereby
be less limited and less dependent on human sources and resources than heretofore. More and more persons are now being

freed from the limitations of personal sense, that is, the limitations of their personal selfhood, than has ever been true in the history of the world. But many as they are, it is not enough. The possibilities are such that every person can be the outlet for this love, Grace, power, and benediction, and there is no longer any reason to restrict it to a few teachers or leaders, to a few saviors or messiahs, or a few saints or seers.

At one time, it was believed that only those called to the religious life could enjoy this conscious union with God and that through them their flocks could benefit vicariously. Today we know that every man, woman, and child on the face of the globe can leave their "nets" and bring themselves into that union, thereby becoming a center or force through which God's grace flows out into their community, speeding the day when the kingdom of heaven will be manifest on earth.

There comes a time in the experience of every person when human circumstances are such that he realizes he cannot go any further in the unfoldment of a happy, successful, or prosperous life without the aid of something beyond humanhood; and it is in such moments that he may turn to a search for what he calls God. Some few there are who find God, but there are many more who do not.

Probably the very word God keeps many persons from finding Him because that word has been given so many meanings of a superstitious nature that the way is often lost. In other words, instead of seeing man made in the image and likeness of God, what we usually do is to see God made in the image and likeness of man.

If we are to be successful in our search for God and attain conscious oneness with our Source, we must go beyond the mythical God of rewards and punishments, beyond faith in some far-off Being who is but the figment of imagination and superstition. Probably if there were not so many false teachings about God, it would not be so hard to find Him. If we were wise enough to follow scriptural and mystical teachings, we would learn not to look outside for God, but to turn within until the revelation of the true God came from within our own being.

Did not Jesus teach that the kingdom of God is within, but have we not been making the mistake of praying to a God separate and apart from our own being? Is not every sense of discord in our experience, mental, physical, financial, and emotional, but a sense of separation from God? This sense of separation that we entertain is not of our making. That was done by religionists long, long ago. It was done by philosophers and by persons who were seeking God somewhere outside their own being, by those who were seeking good to be added to them.

The first lesson that we must learn, therefore, is that God is "closer . . . than breathing, and nearer than hands and feet." When we learn that, we begin to expect an unfoldment or revelation from within rather than a contact with Something outside of our being, unknown and afar off.

We must make the transition from the person who is seeking truth, seeking good, and seeking life eternal to that individual identity which is itself the source and center of infinite good, to the revelation of that individual identity which is the blessing—not receiving a blessing, but being it.

As we come into the realization of the true nature of our being and the true nature of God's being as individual being, in that proportion have we risen above the circumstances and conditions of human existence. At first this may leave us floating through space and wondering where we are going to land before we discover what this power of the Invisible is that acts upon our life and transforms our consciousness.

How many times have I said and written that, before we can

attain that which we are seeking, we must come to a place where we can see that which is invisible, hear that which is inaudible, and know that which is unknowable? "The things of the Spirit of God . . . are foolishness unto" [2] man.

This transformation of consciousness from the thinking mind to the intuitive will not come through the intellect, but rather it will define itself to what is called the Soul-faculties, the inner awareness. Jesus' statement, "Having eyes, see ye not? and having ears, hear ye not?" [3] is a reminder that we do not see spiritual truth or hear spiritual truth with the eyes or the ears. There is an inner consciousness, a spiritual faculty, that receives and interprets truth to us. We may call It [4] God, we may call It divine Love, universal Life, or the Spirit of God. Regardless of what name or term we use, however, we are acknowledging that there is a center of inspiration. We are acknowledging that of our own selves we can do nothing, that it is the Father within that does the works, that the Christ lives our life, meaning the Spirit of God in our individual being or individual awareness.

As we acknowledge that there is this infinite Source of inspiration and all good, we go on to the next step and realize that to the degree that that infinite good comes into our experience do we bring forth the beauty and bounty of that Infinity. Without It, we would be nothing; without It, we could do nothing.

Such a teaching is transcendental, and it is a reversal of the ordinary human sense of existence. For example, the world concept of supply is that we go out and get it, we work for it, plan, scheme for it, or steal; but in some way or other, we do get it.

[2] I Corinthians 2:14.   [3] Mark 8:18.
[4] In the spiritual literature of the world, the varying concepts of God are indicated by the use of such words as "Father," "Mother," "Soul," "Spirit," "Principle," "Love," and "Life." Therefore, in this book the author has used the pronouns "He" and "It," or "Himself" and "Itself" interchangeably in referring to God.

This teaching reverses that and says that the flow of the Spirit of God in us is the secret of supply. But this is something we could hardly go out and tell to the man on the street.

The world also believes that material remedies are absolutely essential, so would it not be foolish to try to tell anyone who places his faith in such remedies that, as effective as they may be, there is a more effective way? How many of them could understand that and accept such an idea? Why, it would be as ridiculous as saying that it is not necessary to pray to God for our good. I know because, when I have made that kind of a statement, I have seen the shock on the faces of persons who were well trained in religious beliefs. Not pray to God for our good? Unthinkable!

But how can we ask God for something that God must know we already need? Is not God omniscience, all-knowledge, all-wisdom? And if He is, is not the prayer that asks, begs, and beseeches God for the things of "this world" sin? The prayer, however, that turns to the Father and asks, "Open my eyes; illumine me; give me light. Be a light within me; shine through me; express. Fit me to be a better vehicle for Thy grace, a better servant of Thy will," comes nearer to the higher form of prayer which is communion with God.

It is like the relationship that exists between two persons who understand each other thoroughly, and who sit on a mountain or by a stream, looking at the scenery, enjoying the great delights of the mountains, the valleys, or the sea without any words passing between them, but looking at each other once in a while in mutual joy at this great privilege of beholding the work of God, two persons so completely in tune that just an occasional reminder, "Isn't the moon beautiful? Aren't the stars shining brightly tonight?" or a few words like that, and there is communion.

True prayer is like that. It is when one communes with God

and feels the divine Presence in him and through him, and in and through all people, and everything round about, and just smiles occasionally and exclaims, "Father, isn't this a heavenly earth we have here! Isn't this a beautiful world! Aren't people wonderful!"

That is the prayer of communion, and it comes about after we have attained a measure of life by Grace, a life in which God is fulfilling Itself as our experience.

It is not that God knows our material needs and supplies them. God knows nothing of our need for automobiles, typewriters, or washing machines. He probably does not even have an awareness of our need for employment. But God speaks to us in terms of fulfillment, and that fulfillment is always in terms we can understand. God speaks to us, and the mind interprets it in terms of dollar bills, books, employment, or companionship. God speaks as Spirit. We hear the Spirit, but we interpret It according to our needs, to that which makes for our fulfillment.

John tells us that God is love. If God is love, why ask God for love? God is love. God has no power to withhold love any more than God has power to withhold crops from the ground, or fish from the sea, or birds from the air. It is the function of Life to fulfill Itself, and that in infinite and abundant measure.

During the great depression of the thirties, churches all over the world were open day and night for those who wanted to pray to God for supply, and you know as well as I do that there was no lack of supply. The oceans were full of fish; Maine never was without a surplus of potatoes; the South never ran out of cotton; the Middle West always had more than enough cattle and wheat. As a matter of fact, these things were produced so abundantly that every day of the week thousands of railroad trains and scows were sent out laden with food to be thrown into the ocean or to be burned up. Crops were plowed under, and farmers were paid not to raise them; and all the time the churches were open day and night, filled with people praying for more supply. What would the world have done if God had been able to increase the supply? It would have had twice as much food to throw in the ocean and twice as much to burn up.

There was no sense in praying to God for supply then, and there is no sense in doing so now—unless we want to pray to Him to bring it to our back door for us in a truck. God is already producing more than the people of this earth are using. Yet, at this very moment, all over the world there are those who are praying for God to increase the supply on earth. If God doubled the amount of goods on earth, the people who are praying for it probably would not get any of it. All the prayers that have ever been sent up to God for more food or more clothing were just so much wasted wordage and wasted time.

There is a way to bring the infinity of supply into our experience, however, but that way is not by repeating a lot of words or singing sentimental songs, and by so doing believing that God is somehow going to begin giving us what up to now He has been withholding from us. No! No! That is not the way.

The way to restore normalcy, harmony, and abundance is not to pray to God to increase the supply, which is already greater than we can use, but rather to become consciously at-one with that Source so that it can flow. It is like the electricity which we use every day. There must be a contact with the source of the power before that power can flow and operate. The room in which we are sitting may be filled with electrical outlets; the walls may be lined with electrical wires; but it would do no good to sit around praying for electricity. The appliance must be plugged in before the power can flow.

So it is with us. God is the very life of our being, the very love and source of our being, but we must tune in. We must recognize and realize our at-one-ment. Our prayer then will never be a reaching out. It will never be an attempt to gain more truth, more life, or more love. It will never be a seeking of any form of demonstration—except one, and that is the demonstration of God's presence.

And so it is useless to pray any prayer in the sense of a desire to get, to accomplish, to achieve, or to demonstrate. The only legitimate prayer that will be left to us is a "Thank You, Father," and a sitting in the silence in sweet communion with the gentle Presence that is already within our own being. This Presence will not be added to us—no, no, no! It will be revealed as within our own being.

Do you see why desire is wrong? It is an acknowledgment of a lack. Jesus said, "Ask, and it shall be given you; seek, and ye shall find; knock, and it shall be opened unto you." [5] Beg, plead, knock, ask! But ask for Spirit, for spiritual illumination. Ask for God-realization, and pray for it. Ask for the gifts of the Spirit. Ask the Spirit for spiritual things. Paul said, "For we know not what we should pray for as we ought: but the Spirit itself maketh intercession for us." [6] Acknowledge then when you go to pray that you do not know what to pray for, and therefore what you are praying for is spiritual light, spiritual illumination.

Suppose that God could be so personalized as to be available to you here and now, what would you pray for? Something called a home, money, companionship, or a parking space? Or for the presence of God? If you were holding God's hand, would you not know that in the intimacy of that association God would know your need and provide for it? So the only thing you would pray for is God.

God really is just as available and tangible as though He were

[5] Matthew 7:7.   [6] Romans 8:26.

standing here visibly holding your hand. Why? Because God is omnipresent. God is omnipresence itself. God is the life and the fulfillment of all being. So if you have God, why do you have to ask for God *and* a parking place? If you have God, why do you have to ask for God *and* employment? Oh no, no! It would be enough to ask for God and get It. That would be enough for anyone—as all who have experienced God have found out. In the presence of God, there is nothing left for which to pray.

You profane prayer if you bring into it a concern, worry, fear, or a desire for anything or anybody. How can you believe in God and fear or doubt for the outcome?

From this moment on, then, you lose the privilege of praying for any person, any thing, or any condition. Your whole prayer becomes a continuous song of gratitude that God is love, that God is here, and that God is now. God is the all-knowing intelligence, the principle of our existence, the all-loving parent. Prayer thereby becomes a recognition of God's presence, a communion with God, a resting back in God's bosom, a holding of God's hand, a feeling of the divine Presence. That is prayer, and nothing else is.

Do you begin to see the reason for constant and frequent meditation? Do you see now why you require stillness of mind instead of taking thought? Do you see why in your meditation you must develop a listening attitude, a state of receptivity in which you do not think thoughts as much as wait for thoughts to come from the depths of your own being? Truth does not have to come from up in the sky. You do not have to strain for it. You do not have to make a mental effort for it. You merely have to let it gently flow forth.

Realize that all your good is to flow out from you. None of it can come to you. Divorce yourself from any outer dependence, whether person, place, or thing. See yourself in such a light that you can really and truly understand that if you walked out of your house in the morning without a dime in your pocket, you could fulfill yourself quickly with everything needful because it would not have to come to you but would flow out from you. If a bomb burst over the city, you would still go on eating three meals a day and have a place to sleep and be able to care for others. Out of what? Out of the depth of the infinite nature of your own Christhood. You could do as the Master did, walk out on the street and heal the sick and feed the multitudes. Out of what? Out of your Christhood. That is the lesson we all must learn: our Self-completeness in God and through God, our Self-completeness as the very Christ of God.

The truth which is your being becomes the light for all those who do not yet know that the kingdom of God is within them, and as they search for it they will find it through you. Not from you—no! You will be but the light revealing the light within them. You will never give them truth. The truth you will impart is the truth that is within them.

To a person of mortal, material consciousness it would seem impossible that a change could take place in his life by means of Something he had never seen, heard, tasted, touched, or smelled. But with that first experience would come more and more experiences, and as one change followed another, the day would come when somebody would say, "You know, you are not the same person I formerly knew." The transition from mortal, material sense to some measure of spiritual consciousness would have begun.

As these first experiences come, you realize that it is possible to bring about harmony, joy, and peace in the outer realm through spiritual means. However, you are still thinking in terms of dollar bills when you think of supply, only now you hope to accumulate them spiritually instead of materially. You are still thinking of a heart, lungs, liver, and gall bladder that operate in such and such a fashion, only now instead of bringing about their proper functioning through physical means, you are going to bring it about through spiritual means.

That was but the beginning of your transition from mortal, material sense to spiritual consciousness. But it was a transition, and that "old man" was beginning to "die," and a new one was being born, dependent on spiritual means for attaining material good.

The day eventually comes, however, when another transition has to be made, and the realization dawns that neither supply nor the body is material. Even the universe is not a structural universe.

"My kingdom is not of this world" [7]—no, not in any sense of the word. There are joys of which the people of this world have never even dreamed; there is a sense of health of which nobody in mortal or material sense, or even in the mental or half-way spiritual sense has ever conceived. There is another world, a new world. "My kingdom is not of this world": *My* [8] kingdom is the kingdom of heaven. There really is a heaven, and when the old earth and the old heaven are washed away, you come into the new earth and the new heaven and find that they are purely spiritual.

Now you enter a consciousness in which Spirit is your only health, your only supply. Now you do not think of using Spirit to get a human companion. You do not use Spirit to make the heart beat faster or slower, or to bring the pulse or blood pressure up or down. Here again is another transition; and in this second stage this man who has been "dying" for a long time is completely "dead." Now is he resurrected, probably more than

[7] John 18:36.
[8] The word "My," capitalized, refers to God.

resurrected: ascended into a divine state of consciousness in which the values are no longer earthly.

That transitional experience will go on and on and on until the ascension above all sense of this world. Then, there will be no more reincarnation because there will be no place into which to be reborn. The complete and perfect virginal, spiritual birth, or sense of being, will have been achieved. This is the "dying daily" and the rebirth that goes on continuously until the complete ascension.

Grace

———•———

My grace is sufficient for thee.

II Corinthians 12:9

Included in the word "Grace" is all that is meant by the word "gift." The gift of God is a sufficiency. The nations of the world seek after what they shall eat, what they shall drink, wherewithal they shall be clothed. They are continuously taking thought or being concerned about their affairs of tomorrow. This is not true in "My kingdom," which is not of this world. In the kingdom of Grace, God is the creative principle, the infinite power. The word "Grace" implies that which maintains and sustains: infinite good, and above all, love. Therefore, love must be the measure of the capacity of our good.

Grace is fulfillment, and Grace does not bring partial success or partial happiness, nor does it demand of us that which we cannot fulfill. Grace brings a task to us, but with it, Grace brings the understanding, the strength, and the wisdom to perform it; and Grace also brings whatever is necessary for its fulfillment, whether transportation, funds, books, teachers, or teachings.

Under Grace, tomorrow is not our concern, but God's; and whatever is given us to do must be done to the highest of our present understanding. It makes no difference whether it is shopping, selling, teaching, or healing, God has placed that responsibility upon us. God has given us that task, that joy, that privilege, and we execute it to the best of our ability, and then, if necessary, wait expectantly for the next task to be given to us. To doubt that it will be given, to doubt that it will carry with it all the strength and resources necessary to carry it to fruition, to doubt that it will bring with it joy and success is to have no understanding of the meaning of Grace.

Everything that comes by Grace comes as fulfillment, so there is never an occasion to say, "Oh, Father, You have provided a good job for me in New York, but what about the fare to reach there?" Or, "Father, You have provided an inspirational and uplifting class for me to attend, but nobody to leave at home with the family." No, that never happens! Whatever comes by Grace comes as fulfillment.

The ravens are fed, and the lilies are clothed through Grace —not through man. Man can be the instrument, but man cannot grow a garden. God does that. God, acting and appearing as man, is the avenue or instrument through which the necessary work is done.

If you called upon a spiritual teacher for help, would you not be greatly surprised if that teacher said, "Don't you see what a wonderful teacher I am?" You would be shocked at that, because you know that the teacher is but an avenue for God's grace. As a matter of fact, if that teacher were not there and you were seeking your good through God, another teacher would be provided; and if there were none left on earth, whatever was necessary for your spiritual unfoldment would come to you directly from within your own being. However, as long as an instrument, an avenue, or a channel is necessary, if you keep looking to God, divine Grace, for your good, God will raise up whoever is necessary for you. Yes, even in the wilderness, God will raise up a spiritual teacher for you. God has mysterious ways of bringing your good to you when you look to Him, and to Him alone.

Some years ago in a city on the West Coast, a man came to me in regard to a business matter, and in the course of the conversation asked about the nature of my work. It is not easy to explain this to a person who has no knowledge of mysticism,[1] but I told him that it was a teaching, a way of life.

"Oh, a way of life. Well, how is it that I haven't heard of your being in town?"

"Probably because we do not advertise."

"But I have been seeking just that, a way of life. I am not satisfied with the way things are, and I am seeking something else, but I don't know where to look, or how, and here you are in town with what may be the answer, and how do people know you are here?"

[1] The message of The Infinite Way is a purely mystical one even though metaphysical principles are used in the practical application of its teachings. The Infinite Way accepts the definition of the word "mysticism" as given in Merriam-Webster's *Unabridged Dictionary,* Third International Edition, as follows: "the experience of mystical union or direct communion with ultimate reality reported by mystics . . . a theory of mystical knowledge; the doctrine or belief that direct knowledge of God, of spiritual truth, of ultimate reality, or comparable matters is attainable through immediate intuition, insight, or illumination and in a way differing from ordinary sense perception."

"Well," I replied, "when the need is there, they find us."

"But how could I have found you?"

And I said, "You have."

Do you see? There was no advertising on our part, and yet it brought him; and he was not searching for The Infinite Way or for me. He was seeking a way of life; but in seeking a way of life, without thinking of an avenue, he was led to an avenue. It may prove to have been the very one he wanted and needed, but even if it does not, no harm has been done because it will set him on the path that will ultimately lead him to his way. He did not have to pray for a thing; he did not have to pray for a person: all he had to do was to lift himself to the desire for a way, for good, and then he found it. As long as you are not seeking person, place, or thing, as long as your desire is to be fed spiritually, the realization of divine Grace will interpret itself on your level of understanding.

To me, divine Grace is the realization that God meets the needs of His children, and therefore it is not necessary to go out and proselyte in an attempt to force them to a realization of that Grace. God knows the needs of His children, and when His children are ready for a spiritual teaching He will lead them to the particular teaching necessary for their unfoldment. Let each follow the light as it is given to him of God, and then he will live by Grace. God brings to all those in the world the unfoldment necessary for their demonstration, and to me, that is another phase of Grace.

It is divine Grace if you can feel that whatever the task given to you, the presence of God is there to fulfill it with you or for you. It is divine Grace to go about your work knowing, not that you have to do it, but that you are the instrument through which it is done.

Grace is the realization that you can perform every task allotted to you. You can execute every duty given to you. You can carry through with any work and every work because the responsibility is not yours. The idea is God's; the wisdom is God's; the strength is God's; the necessary love, substance, and activity are God's. And that, too, is divine Grace.

It is divine Grace that you are enabled to fulfill every demand upon you, and this Grace leaves you free and joyous to experience what is called this human life; but this life, understood through Grace, is not a human life at all: it is really divine.

Grace also includes forgiveness. Sometimes we hold ourselves in bondage to the belief of deserved punishment for sins of omission or commission, and often we hold others in bondage to these same beliefs. But under this life of Grace, there is forgiveness without any consideration for whether one has deserved, earned, or been worthy of it. The forgiveness is there because Grace reveals that the transgressor has not done this thing to you: he has done it unto himself, through ignorance.

"Father, forgive them; for they know not what they do." [2] You might think that the Master meant that they knew not what they did to him. He did not mean that at all. He meant that they did not know what they were doing to themselves. To him, nothing could happen. He had come under divine sonship. God was his eternal life, and no one could take that from him. God was his supply: he had already demonstrated that he could feed the multitudes. No one could take that power and ability away from him. He knew that they could do nothing to him; and the only possible meaning of "Father, forgive them" was that they did not know what they were doing to themselves.

The true sense of forgiveness is a realization that no one can harm you. All anyone can do is do something, but he does it to

[2] Luke 23:34.

himself—not to you. Why? Having accepted God as your being, what can happen to you? Can you be deprived of life, health, liberty, freedom, or supply? No! No! No one can take your supply from you because it does not come from man: it comes from God. No one can deprive you of anything; no one can harm you. You and your Father are one. Can anyone break that relationship? No! Then no one can do anything to you, and so when you say, "Father, forgive them," you are really saying that they do not know what they are doing to themselves in accepting the belief in a selfhood apart from God, in accepting into their consciousness hate, envy, jealousy, fear, or malice.

No one can be brought to harm who understands his divine sonship, who has recognized his life through Grace, the gift of God. Anyone who recognizes God to be a sanctuary, his abiding place, can never come under the injuries wrought by wars, bombs, or accidents.

It is only in your sense of separation from God that such things can happen. Neither height nor depth—being up in an airplane or being down in a submarine—can separate you from the life of God or from the love of God. Love means care; love means protection; love means security; and love means safety. So what difference would it make, up or down? What difference would it make, bombs or no bombs? Is there any peril or sword that could separate you from the love of God? Yes, there is! Yes, there is! Your acceptance of a sense of separation from God will do it! Your sense of having a life of your own that can begin and end will do it! Your sense of gaining something at somebody else's expense will do it! Your belief that destroying some other nation will enrich yours or make your nation secure will do it!

Those who thought they could benefit by the destruction of the Germans and Germany lived to find out that it was a very short and not a very sweet victory; and those who later felt that they were going to benefit by the destruction of Hitler and the Nazis, of Japan, or of Russia must have learned that safety and security can never be found in another's destruction. Safety and security can be found in only one way: through Grace.

Grace is love, and love worketh no injury to any man. But you must bring yourself in love to a dependence on the gift of the grace of God, not on the power of the sword or bombs, or on the power of unfair competition.

When you turn to a spiritual unfoldment, you learn one thing: there is no way of getting anything from anyone; there is no way of getting anything out of anything; and there is no hope for those who expect to *get*. Life, spiritually understood, is not a getting process: it is a giving process. You will get out of life whatever you put into it, no more and no less. It may be a life of peace, but there will be no peace or prosperity for those who are expecting to get something. It may be a life of war and depression, but there will be no war or depression to the person who is putting into life his love, his forgiveness, and his dependence on Grace. To that person, none of these things will come nigh his dwelling place.

If you could learn the secret of Grace, which is a complete reliance on this infinite Power within, you would find a spiritual freedom in the outer realm that no man could take from you. Under a life of Grace, there would come a total freedom from the capacity to injure or to be injured. Divine Grace would reveal to you your divine sonship, and that same Grace would maintain and sustain that divine sonship under any and all circumstances.

EIGHT

Living the Life of Grace

———•———

God is infinite, and God manifests Itself in infinite forms and in
infinite ways. God is consciousness, and we therefore become
aware of all those things necessary to our unfoldment through an
activity of consciousness. We see, hear, taste, touch, and smell,
but these are all activities of consciousness manifested at different levels.

Often in meditation it is possible to see visions or to hear the
still small voice; and then there are times when the Presence
makes itself known through the activity of smell, and even of
touch. We may feel a touch on the shoulder, the head, or on the
cheek. At other times, the fragrance of flowers may be noticed.
There is no way to limit God and feel that He can appear in one

way only. God can appear in any form, and probably we can understand that best by recalling that when Joan of Arc was asked, "Does God speak to you in French?" her reply was, "I do not know in what language God speaks, but I hear Him in French."

Does God speak as perfume or odors, voices, or a touch? No! But we can comprehend God in these ways. That is our interpretation of God's presence. Let us learn to accept God in whatever way and in whatever form God may appear to us. How do we know that it is God? How do we know that it is not imagination? By the fruitage, by the results.

When we are indulging in vain imaginings about our spiritual activities and spiritual work, it leaves us up in the air, dangling in space, with no tangible results. But when our experience is actually an experience of God, we can know it by its fruits, and the fruits of the Spirit are joy, peace, prosperity, health, harmony, and love. When the Presence announces Itself, there comes with It a sense of serenity, tranquility, a peace which may translate itself into form.

Everything has form: even thought. All substance must have a form although not a form always visible to our human sense, and the higher we go in spiritual realization and unfoldment, the more we see the spiritual sense of form rather than its material sense, and the more aware we are of spiritual reality. For example, a person with a purely material sense of life looks out and sees faces and figures, hats, dresses, suits, eyeglasses, and earphones. But as he rises higher and higher, he becomes less aware of these things and more aware of a look in the eye, a smile on the lips, a flick of the finger. He becomes less conscious of men and women as such, and more aware of those outer symbols that express inward being. Then there comes a state when he continues to rise above even that, and he is almost unaware of people as human beings. At that stage, he senses or realizes the spiritual nature of their being.

Our entire existence represents states and stages of consciousness. In one state of consciousness, we do things one way, but as we evolve or develop spiritually into another state of consciousness, we do them in another way. For example, until we learn that God's grace is sufficient for us, we think that we have to labor, to plot and plan for our future. We worry, fear, and doubt. Perhaps we have all kinds of human anxieties and thoughts and fears about ourselves and our families and our future; and here an idea is presented to us that God's grace is sufficient for us. We stop short and wonder, "Is that true? Does that really mean what it says? Does it really mean that God's grace is enough without my doing all this worrying, planning, thinking, and scheming? Is that really true? Have I been wasting time and energy in useless thought-taking when all the time there is a divine Grace at hand that can provide for my sufficiency?"

After you have done some thinking about this, you finally come to the conclusion that you will have to prove it for yourself. Your problems are still with you, probably more than yesterday, but with each one, you bring to conscious remembrance this truth: "Thy grace is sufficient for me. I had better stop worrying and being anxious for a while. I will put off taking thought for today. Right now, I rest in the truth that God's grace is sufficient for me."

So you relax, you rest, and you feel at peace, but that does not mean that tonight, tomorrow, or the day after, you are not going to have more anxious moments, more concern, more lack, more fear, or more pain. Then again you remind yourself that God's grace is sufficient, that you must rest in that Grace with no anxiety, fear, doubt, or thought. You may go along that way for months—three, four, five, or six—and all this time you are meeting every appearance of discord with the remembrance that God's grace is sufficient, even though the outward appearance would deny it.

Just a few days, weeks, or months later, and lo and behold, you may begin to feel God's grace coming into expression in your experience. You find good coming to you that you had not humanly planned for; you find harmony and health coming to you that at the moment you may not be able to explain; but with the passage of time, it dawns in your consciousness, "Why, it is true! God's grace *is* sufficient for me." By that time, you have come to a place where you rest more in that sense of peace and no longer need to use as many statements of truth.

Ah, but then perhaps there comes another problem. This time it may be a great responsibility, and you have the feeling that it is beyond your means, your strength, your time, or perhaps your power to cope with it. Along with that comes the remembrance of a passage of Scripture, and you hear: "He performeth the thing that is appointed for me." [1]

That startles you for a minute. "What? What? He performeth?" You think you have been given this job or this work to do, or you have been given this responsibility, and yet Scripture says that He performeth it. There again, while you go about the performance of your tasks, you are reminded, "Very well, I can do it because actually He is performing it through me." Again that responsibility drops away. That rest comes, and soon you find that it is true: there is a *He* at the center of your being. He that is within you is greater than any responsibility, duty, or demand that can come upon you from the world.

So while at first you may have been diligent in the use of statements of truth and may have brought them to your awareness

[1] Job 23:14.

over and over and over again, now you find that only occasionally do you have to remind yourself of them because now the
words have given way to the actual awareness itself, and when
you have the awareness, you do not need the words.

This bringing of statements of truth to conscious remembrance
is called contemplative meditation. When you undertake this
form of meditation, you may at first be bringing to conscious remembrance every statement of truth you know. It may take you
a half hour to complete your part of this contemplative part of
the meditation, that is, your voicing of the truth. Then you sit
back and listen, and that part of the meditation may be one minute, two, three, or five. As you continue this form of contemplative meditation, however, you will gradually get to the place
where your part of it takes only five minutes, and God's part
takes a half hour. It just reverses itself. God keeps filling you
with His truth; God keeps filling you with the realization of His
presence; but you have made way for the Spirit by your preparation through your contemplative meditation. Therefore, do not
hesitate to bring to your conscious remembrance every statement
of truth you know until you have built your consciousness to
where that is no longer necessary.

You do not discard: you just evolve. You grow gradually
from one form of meditation to another, and from one state of
consciousness to another, and in time, you come to the place
where it is only occasionally that it seems necessary consciously
to remember some truth. For the most part, truth is imparting
itself to you from the infinity of your being, sometimes in the
form of quotations that you already know, and very often in a
form that you never heard of before.

Eventually you learn what it means to pray without ceasing.
When that time comes, whenever you hear a news broadcast, see
a headline, or somebody brings you bad news, automatically you

just turn it off with the reminder that in God's kingdom harmony alone reigns. Wherever you may be—on the street, in a bus, in your office, or in your home—when you witness sin, disease, lack, limitation, or death, you automatically realize, "No, that can exist only as a picture in the human mind, not as any part of God's kingdom. God's kingdom could never hold any such pictures as that." And so you are praying without ceasing, and yet you are doing it without consciously going around declaring truth, except as the pictures of sense touch you, and you automatically learn to re-interpret them into their spiritual values.

It is possible to reach the heights attained by Jesus when, without his even knowing that she was there, the woman who pressed through the throng and touched the hem of his robe was healed. Jesus was living in such a high state of spiritual consciousness that he was not even aware of a sick woman near him. Because of his years of training, he was able to lift himself into that exalted state so that without any conscious thought, he did not see any error to deny. When you arrive at the state of consciousness where you never see, hear, taste, touch, or smell any form of error, you are then in a state of consciousness where your meditations and your prayers are wordless, but you can be assured that then you will be meditating and praying all the time.

The one infinite divine Consciousness, called God, is your individual consciousness; and while there are no degrees to It, there are degrees of your awareness of It. That is because of the word "I." When the word "I" was used to identify a human being, that was when a mind apart from God was set up, and that is the experience of the Prodigal.

When I say, "I, Joel," I am referring to a certain state of consciousness. True, it is God-consciousness, but it is limited by my concept of what Consciousness is. If I accept the human view that my consciousness is made up of my prenatal experience, my environment, education, and personal experience, and then think of that as my consciousness, it would be a very limited sense of consciousness, one which would limit me forever. And always, throughout my life, I would have to move in the groove of that consciousness. That is the way of the human world. It says that if you had a certain prenatal experience, a particular kind of environment, education or lack of it, and certain personal experiences, you will move in a foreordained groove. For the most part, people do just that until in some way or other spiritual wisdom is brought to them in some fashion, and the revelation given that that is all foolishness.

The truth is that God is the measure of your consciousness. God is the circle and the circumference of your consciousness, and nothing less than the allness of God belongs to you.

With that point of view, your life begins to change. Instead of looking back and attributing your present situation in life to a lack of education, an unhappy childhood, a discordant family life, or to the unpleasant fact that your grandmother was a neurotic or your grandfather an alcoholic, and so on and on, now, all of a sudden, you come to the realization: "Wait a minute! Wait a minute! What has that to do with me? I am the offspring of God, and God is my parent, God is my inheritance, God is my environment. I am not limited to that personal sense of consciousness, or to a subconscious or superconsciousness. I am limited only to whatever limitations there are upon God, and since God is infinite there are none."

Now you begin to live out from a new basis. You are living out from the universal Consciousness which is pouring Itself into you, and you are letting It come into you and pour forth through you. If you do that, what becomes of the inhibitions you believed arose out of your childhood, your education or lack of it, or your wealth or lack of it? All that would be broken down instantly, and your prayer becomes, "Flow, God; flow! Flow into me and through me, and out into this vast world."

This would reveal to you the true meaning of humility. You would know then that you not only have no limitations, but that you can take no praise for your accomplishments, since it is all God pouring Itself through. Then you will really know in all humility that there is absolutely no limitation upon your being.

You are Self-complete through God: not Self-complete because of your education, not Self-complete because you have inherited a fortune, not Self-complete because of some human circumstance or condition; but Self-complete because God is your life, your soul, and your consciousness. With God as the infinite nature of your being, what becomes of limitation? There is none. It all disappears.

The nature of the entire message of The Infinite Way is the revelation of God as individual identity and capacity, God as infinite being, and God as the infinity of individual being. The essence of the entire Message is: "I can of mine own self do nothing.[2] . . . The Father that dwelleth in me, he doeth the works."[3] What work? Limited work? No, infinite work! Infinite because of you or me? No, infinite because of the infinity of God.

Do you not see that until you wipe out all that sense of limitation that has come about by believing that you are limited to a finite mind, a subconscious mind, a superconscious mind, or any other kind of mind, and realize that there is only one mind, and that it is the instrument of God, and it is infinite, you will always be limited. God is the only capacity you have, and therefore, there is no limit to your capacity. Think; pray; meditate on God

[2] John 5:30. [3] John 14:10.

as your intelligence, God as your life, God as the measure of your capacity, God as the infinite nature of your being!

How can you be immortal or eternal? *You* cannot be, except as God is immortal and eternal. There is only one immortality, and the immortality of God is the immortality of your being. How can you be loving? *You* cannot: only God is love. But the measure of your love is the measure of God since **God is** love. To think that you have it in your power to be loving, in and of yourself, or that you have it within your power to be generous, kind, or just would be to believe that you had gone beyond the demonstration of Jesus Christ. It may happen some day, but it **has** not happened yet. Remember, Jesus himself said, "Why callest thou me good? there is none good but one, that is, God." [4]

So with us. When you learn that love is not a personal quality, you are able not only to love infinitely but to be loved infinitely. It is only when you limit love to your personal capacity for love that you find love very, very limited. It is only when you think of justice as being a quality of this man's character or that man's nature that you find it limited. But when you see that love or justice is of God, there is no limitation to it any more. You have then removed the egotism that would think that you can be loving, even though Jesus said that there is none good but one. You cannot be loving, neither can you withhold love because God is love, and God is forever expressing Itself as love to every open avenue. And that you are. There is where the practice must come.

"My grace is sufficient for thee," [5] but it will not come into active expression until that statement of truth passes from being a statement to being an inner conviction:

[4] Matthew 19:17.   [5] II Corinthians 12:9.

*Thy grace is sufficient for me. Thy law is sufficient for me,
and I will have no dealings with any other sense of law—only
the spiritual. Thy strength is sufficient for me. It is not a question
of the strength of my muscles; it is not a question of my strength:
Thy strength is sufficient for me. Thy love is sufficient for me.*

As you come into the awareness that God's love is sufficient
for you, God's love is made evident to you through men and
women. "If a man say, I love God, and hateth his brother, he is
a liar: for he that loveth not his brother whom he hath seen, how
can he love God whom he hath not seen?" [6] In other words,
then, by first looking away from men and women, and realizing
that the only love that can come to you is the love of God, more
than likely it will appear as, or through, men and women and
children and the world at large: as animals, birds, and plants.
It will come to you through God, as God's love expressed as
some measure of form.

God's wisdom, too, is sufficient for you. Is there any need,
then, for being concerned about your wisdom or mine, or our
lack of wisdom? No, you are opening yourself now to God's
wisdom that is sufficient for you. And God's wisdom fills you.
God's love fills you. God's presence is sufficient for you. God's
presence! And you may have been thinking in terms of husband,
wife, sister, brother, friend, or other relatives, but here you are
faced with the truth that God's presence is sufficient for you.
Just think of that: God's presence.

Most persons do not believe that. As a rule, they do not accept it. They talk in terms of God's presence, and then turn
around and cry their hearts out for some other presence—some-

[6] I John 4:20.

times even for the absence of some other presence. But the real truth is that God's presence is sufficient for them, and as they rest back in that conviction, God's presence appears to them as the presence of friends, relatives, husband, wife, child, whoever it may be.

Carry this with you; practice it today, and practice it tonight; practice it tomorrow morning, so that you will be able to have the experience of God's grace unfolding, unfolding, and unfolding.